Decolonizing Modernism
James Joyce and the Development of
Spanish American Fiction

LEGENDA

LEGENDA, founded in 1995 by the European Humanities Research Centre of the University of Oxford, is now a joint imprint of the Modern Humanities Research Association and Maney Publishing. Titles range from medieval texts to contemporary cinema and form a widely comparative view of the modern humanities, including works on Arabic, Catalan, English, French, German, Greek, Italian, Portuguese, Russian, Spanish, and Yiddish literature. An Editorial Board of distinguished academic specialists works in collaboration with leading scholarly bodies such as the Society for French Studies and the British Comparative Literature Association.

MHRA

The Modern Humanities Research Association (MHRA) encourages and promotes advanced study and research in the field of the modern humanities, especially modern European languages and literature, including English, and also cinema. It also aims to break down the barriers between scholars working in different disciplines and to maintain the unity of humanistic scholarship in the face of increasing specialization. The Association fulfils this purpose primarily through the publication of journals, bibliographies, monographs and other aids to research.

Maney Publishing

Maney Publishing is one of the few remaining independent British academic publishers. Founded in 1900 the company has offices both in the UK, in Leeds and London, and in North America, in Boston. Since 1945 Maney Publishing has worked closely with learned societies, their editors, authors, and members, in publishing academic books and journals to the highest traditional standards of materials and production.

Decolonizing Modernism

James Joyce and the Development of
Spanish American Fiction

❖

José Luis Venegas

l

LEGENDA

Modern Humanities Research Association and Maney Publishing
2010

Published by the
Modern Humanities Research Association and Maney Publishing
1 Carlton House Terrace
London SW1Y 5AF
United Kingdom

LEGENDA is an imprint of the
Modern Humanities Research Association and Maney Publishing

Maney Publishing is the trading name of W. S. Maney & Son Ltd,
whose registered office is at Suite 1C, Joseph's Well, Hanover Walk, Leeds LS3 1AB

ISBN 978-1-906540-46-3

First published 2010

Printed in Great Britain

Cover: 875 Design

Copy-Editor: Richard Correll

CONTENTS

❖

TO MY MOTHER

ACKNOWLEDGEMENTS

❖

The origin of *Decolonizing Modernism* dates back to my years as an undergraduate student at the University of Seville. It was within the eighteenth-century walls of the Real Fábrica de Tabacos, the stately building that houses the School of Modern Languages and Literatures, that I began reading Joyce with consuming interest. It was also within those walls that I started collecting the scholarly debts that I must acknowledge now. I am deeply grateful for the intellectual generosity and support of Francisco García Tortosa, José María Tejedor and Ricardo Navarrete. Their passion for matters Joycean and the rigor and erudition of their transcultural and translational work on the Irish writer's fiction have been inspirational throughout the years that took me to complete this project. At the University of North Carolina at Chapel Hill, the guidance of Diane Leonard has been simply invaluable. This study has truly benefited from her useful recommendations and suggestions. My thanks also go to Juan Carlos González Espitia and Nicholas Allen for their careful reading of parts of the manuscript and their helpful criticism.

The Duke–University of North Carolina 'Modernity/Coloniality' Working Group provided me with a valuable forum where a substantial part of the theoretical ideas that inform *Decolonizing Modernism* took shape. Although all the members of the group contributed to my thinking in meaningful ways, I want to express my most sincere gratitude to Walter Mignolo. He has shown unrelenting interest in this project since its inception. The argument and final structure of *Decolonizing Modernism* owe no small part to our conversations, debates and emails. I would also like to thank Declan Kiberd. His Joyce seminar at Duke during the Spring of 2004 allowed me to perceive the affinities between his views on Irish Modernism and my own research on Joyce in Spanish America. Those affinities made me even more aware of the necessity of an encounter between Irish and Latin American literary studies, an encounter that this book sets out to accomplish.

Without the support and encouragement of my families on both sides of the Atlantic, this book would not have been completed. John and Lynn, thank you for your warmth and unstinting generosity. My sisters, Ana and Inmaculada, remain my biggest supporters, and my father, José Luis, my most valued interlocutor for matters both academic and personal. This book is dedicated to the memory of my mother, Ana, who could not see it completed, but who inspired every page of it with her love.

The final word of gratitude is owed to my loving wife, Jessica, who has always believed in me and guided me with her caring touch.

Sections of Chapter 2 appeared in a different form in my article 'Eliot, Borges, Tradition, and Irony', *Symposium*, 59, 4 (2006), 237–55.

All translations in the text are my own.

JLV, July 2009

INTRODUCTION

❖

The Place of Modernism in Spanish America

> Es comprensible que [los europeos] insistan en medirnos con la misma vara con que se miden a sí mismos, sin recordar que los estragos de la vida no son iguales para todos [. . .]. La interpretación de nuestra realidad con esquemas ajenos sólo contribuye a hacernos cada vez más desconocidos, cada vez menos libres, cada vez más solitarios.
>
> [It is understandable that Europeans insist on measuring us with the same yardstick with which they measure themselves, without recalling that the ravages of life are not the same for all (. . .). To interpret our reality through schemas which are alien to us can only contribute to making us even more unknown, even less free, even more solitary.]
>
> GABRIEL GARCÍA MÁRQUEZ, Nobel Prize Speech

In one of his letters to the painter Sergio Sergi, Julio Cortázar remarked that his summer vacation of 1947 was fairly apathetic and that he spent most of his time sunbathing, drinking Coke and reading James Joyce's *Ulysses*.[1] Cortázar, who had recently returned to Buenos Aires after a short stint as a professor of modern French and English poetry at the University of Cuyo in Argentina's western region of Mendoza, vividly evokes the figure of the peripheral intellectual committed to consuming (quite literally in the case of his soda choice) the products of the First World. That this writer, already an accomplished translator of works by G. K. Chesterton, André Gide, John Keats and Daniel Defoe, went on to publish a Joycean text such as *Rayuela* (1963), during a voluntary exile in Paris that would last until his death, seems to provide strong evidence for considering him an exemplary case of the provincial artist who abandons local attachments to come to the metropolitan centre and embrace cosmopolitan values.

A few years after the publication of *Rayuela*, the Uruguayan critic Emir Rodríguez Monegal suggested that the assimilation and reproduction of European models that Cortázar's work appears to exemplify may appropriately define the development of Spanish American fiction between the late 1950s and the 1970s. In one of the first systematic studies of the Latin American *nueva novela, El boom de la novela latinoamericana* (1972), Rodríguez Monegal argues that James Joyce's *Ulysses* became the 'invisible central model' of the internationally acclaimed fiction of the 'boom': Jorge Luis Borges, the outstanding precursor of this innovative trend, achieved a 'scale reduction' of Joyce's novel in his short stories, and Julio Cortázar's *Rayuela*, José Lezama Lima's *Paradiso*, Carlos Fuentes's *Cambio de piel* and Guillermo Cabrera Infante's *Tres tristes tigres* all took the shape of 'Joycean books'.[2] According to this critic, the literary merit of these texts, which he groups under the category of 'novels of language', derives from the formal and linguistic complexities they share with Joyce's fiction, as well as from the self-contained autonomy that they attain through 'parody' and 'myth'. He concludes that Joyce's influence shaped an international literary culture in Spanish America that abandoned narrow regionalisms to become part of a global canon.

The innovations in style and technique that Rodríguez Monegal perceives in this cosmopolitan trend largely coincide with those most often associated with Anglo-American modernism. In an important essay published the same year as *El boom de la novela latinoamericana*, Maurice Beebe notes that the main features of modernist literature are its 'formalism' — its emphasis 'on the importance of structure and design'; its irony, 'characterized by an attitude of detachment and non-commitment'; its use of myth 'as an arbitrary means of ordering art'; and its 'reflexivism': 'Modernist art turns back upon itself and is largely concerned with its own creation and composition'.[3] Indeed, later commentators have made explicit the relationship between literary modernism and the new narrative in Spanish America suggested by Rodríguez Monegal. For instance, Morton Levitt's *Modernist Survivors* includes a chapter on Joyce's influence on the 'boom' novelists ('"The Fortunate Explosion": Contemporary Fictions in Latin America') where it is argued that the narrative production of these novelists is 'an extension and elaboration of European Modernism that is in the spirit at once of Joyce and his fellows and of this new continent'.[4] Levitt adds that Joyce and other modernists such as Virginia Woolf and William Faulkner 'enabled this new generation of writers to transform their separate, local literary inheritances into fictions which are truly universal'.[5]

Decolonizing Modernism concentrates on a body of texts typically associated with the 'boom' and framed by the publication of Borges's *Ficciones* (1944) and that of Fernando del Paso's *Palinuro de México* (1977) to endorse and further develop Emir Rodríguez Monegal's contention that Joyce's *Ulysses* is indeed a central model for the development of contemporary Spanish American narrative. To support this claim, I will analyse the use of allusion, myth and parody in a select group of novels and short stories frequently termed 'Joycean'. But by focusing on these formal aspects, I will contest rather than defend the adequacy of Anglo-American modernism as the standard literary–historical category against which we should read and compare *Ulysses*, *Ficciones*, *Rayuela* and *Tres tristes tigres*, among other texts. In doing so, I seek to challenge the belief that experimental prose written in Spanish America dissolves the links between art and place, between literary expression and specific historical and geographical settings. Certainly, narrative fragmentation, structural complexity and linguistic self-reflexivity, common features that define both literary modernism and contemporary Spanish American fiction, generally convey a feeling of repudiation and aloofness toward history and society. Consider, for instance, the disembodied meditations that fill the pages of Virginia Woolf's *The Waves* or the ethereal consciousness through which the events narrated in Marcel Proust's *In Search of Lost Time* are filtered. But non-representational literature, especially in postcolonial settings, can also grow out of a commitment to elaborate an inchoate cultural landscape, challenging inherited styles, themes and ideas and imagining alternative forms of expression. Indeed, the process that Ngugi wa

Thiong'o called the 'decolonization of the mind' involves 'un-learning' an imposed culture and then engaging in the daunting task of building a liberated consciousness and a new order of things, utopian realities for which experimental fiction can provide a preliminary blueprint. It might be, then, that the narrative innovations of peripheral writers have their roots not only in a compulsion to be modern, to keep up with metropolitan tendencies, but also in a desire to imagine what Stephen Dedalus evokes in *A Portrait of the Artist as a Young Man* as 'the loveliness which has not yet come into the world'.[6]

In this sense, it may not be merely a coincidence that Joyce wrote the revolutionary prose of *Ulysses* during the years in which a rapid succession of crucial political and cultural events ended centuries of colonial control of Britain over Ireland. Nor is it a matter of chance that the emergence of the *nueva novela* in Spanish America coincided with a whole constellation of philosophical ideas and political events — including the 'Theology of Liberation' and the Cuban Revolution — that challenged the region's historical dependency on European intellectual and artistic movements. I am interested, therefore, in revealing the ways in which formal techniques usually labelled 'modernist' — myth as a structural device, parody, linguistic experimentation and fragmented temporalities — become part of a strategy to grapple with rapidly changing cultural landscapes where imperial models of subjectivity, representation and language should be cast off to achieve cultural decolonization. Therefore, I will not interpret the parallels, tangencies and connections between Joyce and Spanish American fiction as evidence of a universal literary paradigm originating in Europe and then spreading outwardly to the peripheries, but as a network of related yet localized aesthetic responses to specific historical and cultural conjunctures. That is, I propose to return to the scene that opened these pages and look at Cortázar reading *Ulysses* not as an example of a marginal artist absorbing the teachings of a First World master, but as an encounter between two peripheral intellectuals. If Cortázar contended that he arrived in Paris only to discover that he was South American, not European — he once told Cuban writer Roberto Fernández Retamar that, paradoxically enough, it was in France that he found his 'true Latin American condition' (*su verdadera condición de latinoamericano*) — it might be that he also found in *Ulysses* a book that resonated with his own struggle to accentuate received forms and themes with the sense of displacement and marginality experienced by the provincial artist — with what he memorably called *el sentimiento de no estar del todo*. Taking my cue from the cultural and literary implications of this encounter on the margins, I should like to interpret the aesthetic intersection between Joyce and the Spanish American new narrative as a direct questioning of Eurocentric cultural referents — that is, as a nodal point that resists and exceeds the unilinear historical narrative that leads from the local to the global, the primitive to the modern, the particular to the universal, or, to put it in terms familiar to Latin American cultural discourse, from barbarism to civilization. In sum, this study sets out to explore the possibility of an alternative literary history, one that does not replicate the unfolding master-narrative of modernity in its universal, progressive and developing garbs.

It is in this spirit that I will analyse 'modernist' literary strategies: not to endorse the kind of linguistic universalism that triumphantly erases the scars of history, but to show that formal innovation can be used by postcolonial artists to carve out a distinctive place of enunciation, to transmit their unbending determination to transform an acquired speech into an instrument of cultural liberation.[7] Connecting the techniques of literary modernism with cultural marginality — with a 'sense of place' caught at the crossroads between the familiarity of local attachments and the foreignness of metropolitan fashions — certainly demands the 'deterritorialization' of hegemonic structures of sense and expression that Gilles Deleuze and Félix Guattari associate with 'minor literature'.[8] However, while 'minor literature' embraces fragmentation and polyphony, breaking established forms and revolting against every closure of the 'major language', it must also involve a certain degree of 're-territorialization' that allows us to identify distinct local traditions within global literary geographies. Such spatial perspective shakes up the sequential unfolding of the stages of literary change, turning the global literary map into a network of transnational affiliations linked by shared local concerns and not by universal standards of time. This spatial logic estranges the category of 'modernism' itself and configures what Laura Doyle and Laura Winkiel term 'geomodernisms'. Geomodernisms signal 'a locational approach to modernisms' engagement with cultural and political discourses of global modernity', thus providing a suggestive frame to rethink the dialogue between Joyce and Spanish American fiction beyond the confines of Eurocentric literary history.[9]

By taking this approach to 'Joycism' in Spanish America, my main goal is to offer a corrective reassessment of what Neil Larsen has felicitously called the 'canonical decolonization' of modernism, proposing a geopolitical decolonization instead.[10] According to Larsen, the act of recognition that granted literary celebrities such as Borges and Cortázar the status of canonical modernists during the 1960s and 1970s is ultimately an imperialistic critical move. The result of this act of recognition is that a 'parity of North and South is proposed, but this parity is strictly *literary*, defined against a universal aesthetic standard embodied in modernism'.[11] Indeed, it would be hard to avoid flattening out the differences between centres and margins, between North and South, if one postulates a general category whose range of reference stretches in space from England to South America and in time from the early 1900s to the late 1960s. As we shall discuss, this neutralizing strategy also characterizes critical approaches to Joyce that neglect his 'Irishness' in order to convert his narrative into the model of the 'universal aesthetic standard' of modernism. The geopolitical decolonization of modernism that I propose does not rely on the capacity of a core literary system, or a central category such as 'modernism', to engulf and absorb ex-centric literary production; instead, it challenges temporal classifications that adhere to an unfolding narrative of development, to a single line of progress that wrenches texts from places and defines them according to their proximity, compliance, or assimilation of 'universal' principles that invariably radiate from the great centres of civilization and culture. As Fernando Rosenberg has brilliantly argued with regard to the Latin American avant-garde of the 1920s and 1930s, 'if we are to aspire to dismantle all sorts of diffusionist accounts that leave Latin America in an epistemologically subrogate position, vanguardism must not be read as part of a single line of progress that only belatedly catches up with Latin America'.[12] Within the refocused literary topography that, following Rosenberg, I intend to chart here, Joyce ceases to cross paths with Borges, Cortázar, Lezama Lima, Cabrera Infante and del Paso amidst the monuments of a *civitas verbi* whose centre lies in Paris or London and whose circumference is everywhere; instead, these writers meet halfway between Dublin's backstreets and the *orillas* of Buenos Aires, in the entranceways of liminal sites teetering between the weight of an inherited culture and the amorphous energy of emancipatory longings. In the last analysis, therefore, my reassessment of 'Joycism' in Spanish America attempts to elucidate a type of literary cosmopolitanism that is not defined from a privileged vantage point, but is rather knit by the threads connecting firmly situated and historically grounded points of resistance to globalizing paradigms.

Perhaps the most persuasive argument for a 'Spanish American modernism' inspired by Joyce is found in Gerald Martin's *Journeys through the Labyrinth*.[13] Martin, like Rodríguez Monegal, considers Joyce's *Ulysses* to be the main catalyst for the modernization of Spanish American narrative.[14] The Irish novelist is considered to be a 'First World' writer whose formal innovations reached Latin America at a moment when this peripheral culture was ripe for the assimilation of the daring techniques of European modernism.[15] It is at this point that 'the final flowering of Latin American Modernism in the shape of the "boom" novel'[16] took place, the publication of Cortázar's *Rayuela* marking 'the precise moment at which "Joycism" appeared to assume the main thrust of Spanish American fiction'.[17] In Martin's view, the Joycean audacity of works such as *Rayuela* and *Palinuro de México* is the artistic indication that Latin America has finally achieved literary modernity and that it 'really is a part of Western civilization and that its cultural identity was of such a nature as to provide both a replication of the Joycean trajectory and optimum conditions for its assimilation'.[18]

It should be noted, however, that Martin does not advocate a fully 'diffusionist' pattern of literary evolution whereby 'Spanish American modernism' merely reflects metropolitan aesthetic innovations. With the success of the boom, literary influences began emanating from Latin America as well, transforming the contours of European narrative. 'Indeed, whereas most Latin American fiction between the 1940s and the 1960s is recognizable as "Joycean" or "Faulknerian", it is equally arguable that since the 1960s many of the most important writers — Italo Calvino, Milan Kundera, Salman Rushdie, Umberto Eco — have had to become "Latin American" novelists'.[19] This approach embraces a more global, less hierarchical model of literary analysis, for it seems to debunk the conviction that European literature is the norm to be copied and assimilated in the peripheries. Foremost among contemporary proponents of this transnational form of analysis is Franco Moretti, who in his programmatic 'Conjectures on World Literature' boldly defends an understanding of literature without reference to national spaces. Despite its postulation of a global dimension where national differences cease to have relevance for artistic creation, it could be argued that Moretti's model ultimately privileges the hegemonic designs of European literature. According to his literary geography, those writing from the periphery can access the world literary system only through a process of 'incorporation'. Speaking of the novel, Moretti claims that 'in cultures that belong to the periphery of the literary system (which means: almost all cultures, inside and outside Europe), the modern novel first arises not as an autonomous development but as a compromise between a Western formal influence (usually French or English) and local materials'.[20] It is as if the formal patterns manufactured in Europe, particularly France and England, were universally valid as representational devices, and historical specificities only had a bearing on the content, but not the form, of the literary text. From this perspective, one might wonder whether Borges was canonized as a modern literary master because his 'otherness' as a peripheral writer was acknowledged or simply because his fiction could be easily 'incorporated' into a literary system governed by metropolitan norms and forms. The same applies to the 'Latin Americanness' of Calvino or Eco. Wouldn't this reversal of unidirectional literary influences have more to do with the fact that Cortázar or García Márquez were perceived primarily as 'Joycean' and 'Faulknerian' and not as 'Latin American' writers? On close scrutiny, therefore, Moretti's and Martin's revisions of cultural hierarchies and old models of literary influence appear to be ruled by a persistent Eurocentric logic.

I propose that analysing the presence of Joycean features in Spanish American narrative can help us elucidate a different approach to artistic cosmopolitanism, one that is not organized around a single regulatory ideal (Western novelistic form), but rather stems from the local histories of what Moretti calls the 'periphery'. The cultural dialogue among marginal histories, among intersecting impulses to demarcate local experiences against 'universal' values and principles, has the potential to configure an ex-centric web of literary relations, a system of communicating vessels that crisscross as they circumnavigate privileged centres. Framed within this literary geography, the interrelation between Joyce and the *nueva novela* performs a radical questioning of 'literature' and its complicity with hegemonic power structures. In *Against Literature*, John Beverley has persuasively shown that the institutional value of literary discourse in Latin America derives from its colonial origins and its instrumentality for neocolonial projects of nation formation.[21] Without contesting the truth of this claim, I should like to argue that Spanish American 'Joycism' demystifies hegemonic notions of 'literature' not by turning to more 'authentic' or testimonial kinds of writing, but by subverting, recycling and, most importantly, reconceiving European literary forms and methods of representation — by approaching canonical works less as monolithic models to be revered, copied, or even rewritten with a local flavour, than as a gallery of mirrors which, when repositioned rightly, can reflect the luminous contours of an emancipated culture. Therefore, rather than maintaining that literature in the periphery arises from the encounter of Western form and local reality, I contend that local reality demands a transformation of Western form. In subsequent chapters, I will focus, for instance, on how Borges and Cortázar do not assimilate 'Joycean' formal methods such as parody and myth to represent their 'local reality' in new and unsuspected ways, or even to transcend the 'backwardness' of that reality. Their marginal status within the literary world system is not only registered at the level of content, thus leaving the universal validity of metropolitan form unquestioned; instead such marginality is signalled most forcefully and profoundly by showing that received forms are unable to fully represent local experiences unless they are refashioned, retooled, tampered with. Thus, parody for Borges interrupts rather than perpetuates the connection between an original and its copy. And myth for Cortázar is not a mechanism of structural control ensuring representation, but a dislocation of the assumptions that make representation possible at all. In addition, this subversive use of myth and parody doubles as a radical act of interpretation that by throwing into relief Joyce's own marginality challenges his status as a modernist icon. In fact, as I shall discuss, Borges's and Cortázar's unconventional deployment of form, their use of salient 'modernist' features to dismantle the possibility of 'universal aesthetic standards', involves an almost perfect reversal of what Larsen terms 'canonical decolonization'.

A perusal of recent criticism on contemporary Spanish American fiction reveals that the underpinnings of 'canonical decolonization' remain largely uncontested. To a large extent, Rodríguez Monegal's and Martin's assessments of Joyce's role in the development of the boom have informed the critical guidelines of the ongoing debate on 'Spanish American modernism'. Critics such as Raymond L. Williams and Donald L. Shaw agree that 'modernism' is a valid term to study the evolution of the region's fiction from the 1940s to the 1970s. In their opinion, the narrative techniques and philosophical attitudes that ripened during these years largely coincide with those of Anglo-American modernism. In a number of recent publications, Williams has observed that the 'rise of the Modernist novel' brought with it a renovation of the regionalist realism and naturalism that dominated Spanish American letters until the publication of Borges's *Ficciones* in 1944.[22] It is his conviction that the 'modernist' novels of Fuentes, Cortázar, García Márquez, Donoso and Lezama Lima fulfilled in the 1960s a 'desire to be modern' (a phrase he borrows from Octavio Paz) that had persisted among Spanish American intellectuals since the nineteenth century. 'In their desire to be modern', Williams explains, 'the Latin-American novelists of the 1940s and 1950s were well aware of the basic tenets of Modernism, and their understanding of the aesthetics of Modernism dramatically transformed Spanish-American fiction'.[23] The assimilation of the stylistic strategies of Anglo-American modernism afforded novelists such as Miguel Ángel Asturias, Agustín Yañez and Alejo Carpentier the possibility of finally becoming 'modern', thereby leaving behind the backwardness of provincial literature and completing a process of intellectual maturation that began in the nineteenth century with the achievement of political independence from Spain. Although texts such as *El Señor Presidente* (1946) and *Al filo del agua* (1947) still revolve around specific regional settings and circumstances, this critic contends that their use of modernist aesthetics invest them with 'universal interest' that transcends narrow nativist concerns.

Donald Shaw also believes that to study 'Spanish-American fiction in the context of Modernism/Postmodernism can be very beneficial'.[24] According to Shaw, Spanish American narrative acquired modernist characteristics as early as the late 1920s, with the 'dehumanized' and subjectivist novels and short stories of Eduardo Mallea, Felisberto Hernández and María Luisa Bombal, among others. The work of these authors marked the abandonment of regionalism and the 'beginnings of Modernism in fiction, which plainly led via Borges directly to the Boom'.[25] Like Rodríguez Monegal, Shaw consistently stresses the technical and linguistic continuity between Anglo-American modernism and the 'boom', arguing for the inclusion of Ernesto Sábato, Julio Cortázar and Carlos Fuentes within the canon of High Modernism. Shaw observes in this 'peripheral' manifestation of modernism the overcoming of 'local reality' and the successful assimilation of 'Western form' — to use Moretti's terms — by a select group of Spanish American writers, an assimilation that authorizes the use of categories culled from Western literary history to analyse their work.

A latent theoretical conviction underlying the use of the term 'modernism' to describe contemporary Spanish American narrative is that there is a transnational norm that should be met in order to reach aesthetic 'modernity'. Pascale Casanova's useful term, 'Greenwich Meridian of literature', can help us refine our understanding of this aesthetic-temporal principle:

> Just as the *fictive* line known as the prime meridian, arbitrarily chosen for the determination of longitude, contributes to the *real* organization of the world and makes possible the measure of distances and the location of positions on the surface of the earth, so what might be called the Greenwich meridian of literature makes it possible to estimate the relative aesthetic distance from the center of the world of letters of all those who belong to it.[26]

Studied from this point of view, literary history unfolds as a teleological sequence, relegating what is 'backwards' and 'local' to the past of what is 'modern' and 'universal'. Casanova argues that 'one may say that a work is contemporary; that it is more or less current (as opposed to being out of date — temporal metaphors abound in the language of criticism), depending on its proximity to the criteria of modernity'.[27] If modernist aesthetics, a set of art forms that emerged in Europe in the early twentieth century, is established as the standard to determine literary modernity in Spanish America, then to be modern is, to a large extent, to be European. This critical perspective implies that producing modernist works in the periphery demands overcoming a differential gap that is not only chronological, but also cultural. Spanish American 'modernism' 'catches up with' Western literature, and in doing so it confirms that the contemporaneity that it achieves depends on a self-transcending temporality which perpetually determines what kind of cultural phenomena qualify as 'modern'.

This conception of literary history is shaped by an understanding of modernity that derives from Kant and the Enlightenment. As is well known, Kantian modernity is a northern European philosophical concept that was nonetheless presented as a universal truth, as the endpoint of the path toward historical progress ploughed by an autonomous, 'emancipated' reason. 'Progress', 'universality', 'development' and 'rationality' are all ideas that emanated from Europe to constitute a normative discourse of universal proportions, a set of principles and values, or even an evolving force, as Hegel would put it, which societies worldwide had to embrace in their quest for 'self-knowledge'.[28] Hence, it should not surprise us that Spanish American artists and intellectuals have frequently perceived modernity and progress as elusive ends to struggle for. For instance, the Mexican essayist and poet Octavio Paz acknowledged in a variety of his writings that the promises of 'modernity' became the obsessive horizon of his poetic endeavours. In a passage that can be taken as paradigmatic of the Spanish American 'desire to be modern', Paz claims that the search for the present implies looking for the 'real reality' ('la realidad real'). This 'real reality' resides, for Spanish Americans, in 'el tiempo que vivían los otros, los ingleses, los franceses, los alemanes. El tiempo de Nueva York, París, Londres. Había que salir en su busca y traerlo a nuestras tierras' [the time of the others, of the English, the French, the German. The time of New York, Paris, London. We had to go out looking for it to bring it to our countries].[29] Paz adds that shortly after he became aware of this temporal gap between Spanish America and the First World, he started writing poetry as a quest for modernity, a gesture that parallels the repeated attempts of the Spanish American nations to modernize themselves. 'De ahí que a veces se hablase de "europeizar" a nuestros países: lo moderno estaba fuera y teníamos que importarlo' [Hence, sometimes we would speak about 'Europeanizing' our countries: the modern was outside and we had to import it].[30]

While the economic dependence of Spanish America is still a palpable reality that perpetuates an uneven relationship with the West, Paz argues that in the cultural terrain the gap with modernity has been narrowing incessantly ever since the legitimacy of enlightened thought was exposed and undermined by the horrors of two world wars. The collapse of Reason signalled the end of history as a narrative of progress and the advent of a temporal relativity that rejects the idea of a stable cultural centre: 'No hay centro y el tiempo ha perdido su antigua coherencia: este y oeste, mañana y ayer se confunden en cada uno de nosotros' [There is no centre and time has lost its old coherence: East and West, tomorrow and yesterday get confused in each of us].[31] This 'post-modern' lack of certainties fosters the conviction that the hierarchies that determine global cultural production have disappeared, and that we cannot really talk about 'artistic underdevelopment'.

In *La nueva novela hispanoamericana* (1969), Carlos Fuentes develops Paz's ideas on artistic creation, claiming that the crisis of European culture opened the doors of modernity to those who until then had been banished from it. Now 'universality' is fully available to the Spanish American writer, who no longer needs to remain loyal to parochial forms of writing. Fuentes writes:

> Los latinoamericanos — diría ampliando un acierto de Octavio Paz — son hoy contemporáneos de todos los hombres. Y pueden, contradictoria, justa y hasta trágicamente, ser universales escribiendo en el lenguaje de los hombres de Perú, Argentina o México. Porque, vencida la universalidad ficticia de ciertas razas, ciertas clases, ciertas banderas, ciertas naciones, el escritor y el hombre advierten su común *generación* de las estructuras universales del lenguaje.[32]

> [Latin American people — I would say elaborating on one of Octavio Paz's insights — are today contemporaneous with all men. And, contradictorily, justly, and even tragically, they can be universal writing in the language of the men of Peru, Argentina or Mexico, since once the fictitious universality of certain races, classes, flags and nations has been superseded, writers and men become aware of their common *generation* of the universal structures of language.]

The disappearance of stable centres of authority places the Spanish American writer within the same temporality as his European and North American counterparts, for they are all now engulfed by a new textual universality that transcends the racial, cultural and economic imbalances that structure the world otherwise. We are all contemporaneous and modern, Fuentes claims, because we are all philosophically ex-centric, our only common frame of reference being language.

From this perspective, the presence of Joycean techniques in the Spanish American novel would be testimony to the erasure of boundaries between the centre and the periphery within the realm of literature. It is no coincidence that Fuentes also proposed a theory of 'multi-vocal' textuality derived from Cervantes and Joyce that complements and supports his notion of contemporary literature as a polycentric phenomenon. In *Cervantes o la crítica de la lectura* (1976), Fuentes articulates a model of reading and writing that seems to be specifically tailored to the Spanish American new novel as he interpreted it in *La nueva novela*. In his view, Cervantes's *Quixote* undermines authoritative readings by presenting the protagonist as an individual whose personality disintegrates as soon as he becomes conscious of his dual and paradoxical role as both reader and fictional character. The enigmatic figure of Don Quixote makes the boundaries between fiction and reality porous to such an extent that the illusion of realism vanishes. Fuentes makes the poststructuralist claim that this porosity also dismantles monolithic interpretations, for the reader, like Don Quixote, is trapped in an inescapable web where he lacks ultimate mastery over the text. It should be obvious that this sort of reading practice is consistent with a conception of reality where obsolete certainties, values and principles have now given way to a linguistic universality where thinking, reading and writing are virtually indistinguishable.

Fuentes connects this 'multi-vocal' reading strategy with the unconventional style of Joyce's *Ulysses* and *Finnegans Wake*. He claims that the Irish writer ushered in the linguistic revolution from which the *nueva novela* stems: 'Joyce abre las puertas de la totalidad del lenguaje, de *los* lenguajes' [Joyce opens the doors of the totality of language, of *languages*].[33] The de-centring festival of languages and styles of Joyce's fiction rewrites the 'true discourse of the West' ('el verdadero discurso de Occidente'), a discourse that now becomes conscious of its artificiality and thrives on its contradictions. Due to the collapse of cultural certainties, the knowing subject of the Enlightenment becomes, like writing itself, fragmented, a phenomenon that Fuentes calls 'desyoización' ('de-I-fication'), an obvious pun on 'yo' and 'Joyce'. According to the Mexican writer, 'la crítica de la escritura en Joyce es una crítica de la escritura individual, de la escritura del yo [...] la novedad de la *Joyceización* es que inscribe la *desyoización*' [Joyce's critique of writing is a critique of individual writing, of the writing of the I [...] the novelty of *Joycification* is that it inscribes the *de-I-fication*].[34]

Fuentes's reading of Joyce closely parallels his characterization of the Spanish American novel in *La nueva novela*. Indeed, 'Joyce' emerges in this study as a cipher of the stylistic innovations of novelists such as Cortázar and Cabrera Infante. The flamboyant playfulness and deconstructive relativism that the Mexican novelist associates with *Ulysses* and *Finnegans Wake* cross national borders in an age of lost beliefs to shape the narrative of *Rayuela* or *Tres tristes tigres*. This 'linguistic universality' embodies a new kind of aesthetics directly related to crises and transformations of European history and society. As Fuentes's arguments suggest, the 'desyoización' of the new novel is coterminous with the familiar poststructuralist critique of Western metaphysics, a critique that opens up a two-way street whereby 'el escritor occidental sólo puede ser central reconociendo que hoy es excéntrico, y el escritor latinomericano reconociendo que su excentricidad es hoy central en un mundo sin ejes culturales' [the Western writer can only be central by realizing that nowadays he is eccentric, and the Latin American writer can attain such centrality by realizing that his eccentricity is nowadays central in a world that lacks cultural axes].[35] This celebration of the margins stands as a powerful theoretical justification for abandoning cultural hierarchies and embracing a literary historiography that erases self-sufficient national barriers. As the Mexican novelist has reiterated in *Geografía de la novela* (1993),

> Al antiguo eurocentrismo se ha impuesto un policentrismo que, si seguimos en su lógica la crítica posmodernista de Lyotard, debe conducirnos a una 'activación de las diferencias' como condición común de la humanidad sólo central porque es excéntrica, o sólo excéntrica porque tal es la situación real de lo universal concreto, sobre todo si se manifiesta mediante la aportación de lo diverso que es la imaginación literaria. La 'literatura mundial' de Goethe cobra al fin su sentido recto: es la literatura de la diferencia, la narración de la diversidad, pero confluyendo, sólo así, en un mundo único, la superpotencia mundo, para decirlo con un concepto que conviene a la época después de la guerra fría.[36]

> [The old Eurocentrism has been superseded by a polycentrism which, following the logic of Lyotard's postmodern critique, should take us to an 'activation of differences' as the common condition of humanity, central only because it is eccentric, or eccentric only because such is the real condition of the concrete universal, particularly if it manifests itself through the diversity of the literary imagination. Goethe's 'world literature' has finally found its correct meaning: it is the literature of difference, the narration of diversity, but converging in one world, the world superpower, to use a concept that befits a post-Cold War era.]

This approach to literary change successfully smoothes over the cultural unevenness between the metropolitan centre and its periphery. Certainly, Fuentes's words resonate with Martin's contention that the assimilation of Joycean aesthetics by Spanish American novelists is conclusive evidence that 'Latin America really is a part of Western civilization'.[37] However, Fuentes's enthusiastic celebration of marginality overlooks the underlying fact that postmodern and poststructuralist cultural manifestations still gravitate around Europe. As Robert Young clearly states, poststructuralism 'does not offer a *critique* by positioning itself outside "the West", but rather uses its own alterity and duplicity in order to effect its deconstruction'.[38] Ernesto Laclau has made a similar point by arguing that 'Postmodernity does not imply a *change* in the values of Enlightenment modernity but rather a *weakening* of their absolutist character'.[39] In other words, the lack of hegemonic literary axes that Fuentes describes is the philosophical consequence of an *internal* critique of

European modernity, and so it should be conceived of as a phase (perhaps a terminal one) of such modernity.

Given that this intellectual genealogy connects contemporary Spanish American narrative with Joyce and modernity in its 'postmodern' or 'poststructuralist' phase, it should not be surprising that 'Joycean' writers such as Cortázar and Cabrera Infante have been frequently censured for not being 'Spanish American' enough. In the 1970s, Alejo Carpentier wrote in *Ecue-Yamba-Ó* that the dilemma that plagued the Spanish American intellectual in those days was how to be a 'nationalist', yet also 'avant-garde', given that embracing technical virtuosity and experimentation was perceived by many as being at odds with a sincere engagement with local reality.[40] The literary critic Manuel Pedro González illustrates this type of critique with his polemical views on the new narrative. In a series of articles published during the 1960s, González condemned the experimental techniques of Joyce's *Ulysses* as a damaging influence on the 'boom' novelists, who by welcoming such influence chose to neglect the immediate reality of the American continent and favour the cultural fashions of the First World.[41] He vehemently contended that the boom employed formal methods that are largely inadequate to capture autochthonous elements, a task for which the regionalist novel remains unsurpassed. This opposition between local concerns and modernist aesthetics has also been sustained by some of the most prominent members of the boom themselves. For instance, José Donoso underlined in his *Historia personal del Boom* the close ties between Anglo-American modernism and the new novel while rejecting the cultural backwardness of regionalist realism. Fuentes himself formulated in unambiguous terms the opposition between regionalism and cosmopolitanism. According to the Mexican novelist, the Spanish American writer is confronted with two options: on the one hand, he could aspire to the 'universality' associated with the styles and themes of the European avant-garde movements; on the other hand, he could remain a 'national writer' doomed to lag behind metropolitan innovations.[42]

Some critics have recently elaborated on González's accusations against the boom, highlighting the limitations of Fuentes's repudiation of 'primitive' realism. According to Doris Sommer, the 'national romance' of the nineteenth century might have been derivative in aesthetic terms, but it had enormous leverage to shape the politics of the emerging Spanish American republics. The illusion of progress towards economic and cultural modernization that this type of fiction conjured up died out after World War II, when the mirage of financial well-being of the inter-war period gave way to chronic underdevelopment in South America. Sommer writes that at this point 'patriotic storylines wilted into the vicious circles that Carlos Fuentes found typical for the new novelists'.[43] In Fuentes's words: 'ni el anhelo ni la pluma del escritor producen por sí mismos la revolución y el intelectual queda situado entre una historia que rechaza y una historia que desea' [neither the hopes nor the pen of the writer can bring about the revolution, so the intellectual remains caught between a history he rejects and a history he desires].[44] The linguistic euphoria that characterizes the new novel may then be a mask that hides a pessimistic abandonment of the intellectual's capacity to change society and history. Banished to a purely textual realm like Don Quixote, the boom novelist makes the mark of the 'Greenwich Meridian of literature', but only after sacrificing the potential of cultural production to infiltrate the world of politics. It seems, then, that the renovation of literary forms threw out the baby of social criticism with the bath water of rudimentary realism. The sheer experimentalism of the 'modernist' Spanish American novel involves the fulfilment of 'universalism', or, to put it differently, of what Paz and Williams identified as the persistent Spanish American 'desire to be modern'. But as Sommer suggests, stylistic sophistication often severs the ties between the text and the world, between literary production and cultural specificity, abdicating the capacity of art to shape society. From this point of view, the 'Joycean' traits of the *nueva novela* can only be explained as a centrifugal force that pulls the Spanish American text away from the particularities of its place of origin and propels it into the depoliticized realm of transnational modernism and postmodernism.

Peruvian novelist José María Arguedas was another outspoken voice that stressed the connection between the 'Joycean' pyrotechnics of the new novelists, on the one hand, and a lack of engagement with the immediacy of social reality, on the other. In the diary entries included at the beginning of *El zorro de arriba y el zorro de abajo* (1971), Arguedas dispels any sense of affinity between his writing and literary modernism, for he claims that as an 'escritor de provincias' [a provincial writer] he can understand Shakespeare, Rimbaud, Poe and Quevedo, 'pero no el *Ulises*' [but not *Ulysses*].[45] Although Arguedas's fiction, notably *El zorro de arriba y el zorro de abajo*, displays 'modernist' formal methods (temporal fragmentation, episodic plot, lack of an omniscient narrator), he refuses to embrace them as the manifestation of an aesthetic 'universality' that muddies the distinction between regionalist writers and their metropolitan counterparts. Instead these methods are deployed to render the sense of uprootedness and frustration experienced by Peru's indigenous communities after the arrival of industrial modernization. In the diary section that opens *El zorro*, Arguedas describes the challenges of finding an appropriate literary form to express the feeling of alienation that capitalist modernity brought to Chimbote, the coastal Peruvian town where the action in the novel takes place. Within this context, he considers his relationship to other Latin American novelists, particularly those of the boom. Even though Arguedas's innovative techniques might coincide to some degree with those of Cortázar or Fuentes, he is quick to make a sharp distinction between the cosmopolitan alliances of these authors and his own provincial perspective. Arguedas writes:

> Este Cortázar que aguijonea con su 'genialidad', con sus solemnes convicciones de que mejor se entiende la esencia de lo nacional desde las altas esferas de lo supranacional. Como si yo, criado entre la gente de don Felipe Maywa, metido en el *oqllo* mismo de los indios durante algunos años de infancia para luego volver a la esfera 'superindia' de donde había 'descendido' entre los quechuas, dijera que mejor, mucho más esencialmente interpreto el espíritu, el apetito de don Felipe, que el propio don Felipe.[46]

> [This Cortázar goads us with his 'geniality', with his solemn conviction that the essence of the national is better understood from the high spheres of the supranational. This is as if I, raised among the people of don Felipe Maywa, immersed into the very *oqllo* of the Indians for a few years during my infancy

to then come back to the 'superindian' sphere from which I had 'descended' among the quechuas, were to claim that I can interpret the spirit of don Felipe better, more essentially, than don Felipe himself.]

This quote is part of Arguedas's reply to an open letter (originally published in *Casa de las Américas* in 1967 and later reprinted as 'Acerca de la situación del intelectual latinoamericano' in *Último Round*) that Cortázar had sent to the Cuban critic Roberto Fernández Retamar. The letter addresses the dichotomy between provincialism and cosmopolitanism to suggest that regionalist literature and the 'universal' aesthetics of the new novel are different albeit complementary responses to the same historical demands. The Argentine writer's main point is that neither his situation as an exile nor the experimental aspects of his fiction signify an aloofness to what it means to be a Spanish American intellectual. Cortázar maintains that it is precisely from France that he became keenly conscious of his Spanish American condition, adding that he manages to articulate his 'Argentinness' by injecting into the foreign culture he has absorbed 'los jugos y la voz de su tierra' [the juices and the voice of his land].[47] He goes on to negotiate his intellectual position with regard to the seemingly opposing poles of 'universalism' and 'nationalism'. On the one hand, he seems to respond to Fuentes and Paz by claiming that apolitical and ahistorical universalisms are comfortable ways to avoid 'las responsabilidades inmediatas y concretas' [concrete and immediate responsibilities].[48] On the other hand, the novelist is also careful to distance himself from what he calls 'los nacionalistas de escarapela y banderita' [the flag-and-badge nationalists],[49] whom he connects to the regionalist literary tradition epitomized by Rómulo Gallegos's *Doña Bárbara*. In his view, a nationalist attitude that refuses to embrace a global perspective can result in a defence of ethnic purity very much like Arguedas's in the diary entries of *El zorro*. Therefore, Cortázar navigates between the extremes of the local and the global and convincingly argues for an intellectual attitude that connects literary experimentalism and social compromise.

It was precisely Fernández Retamar, the addressee of Cortázar's letter, who first explored the social dimension of the Argentine writer's work during a colloquium on *Rayuela* held in Havana shortly after the publication of the novel. Fernández Retamar states that despite the fact that *Rayuela* was completed in Paris, the novel is one of the most important books written *in* America ('uno de los libros más importantes escritos en América').[50] While he is cautious enough not to interpret Cortázar's text as a general statement concerning the condition of the Spanish American intellectual, he highlights the novel's relation to the culture and society of the region. The Cuban critic contends that far from being the plight of a disengaged émigré, the experiences of the protagonist, Horacio Oliveira, embody those of 'un pensador de un país latinoamericano frente al problema de la cultura. Un intelectual que vive del lado de allá y del lado de acá. Es decir, que vive en París, y que vive después otra vez en el Río de la Plata' [a thinker from a Latin American country facing the problem of culture. An intellectual who lives on this side and on that side — that is, who lives in Paris and then returns to the River Plate again].[51]

Fernández Retamar goes on to establish a connection between *Rayuela* and Joyce's *Ulysses*. But instead of grounding his comparison on the verbal audacity and formal innovations shared by both texts, he stresses the parallels between the society and history of Ireland and Spanish America as reflected in the novels. Oliveira's predicament as a Spanish American intellectual resonates with Stephen Dedalus's troubled relationship with Ireland at the turn of the twentieth century. Fernández Retamar writes: 'En cierta forma ese ahogo, esa opacidad de la sociedad argentina actual, y de casi todas las sociedades de la América Latina, se expresan en Oliveira en forma similar a aquel ahogo de la sociedad irlandesa que se manifiesta en Esteban' [In a way, the stifling opacity of contemporary Argentine society (and of almost all societies in Latin America) is expressed by Oliveira in a way that recalls the oppression of Irish society experienced by Stephen].[52] Furthermore, this critic argues against taking *Ulysses* as the 'model' for *Rayuela* as much as he discourages interpreting Joyce's novel as a modern rewriting of Homer's *Odyssey*. According to him, a literary work develops specific ties with concrete historical situations, ties which disrupt transnational and transhistorical models of literary analysis based on 'models' and 'imitations', on 'originals' and 'replicas'.[53]

Fernández Retamar's remarks encourage a comparative reading of Cortázar's *Rayuela* and Joyce's *Ulysses* that departs from Fuentes's linguistic ahistoricism, but also from Arguedas's recalcitrant nativism. Whereas Fuentes perceived in Joyce and the new novel facets of the same 'linguistic universalism', the Cuban critic and poet defends a historicized interpretation of the Joycean features of *Rayuela*. Instead of postulating a transatlantic aesthetics that disregards local conditions, the Cuban thinker emphasizes that a comparison between Cortázar and Joyce should be predicated primarily on the similarities and correspondences between the specific social contexts that determined their writing. This perspective adds an historical dimension to Fuentes's poststructuralist approach, while its transcontinental scope moves beyond the constraints of Arguedas's ethnic exclusivism. Interpreted in this way, the 'contact zone' between Joyce and Cortázar resists rather than favours the erasure of local particularities. Therefore, the critical implications of Fuentes's claim that *Rayuela* is to Spanish prose what *Ulysses* is to English prose[54] are quite different from those of Fernández Retamar's almost identical contention that *Rayuela* 'es para nosotros los latinoamericanos tan importante como el *Ulysses* para los escritores de lengua inglesa' [is for us Latin Americans as important as *Ulysses* for the English-speaking writers'.[55]

In *Para una teoría de la literatura hispanoamericana*, Fernández Retamar claims that analysing and classifying Spanish American literature with the help of theories and concepts originally tailored to the metropolitan literatures ('las literaturas metropolitanas') results in academic colonialism.[56] In his well-known essay, 'Calibán', he illustrates this entrenched bias toward European models with Fuentes's *La nueva novela hispanoamericana*, which he describes as the product of a typically colonial attitude ('una típica actitud colonial'), arguing that the Mexican author applies to the new narrative 'esquemas derivados de otras literaturas (de países capitalistas), reducidas hoy a especulaciones lingüísticas' [schemes derived from other literatures (from capitalist countries), reduced nowadays to linguistic speculations].[57] Fernández Retamar explains that this type of literary colonialism, a 'secuela del colonialismo político y económico' [sequel of political and economic colonialism], stems from the often uncontested belief that metropolitan ideas have universal validity.[58] But this critique of cultural dependence does not involve an isolationist attitude. This critic qualifies his ideas about literary and academic colonialism by stating that he does not advocate 'partir absolutamente de cero e ignorar los vínculos que conservamos con la llamada tradición occidental, que es *también* nuestra tradición, pero en relación con la cual debemos señalar nuestras diferencias específicas' [starting radically from scratch and ignoring the ties with the so-called Western tradition, which is *also* our tradition, but in relation to which we should point out our specific differences].[59]

It is from Fernández Retamar's anti-colonial perspective that I want to rethink Joyce's impact on Spanish American narrative. My argument will draw its strength primarily from careful analyses of form and structure, thus showing how close attention to literary style and technique should not necessarily support ahistorical approaches to literature. The following chapters also intend to add a transatlantic dimension to the ongoing 'recolonization' of Joyce as an Irish writer. As Vincent Cheng has pointedly remarked, Joyce has been 'canonized by an Academy that has chosen to construct a sanitized "Joyce" whose contributions are now to be measured only by the standards of canonical High Modernism'.[60] Likewise, Emer Nolan raises an argument that recalls Fernández Retamar's critique of academic colonialism as she claims that 'the major trends in Joyce criticism have occluded the particularity of Irish historical experience as it determines and is reflected in his fiction'.[61] If we consider Joyce's experimental techniques as a reflection of 'Irish historical experience', then the *formal* links between his fiction and Spanish American narrative might not simply signal a transcultural manifestation of modernism. Therefore, the conversation between Joyce and Cortázar, for instance, might be interpreted as the result of circumnavigating the 'Greenwich Meridian of literature'. To use Elleke Boehmer's words about the interaction between anti-colonial nationalisms at the turn of the twentieth century, the 'contact zone' of literary exchange between these authors, which has been 'conventionally located between the European colonial centre and its periphery will instead be positioned *between* peripheries'.[62]

As Robin Fiddian has observed in an important and stimulating article that unfortunately has not inspired much scholarship, an 'essential element in the collective Spanish-American response to Joyce and, by implication, a key factor in the process of *Joyceización*, has been recognition of Joyce's status as a paradigm of cultural excentricity'. Fiddian adds that 'excentricity' and 'peripherality' are the consequences of colonialism, 'and in this respect Spanish-American intellectuals have not failed to note the similarities between their experience and that of Joyce and his fellow countrymen'.[63] However, as we have noted above, the meaning of 'excentricity' and 'peripherality' can fluctuate, for these terms certainly mean different things for Paz and Fernández Retamar, for example. While Fiddian does not elaborate on what he understands by 'peripherality', César A. Salgado has been more specific in his valuable comparative study of José Lezama Lima and James Joyce, *From Modernism to Neobaroque*. He correctly points out that Lezama's indebtedness to Joyce should not be seen as creative dependence, but as an act of recognition: 'it is the margin seeing the margin, the colonized seeing the colonized, the islander the islander'. Salgado echoes Paz's and Fuentes's theories of modernity and cultural change when he affirms that the literary intersection between Joyce and Lezama is the result of the 'crisis of European centralism after the First World War' and the subsequent dislocation of 'the hierarchy of centre and periphery, high and low, metropolis and margin'. Therefore, this scholar stretches the boundaries of 'High Modernism', as it were, converting it into a category wide enough to include Ireland and Cuba, Europe and the Tropics, Joyce and Lezama. 'Modernism', he maintains, 'becomes a global phenomenon, a poetic exercised in areas politically and geographically remote'.[64]

By arguing that 'the crisis of European centralism' unravelled the dissemination of modernism across the globe, Salgado suggests that it is such centralism and its internal transformations, contractions and expansions that determine and control the shape and development of global cultural geographies. From this standpoint, it is only when European modernity becomes self-conscious and self-questioning about its epistemological foundations that the formerly excluded 'other' is finally incorporated as a supplement. As Carlos J. Alonso has elegantly remarked, 'if at the banquet of modernity [Spanish Americans] were always a second-class invitee, history finally rewarded [them] when sveltness became the apparent universal fashion'.[65] Indeed, that the 'Greenwich Meridian of literature' is no longer located in Paris, London, or New York does not mean that it has ceased to be regulated by the principle of aesthetic modernity, which, however disjointed, dismembered and fragmented it might be in its postmodern guise, still claims for itself universal validity — and still is, then, very much a 'universal fashion'. Thus, expanding the limits of labels such as 'modernism' or 'postmodernism' to encompass Joyce as well as Cortázar and Lezama Lima, for instance, amounts to interpreting their work as a symptom of the booms and busts of modernity — that is, as part of an artistic negotiation of what should be done at a challenging moment of cultural crisis, and not as an effort to coax into existence what Lezama evoked with typical plasticity as 'los retablos verbales que nos dan rebrillo y liberación de la casa metropolitana' [the verbal altarpieces that give us distinct radiancy and liberate us from the metropolitan house].[66] To put it differently, transforming modernism into a common ground of comparison, into a unified poetics that manifests itself globally, makes it difficult to articulate 'particular positions in the world that are not assimilable to a single picture of the world'.[67]

In reconsidering the links between Joyce and Spanish American narrative, I want to draw attention to those 'particular positions' and their transnational contacts 'in the peripheries', a cultural terrain where literary change remains resilient to explanatory models imposed from above — resilient, that is, 'to a single picture of the world'. A literary space where centres and peripheries are interchangeable fails to account for the links between cultural displacement and literary innovation — links that Borges underlined in his essay, 'El escritor argentino y la tradición'. Here he claims that the creativity of South American writers owes much to their 'irreverence' towards the Western culture, an attitude that they share with the Jews and the Irish. According to the Argentine fabulist, the sense of eccentricity of

South American, Irish and Jewish authors allows them to handle 'todos los temas europeos, manejarlos sin supersticiones, con una irreverencia que puede tener, y ya tiene, consecuencias afortunadas' [all European themes, handle them without superstitions, with an irreverence that could have (and already does have) fortunate consequences].[68] It is plausible to infer from these lines that Borges himself did not consider his work to be a part of the mainstream of the Western tradition. Reaching conclusions and providing insights that could be easily applied to his own writing, Borges establishes strong connections between literary innovation and local reality while suggesting a network of peripheral relations (among the South Americans, the Irish, the Jews) that exceeds the unfolding narrative of European literary history. Borges's essay mentions Jonathan Swift, George Berkeley and George Bernard Shaw, Irish writers who, like 'the Argentines, like South Americans in general', pushed European culture in unforeseen directions, creating works that remain hard to classify with standard critical concepts and categories. To this list Borges could have added the name of James Joyce, who in this context would cease to be revered as a canonical 'First World writer' and a modernist 'master' to become an unruly innovator, a mutinous rebel whose riotous style transformed the conventions of traditional writing beyond recognition. Indeed, a comparative approach that departs from an awareness of this shared 'irreverence' among peripheral literary traditions (particularly the Irish and the Spanish American traditions) should call into question the contention that the presence of Joycean aesthetics in Spanish America is proof that 'Latin America really is a part of Western civilization and that its cultural identity was of such a nature as to provide both a replication of the Joycean trajectory and optimum conditions for its assimilation'.[69] While there is undoubtedly some truth in this statement, to support its validity without any qualifications comes short of explaining the relevance of cultural eccentricity for the production, reception and classification of innovative literary interventions.

Enrique Dussel's revision of the concept of 'modernity' can help us hone our understanding of Borges's 'irreverence' as a productive site of cultural crossing between local and global attachments — a site that can allow us to rearrange transnational literary relations beyond the regulatory authority of the Western canon and the 'Greenwich Meridian of literature'. Dussel argues that European modernity resulted from the constitution of a periphery and not from the coming of age or 'emancipation of Man' postulated by Kant. In Dussel's compelling words,

> Modernity is for many (for Jürgen Habermas or Charles Taylor, for example), an essentially or exclusively European phenomenon, but one constituted in a dialectical relation with a non-European alterity that is its ultimate content. Modernity appears when Europe affirms itself as the 'center' of a World history that it inaugurates; the periphery that surrounds this center is consequently part of its self-definition. The occlusion of this periphery [...] leads the major contemporary thinkers of the 'center' into a Eurocentric fallacy in their understanding of modernity. If their understanding of the genealogy of modernity is thus partial and provincial, their attempts at a critique or defense of it are likewise unilateral and, in part, false.[70]

I contend that by reading the intersection of Joyce and contemporary Spanish American fiction from the perspective afforded by modernity's 'occluded periphery'

— a periphery that Borges recognized as an ex-centric literary space of both transgression and innovation — one could expose the limits of modernism as a transnational category of analysis. So, if we frame Joyce and the new novelists within modernism's internal revision of modernity, their work participates 'in this revision regardless of national context';[71] but if we locate them on the edges of modernity, in a space of radical alterity, we will highlight the positionality of their writing, thereby perceiving the dissonant noise of those who master an acquired speech and transform a culture infused with memories of domination and oppression. Developing Fernández Retamar's insight into the connections between *Rayuela* and *Ulysses*, as well as Borges's opinions about the shared irreverence of the South Americans and the Irish, I will read the formal and stylistic analogies, parallelisms and contacts between Joyce and the new narrative as an aesthetic encounter that resists, exceeds and transcends the limits of literary modernity, of its canonical forms and authoritative taxonomies.[72] This act of interpretation means thinking beyond the stages of modernity as the only standard of artistic development and embracing instead, as Joe Cleary has suggested regarding Irish cultural production, 'a less linear and more global and conjunctural mode of analysis' that remains attentive to the local transformations of 'wider global processes' and clears the critical ground for understanding the cultural interaction, exchange and borrowing among 'coeval' post-colonial sites.[73]

One important way in which the first decades of the twentieth century in Ireland — the period when Joyce wrote *A Portrait of the Artist as a Young Man* and *Ulysses* — and the 1940s, 1950s and 1960s in Spanish America — the decades that witnessed the gestation and flourishing of the Spanish American new narrative — can be seen as 'coeval' is by concentrating on the anti-colonial struggles that characterized both historical moments. These changes may be seen as part of a wider attempt to subvert the foundations of the modern world system, ruled by the economic, political and cultural designs of Europe since the sixteenth century, when England and Spain incorporated Ireland and Spanish America (or what was then called the 'Occidental Indies') as their periphery.[74] The years during which Joyce composed *Ulysses*, 1914–22, witnessed the rapid unfolding of a series of crucial political and cultural events that ended centuries of British colonial control over Ireland. The formation of the paramilitary army of the Irish Volunteers and the turbulent Home Rule negotiations at Westminster eventually boiled over into the Easter Rising of 1916 against British rule in Dublin. The utopian longings unleashed by this momentous military uprising resulted in a War of Independence followed by a Civil War, and culminated in the long-awaited Anglo-Irish Treaty of 1922, which granted political autonomy to twenty-six of the thirty-two Irish counties. The observation that *Ulysses* was published in Paris a month before the Treaty was signed in London might be ignored as irrelevant, or it might trigger a deep reflection on the possible connections between the revolutionary aesthetics of Joyce's novel and the contemporary events that hoped to dismantle the colonial structures of Ireland. Thus, the daring techniques and linguistic contortions of *Ulysses* can be regarded as a strategy to grapple with a rapidly changing cultural landscape committed to overthrowing imperial structures of power and culture and creating decolonized social, political and cultural models. If this second reading of *Ulysses* is seriously considered, then the novel marks, as Edna Duffy has put it, 'the moment at which the formal bravura of the Eurocentric high modernism is redeployed so that a postcolonial literary praxis can be ushered onto the stage of a new and varied geo-literature'.[75]

I will show that, to a large degree, this is the *Ulysses* that was read and rewritten in Spanish America from the 1940s, in Borges's epigrammatic short stories, through the 1970s, in Fernando del Paso's novels. As happened between 1914 and 1922 in Ireland, the 1940s, 1950s and 1960s in Spanish America witnessed radical cultural and political transformations that called into question the universal legitimacy of European knowledge. While the most visible of these transformations gravitated around the Cuban Revolution, the watershed political event of the twentieth century in Latin America, there emerged around these years a whole constellation of other philosophical proposals that challenged the cultural dependency of Spanish America on metropolitan cultural models. 'Dependency Theory', 'Liberation Theology' (a doctrine that, incidentally, elicited sympathetic responses among progressive sectors of the Irish Church), and Mexican philosopher Leopoldo Zea's call for an 'emancipation' of the Spanish American mind were all prominent theories that in the 1960s set out to shift the global geography of knowledge production, boldly claiming that philosophical thought could also stem from the occluded peripheries of the modern world system, and not exclusively from a disembodied and universal 'mind' that ultimately represents the imperial designs of the Western subject.[76] These philosophical interventions were in fact part of a larger framework of decolonization that swept across the Third World during the Cold War years and crystallized in the writings of Frantz Fanon, Aimé Césaire and Léopold Sédar Senghor. It was also during these years that the reception of Joyce's writing peaked in cultural journals and magazines in Spanish America and his aesthetics began to make its presence felt on the pages of the 'boom' novels.

Rather than isolating aesthetics from politics, Chapter 1 analyses the impact of these decolonizing formations on Spanish American literature and culture, concentrating on the critical reception of Joyce's work within this context. I identify two basic trends of Joyce criticism in Spanish America during the years of gestation and ripening of the new novel: one of them relies heavily on the canonical, high-modernist Joyce, whose style and formal techniques elevate him above his Irish origins and locate him within a 'universal' aesthetic sphere; the other reads Joyce as a decolonizing artist in polemical dialogue with hegemonic cultural and philosophical paradigms. Indeed, most Spanish American critics writing about Joyce during the formative years of the 'boom' echoed ideas from the Anglo-American academy and described Joyce's work as a cosmopolitan and modernizing aesthetic force. I will discuss how this trend of Joycean scholarship developed into a more general academic framework that characterized the Spanish-American *nueva novela* as a 'modernist' phenomenon. I will illustrate these critical views by focusing on the articles about Joyce published in the prominent Buenos Aires journal, *Sur*, between the mid-1940s and the 1960s. I conclude this chapter by contrasting the emphasis on Joyce's formalism found in these articles with a different, more subdued, less visible critical trend, one that explored the links between the formal experimentation of the Irishman's writing and his experience of cultural displacement. This trend, exemplified by Arturo Uslar Pietri and other critics publishing in *Cuadernos Americanos*, encourages us to re-examine the suitability of the term 'modernism' to refer to the 'boom' and to frame the transatlantic dialogue between Joyce and the Spanish American novel.

Chapter 2 focuses on selected short stories from Jorge Luis Borges's *Ficciones* (1944) and *El Aleph* (1949), while Chapter 3 explores Julio Cortázar's *Rayuela* (1963), given that these two authors have been consistently singled out as the main precursor and the key figure of the new novel, respectively. Borges played a formative role for the 'boom', mainly due to his iconoclastic use of the Western literary tradition. The revolutionary force of his fiction resides in its capacity to assemble an eclectic yet unsubordinated style through quotations and parodies of European texts. In Chapter 2, I concentrate on how Borges's use of parody and his critical treatment of Joyce's *Ulysses* intersect in his essays and short stories to suggest a conception of literary cosmopolitanism that engages critically with prevailing models of national and global culture. Borges's encyclopaedic range of literary reference has been frequently summoned as proof that his work is better understood as forming part of a canon of universal literature. However, when one contrasts his use of parody with T. S. Eliot's modernist poetics and criticism, Borges emerges as an author who, despite the allusive richness of his prose, consistently manages to infuse the text with his situatedness, with his sense of place.

In Chapter 3, I turn to Julio Cortázar's *Rayuela*, the centrepiece of the 'boom' and, according to Gerald Martin, the culmination of 'Joycism' in Spanish America. I read *Rayuela* as a text that stages an anti-colonial critique of modernism through its nuanced treatment of myth. I begin by showing the central position that Joyce's narrative occupied within Cortázar's aesthetic project and go on to suggest possible alternatives to modernism as the common category uniting both authors. I argue that whereas the use of myth as a structural device has been customarily regarded as a basic feature of literary modernism (following Eliot's famous 1923 review, '*Ulysses*, Order and Myth'), myth in *Rayuela*, particularly the Ulyssean myth of homecoming, is deployed not to give 'a shape and a significance to the immense panorama of futility and anarchy' of contemporary Western culture (as Eliot claimed), but to articulate what Enrique Dussel has called an 'exteriority' from the dialectics between self and other, reason and myth, culture and nature that underpins the philosophical discourse of modernity. Cortázar interrupts this dialectic through the denial of otherness associated with the cognitive phenomenon that W. E. B. Du Bois labelled 'double consciousness'. The divided psyche of the novel's protagonist (an Argentine exile in Paris) and the literary and philosophical ideas of the writer Morelli (arguably Cortázar's *alter ego*) dislocate established models (or 'myths') of representation, temporality and subjectivity, thus opening up a 'counter-mythical' revolutionary dimension that *Rayuela* shares with *Ulysses*.

In the final chapter, I interrogate the notions of 'aesthetic disinterestedness' and 'autonomy' that modernist discourse inherited from Kant — that is, the conviction that art is not tethered to individual appetites or particular experiences and can therefore soar above the material world to 'turn back upon itself' and focus solely on 'its own creation and composition', to paraphrase Beebe's definition of literary modernism. I argue that the fiction of major Spanish American 'Joycean' novelists engage in a thorough critique of the 'autonomy' and 'universality' of aesthetic formalism by showing its inability to abstract away 'local interests' and attachments. Detailed analyses of Leopoldo Marechal's *Adán Buenosayres*, José Lezama Lima's *Paradiso*, Guillermo Cabrera Infante's *Tres tristes tigres* and Fernando del Paso's *Palinuro de México* expand my arguments of Chapters 2 and 3 to examine how their deployment of 'Joycean' form subverts Kantian disinterestedness (mainly through attention to bodily sensations) while articulating cultural particularity.

As so often, the intelligence of Borges's texts affords a lucid way to both summarize and further clarify literary arguments. His famous short story, 'Pierre Menard, autor del *Quijote*', demonstrates that the way we historicize *Don Quijote* can deeply affect our interpretation of the novel: the text of Menard and that of Cervantes are 'verbally identical', but the first one, written by a twentieth-century French author is 'almost infinitely richer', since it involves an act of literary, historical and linguistic reconstruction that is absent from Cervantes's early modern prose. A similar conclusion might apply to our concerns here, for our 'understanding of the genealogy of modernity' can alter our interpretation of the intricate interaction between Joyce and Spanish America's new narrative. If our understanding is 'partial and provincial', as Dussel puts it, we would be inclined to perceive in those ties a transnational manifestation of literary modernism; that is, we would see them as proof that Spanish American letters have finally attained a legitimate place within a global literary canon after completing the long and arduous journey that leads from regional literary attachments to the assimilation of the sophisticated techniques of a 'First World' writer as prominent as Joyce. But if our comparative analysis takes full account of the creative potential of modernity's 'non-European alterity', to cite Dussel again, we could then interpret the literary dialogue that occupies us here as taking place in the underside of the Western canon, in its long-silenced periphery, which thus becomes a site of uncharted crossings where literary innovation arises from a daring 'irreverence' toward metropolitan literary models. It is this second reading that I will explore in the subsequent chapters.

Notes to the Introduction

1. Julio Cortázar, *Cartas*, ed. by Aurora Bernárdez, 3 vols (Buenos Aires: Alfaguara, 2000), I, 224. He writes that he spent 'unas vacaciones bastante abúlicas, tomando sol y Coca-Cola (bebida infecta) y leyendo el *Ulysses*'.
2. Emir Rodríguez Monegal, *El boom de la novela latinoamericana* (Caracas: Tiempo Nuevo, 1972), p. 89.
3. Maurice Beebe, '*Ulysses* and the Age of Modernism', *James Joyce Quarterly*, 10, 1 (1972), 172–88 (p. 175).
4. Morton Levitt, *Modernist Survivors* (Columbus: Ohio State University Press, 1987), p. 182.
5. Ibid., p. 184.
6. James Joyce, *A Portrait of the Artist as a Young Man*, ed. by Chester G. Anderson (New York: Penguin, 1968), p. 251.
7. Whether Spanish America and Ireland should be considered postcolonial sites has triggered heated theoretical debates in recent years. This controversy largely derives from the discontinuities and asymmetries between the historical situation of these two geopolitical areas,

on the one hand, and those that have been the traditional object of analysis of postcolonial studies, on the other. It has become a virtually uncontested critical assumption that postcolonial studies originated in the late 1970s and early 1980s, following the publication of Edward Said's influential *Orientalism* (New York: Pantheon Books, 1978). As it developed, this new field of critical inquiry focused on the Asian and African ex-colonies of the former British Empire, areas whose socio-political structures differed greatly from those of Ireland and Spanish America. Whereas in countries such as India the language and culture of the colonizer remained within the province of bureaucratic administration, in Ireland and Latin America they permeated all layers of society. Other differences stem from the duration of colonial rule and the timing and means of decolonization. See Stephen Howe, *Ireland and Empire: Colonial Legacies in Irish History and Culture* (Oxford: Oxford University Press, 2000); and Liam Kennedy, *Colonialism, Religion and Nationalism in Ireland* (Belfast: Institute of Irish Studies, Queen's University of Belfast, 1996) for 'revisionist' arguments against a postcolonial conception of Ireland. For arguments for the colonial model as a frame that aptly captures the Irish–British relations over the centuries see Declan Kiberd, *Inventing Ireland* (Cambridge, MA Harvard University Press, 1996); Luke Gibbons, *Transformations in Irish Culture* (Cork: Cork University Press, 1996); David Lloyd, *Anomalous States: Irish Writing and the Postcolonial Moment* (Durham, NC: Duke University Press, 1993) and *Ireland after History* (Notre Dame, IN: University of Notre Dame Press, 1999); and Seamus Deane, *Strange Country: Modernity and Nationhood in Irish Writing since 1790* (Oxford: Oxford University Press, 1997). Within Latin American studies, Jorge Klor de Alva, in his widely controversial article 'Colonialism and Postcolonialism as (Latin) American Mirages', *Colonial Latin American Review*, 1, 1/2 (1992), 2–23, regards the application of the term 'post-colonial' to Spanish America as a serious case of academic imperialism. For a response to Klor de Alva's arguments, see Walter Mignolo, 'Occidentalización, imperialismo, globalización: herencias coloniales y teorías postcoloniales', *Revista Iberoamericana*, 61, 170/71 (1995), 26–39.

8. Gilles Deleuze and Félix Guattari, *Kafka: Toward a Minor Literature*, trans. by Dana Polan (Minneapolis: University of Minnesota Press, 1986).

9. Laura Doyle and Laura Winkiel, 'Introduction', in *Geomodernisms: Race, Modernism, Modernity*, ed. by Laura Doyle and Laura Winkiel (Bloomington and Indianapolis: Indiana University Press, 2005), pp. 1–14 (p. 3).

10. The term 'geopolitics' was originally coined by Rudolf Kjellén to refer to the links between political power and geographic space. For my purposes, 'geopolitics' relates to the global connections between knowledge and place, and more specifically to the ways in which those spatio-epistemological connections can contest universalizing paradigms and norms. On geopolitics and knowledge, see Walter Mignolo, 'The Geopolitics of Knowledge and the Colonial Difference', *South Atlantic Quarterly*, 101, 1 (2002), 57–96.

11. Neil Larsen, *Reading North by South: On Latin American Literature, Culture, and Politics* (Minneapolis: University of Minnesota Press, 1995), p. 7.

12. Fernando Rosenberg, *The Avant-Garde and Geopolitics in Latin America* (Pittsburgh: University of Pittsburgh Press, 2006), p. 16.

13. I make a distinction between *modernismo* and 'modernism': the first term refers to the poetic movement represented by José Martí, Julián del Casal, Rubén Darío; the second refers to the 'new novels' of contemporary writers such as Cortázar, García Márquez, del Paso and Fuentes. For a thorough discussion of the critical term *modernismo* in Hispanic literature, see Ned J. Davison, *The Concept of Modernism in Hispanic Criticism* (Boulder, CO: Pruett Press, 1966) and Ivan A. Schulman, 'Reflexiones en torno a la definición de modernismo', in *Estudios críticos sobre el modernismo*, ed. by Homero Castillo (Madrid: Gredos, 1984), pp. 325–57. John Butt provides a useful contrastive analysis of the terms 'modernism' and *modernismo* within the context of Peninsular literature in 'Modernismo y *Modernism*', in Castillo, ed., *Estudios críticos sobre el modernismo*, pp. 39–58. The collection of essays *Modernism and Its Margins*, ed. by Anthony Geist and José Monleón (New York: Garland, 1999), offers a wide range of perspectives on the theoretical problems associated with the definition of aesthetic modernity in Spain and Latin America.

14. Martin argues that Faulkner should be taken as a mediator of Joycean innovations at a time (the 1930s, the 1940s and the 1950s) when Joyce's writings were not as readily available as Faulkner's to a Latin American readership. James Irby's 'La influencia de William Faulkner en

cuatro narradores hispanoamericanos' (unpublished master's thesis, Universidad Autónoma de México, 1956) remains the canonical analysis of Faulkner's impact on Spanish American fiction. More recently, Deborah Cohn has analysed the connections between Faulkner's regionalist perspective and the new narrative in Spanish America in *History and Memory in the Two Souths: Recent Southern and Spanish American Fiction* (Nashville, TN: Vanderbilt University Press, 1999).

15. Gerald Martin, *Journeys through the Labyrinth: Latin American Fiction in the Twentieth Century* (London: Verso, 1989), p. 204.

16. Ibid., p. 130.

17. Ibid., p. 240.

18. Ibid., p. 141.

19. Ibid., p. 7. Douwe W. Fokkema made a similar point in *Literary History, Modernism, and Postmodernism* (Amsterdam: John Benjamins, 1984). Fokkema stated that Jorge Luis Borges was the originator of the postmodernism, 'the first literary code that originated in America and influenced European literature' (p. 38).

20. Franco Moretti, 'Conjectures on World Literature', *New Left Review*, 1 (2000), 54–68 (p. 58). Moretti has developed his views on literary history in a series of influential publications, including *Modern Epic: The World-System from Goethe to García Márquez*, trans. by Quintin Hoare (London: Verso, 1996); *Atlas of the European Novel, 1800–1900* (London: Verso, 1999); and *Graphs, Maps, Trees: Abstract Models for a Literary History* (London: Verso, 2005). For a critique of Moretti's central arguments, see Efraín Kristal, ' "Considering Coldly...": A Response to Franco Moretti', *New Left Review*, 15 (2002), 61–74, and Fernando Cabo Aseguinolaza, 'Dead, or a Picture of Good Health? Comparatism, Europe, and World Literature?', *Comparative Literature*, 58, 4 (2006), 418–35 (esp. pp. 424–30).

21. John Beverley, *Against Literature* (Minneapolis: University of Minnesota Press, 1993).

22. See 'Introduction to the Spanish American Modernist and Postmodernist Novel', in *The Postmodern Novel in Latin America: Politics, Culture, and the Crisis of Truth* (New York: St Martin's Press, 1995), pp. 1–20; *The Modern Latin-American Novel* (New York: Twayne Publishers, 1998); 'Modernist Continuities: The Desire To Be Modern in Twentieth-Century Spanish-American Fiction', *Bulletin of Spanish Studies*, 79, 2/3 (2002), 369–93; and *The Twentieth-Century Spanish American Novel* (Austin: University of Texas Press, 2003).

23. Williams, 'Modernist Continuities', p. 383.

24. Donald Shaw, 'When Was Modernism in Spanish-American Fiction?', *Bulletin of Spanish Studies*, 79, 2/3 (2002), 395–409. See also his *La nueva novela hispanoamericana: boom, posboom, posmodernismo* (Madrid: Cátedra, 1999), especially pp. 365–77, and 'More about Modernism in Spanish America', *A Contracorriente*, 4, 2 (2007), 143–52.

25. Shaw, 'When Was Modernism in Spanish-American Fiction?', pp. 407–08.

26. Pascale Casanova, *The World Republic of Letters*, trans. by M. B. DeBevoise (Cambridge, MA: Harvard University Press, 2004), p. 88.

27. Ibid., 88.

28. Georg W. F. Hegel, *Lectures on the Philosophy of History*, trans. by H. B. Nisbet (Cambridge: Cambridge University Press, 1975). On his views on the 'New World', which he considered to be 'outside of History', see pp. 162–70.

29. Octavio Paz, 'La búsqueda del presente', *Vuelta*, 170 (1991), 10–14 (p. 11).

30. Ibid., p. 12.

31. Octavio Paz, *Corriente alterna* (Mexico: Siglo Veintiuno, 1978), pp. 23–24.

32. Carlos Fuentes, *La nueva novela hispanoamericana* (Mexico: Joaquín Mortiz, 1969), p. 32.

33. Carlos Fuentes, *Cervantes o la crítica de la lectura* (Mexico: Joaquín Mortiz, 1976), pp. 103–04.

34. Ibid., p. 108. Fuentes's assessment of Joyce's writing is influenced by poststructuralist thought, as his references to Jacques Derrida and Hélène Cixous demonstrate (pp. 103, 107). For a detailed discussion of the interconnections among Fuentes, Joyce and poststructuralism, see Wendy Faris, ' "Desyoización": Joyce/Cixous/Fuentes and the Multi-Vocal Text', *Latin American Literary Review*, 19 (1981), 31–39.

35. Fuentes, *La nueva novela hispanoamericana*, p. 32.

36. Carlos Fuentes, *Geografía de la novela* (Mexico: Fondo de Cultura Económica, 1993) p. 167.

37. Martin, *Journeys through the Labyrinth*, p. 141.
38. Robert Young, *White Mythologies: Writing History and the West* (London: Routledge, 1990), p. 20.
39. Ernesto Laclau, 'Politics and the Limits of Modernity', *Social Text*, 21 (1989), 63–82 (p. 67).
40. Alejo Carpentier, *Ecue-Yamba-Ó* (Buenos Aires: O. Sello, 1977).
41. See Manuel Pedro González, 'El *Ulysses* cuarenta años después', in *Ensayos críticos* (Caracas: Universidad Central de Venezuela, 1963), pp. 5–21; 'La novela hispanoamericana en el contexto de la internacional', in *Coloquio sobre la literatura hispanoamericana*, ed. by Fernando Alegría and others (Mexico: Tezontle, 1967), pp. 35–67; and 'Consideraciones sobre la novela', in *Notas críticas* (Havana: UNEAC, 1969), pp. 189–94.
42. Fuentes, *La nueva novela hispanoamericana*, p. 29.
43. Doris Sommer, *Foundational Fictions: The National Romances of Latin America* (Berkeley: University of California Press, 1991), p. 2.
44. Fuentes, *La nueva novela hispanoamericana*, p. 29.
45. José María Arguedas, *El zorro de arriba y el zorro de abajo*, ed. by Eve-Marie Fell (Nanterre, France: ALLCA XX, 1990), p. 21.
46. Arguedas, *El zorro de arriba y el zorro de abajo*, pp. 13–14.
47. Julio Cortázar, 'Acerca de la situación del intelectual latinoamericano', in *Último Round*, 2 vols (Mexico: Siglo Veintiuno, 1980), II, 265–80 (p. 276).
48. Ibid., p. 268.
49. Ibid., p. 266.
50. Roberto Fernández Retamar, in *Cinco miradas sobre Cortázar*, ed. by Ana María Simo and others (Buenos Aires: Editorial Tiempo Contemporáneo), p. 21.
51. Ibid., p. 31.
52. Ibid., p. 33.
53. Ibid., p. 64.
54. Carlos Fuentes, '*Hopscotch*: The Novel as Pandora', *Review of Contemporary Fiction*, 3, 3 (1983), 86–88 (p. 88).
55. Fernández Retamar, *Cinco miradas sobre Cortázar*, p. 25.
56. Roberto Fernández Retamar, *Para una teoría de la literatura hispanoamericana* (Santafé de Bogotá: Instituto Caro y Cuervo, 1995).
57. Roberto Fernández Retamar, *Calibán y otros ensayos* (Havana: Editorial Arte y Literatura, 1979), pp. 69–70.
58. Ibid., p. 82.
59. Ibid., p. 87.
60. Vincent Cheng, *Joyce, Race, and Empire* (Cambridge: Cambridge University Press, 1995), p. 3. Besides Cheng, other authors have recently challenged the construction of Joyce as a 'High Modernist'. See Seamus Deane, 'James Joyce and Nationalism', in *Celtic Revivals: Essays in Modern Irish Literature, 1880–1980* (London: Faber, 1985), pp. 92–107; Declan Kiberd, *Inventing Ireland*, pp. 327–55 and *Irish Classics* (Cambridge, MA: Harvard University Press, 2001), pp. 463–81; Emer Nolan, *James Joyce and Nationalism* (London: Routledge, 1995); Enda Duffy, *The Subaltern 'Ulysses'* (Minneapolis: University of Minnesota Press, 1994); M. Keith Booker, *'Ulysses', Capitalism, and Colonialism: Reading Joyce after the Cold War* (Westport, CT: Greenwood Press, 2000); Marjorie Howes and Derek Attridge, eds, *Semicolonial Joyce* (Cambridge: Cambridge University Press, 2000); and Richard Begam, 'Joyce's Trojan Horse: *Ulysses* and the Aesthetics of Decolonization', in *Modernism and Colonialism: British and Irish Literature, 1899–1939*, ed. by Richard Begam and Michael Valdez Moses (Durham, NC: Duke University Press, 2007), pp. 185–208. For a critical survey of postcolonial approaches to Joyce's work see Vincent Cheng, 'Of Canons, Colonies, and Critics: The Ethics and Politics of Postcolonial Joyce Studies', *Critical Inquiry*, 35 (1996/97), 81–104.
61. Nolan, *James Joyce and Nationalism*, p. xii.
62. Elleke Boehmer, *Empire, the National, and the Postcolonial, 1890–1920* (Oxford: Oxford University Press, 2002), p. 2.
63. Robin Fiddian, 'James Joyce and Spanish American Fiction: A Study of the Origins and Transmission of Literary Influence', *Bulletin of Hispanic Studies*, 65 (1989), 23–39 (pp. 23–24).

64. César A. Salgado, *From Modernism to Neobaroque: Joyce and Lezama Lima* (Lewisburg, PA: Bucknell University Press, 2001), p. 27.

65. Carlos J. Alonso, *The Burden of Modernity: The Rhetoric of Cultural Discourse in Spanish America* (New York: Oxford University Press, 1998), p. 154.

66. José Lezama Lima, 'La expresión americana', in *Obras completas*, 2 vols (Mexico: Aguilar, 1977), pp. 279–390 (p. 347).

67. Natalie Melas, *All the Difference in the World: Postcoloniality and the Ends of Comparison* (Stanford, CA: Stanford University Press, 2007), p. xii.

68. Jorge Luis Borges, *Obras completas*, 4 vols (Buenos Aires: Emecé, 2005), I, 288.

69. Martin, *Journeys through the Labyrinth*, p. 141.

70. Enrique Dussel, 'Eurocentrism and Modernity (Introduction to the Frankfurt Lectures)', *boundary 2*, 20, 3 (1993), 65–76 (p. 65).

71. Salgado, *From Modernism to Neobaroque*, p. 27.

72. The alternative literary history that this study proposes positions itself within a recent trend of cultural studies that sets out to vindicate the epistemological validity of the 'darker side' of modernity as a legitimate discursive space. See Enrique Dussel, *The Invention of the Americas: Eclipse of 'The Other' and the Myth of Modernity*, trans. by Michael D. Barber (New York: Continuum, 1995) and *The Underside of Modernity: Apel, Ricoeur, Taylor, and the Philosophy of Liberation*, ed. by Eduardo Mendieta (Atlantic Highlands, NJ: Humanities Press, 1996); Walter D. Mignolo, *Local Histories/Global Designs: Coloniality, Subaltern Knowledges, and Border Thinking* (Princeton, NJ: Princeton University Press, 2000) and *The Idea of Latin America* (Malden, MA: Blackwell, 2005); and Sylvia Wynter, 'Unsettling the Coloniality of Being/Power/Truth/ Freedom: Towards the Human, After Man, Its Overrepresentation: An Argument', *CR: The New Centennial Review*, 3, 3 (2003), 245–337.

73. Joe Cleary, 'Toward a Materialist–Formalist History of Twentieth-Century Irish Literature', *boundary 2*, 31, 1 (2004), 207–41 (pp. 210–11).

74. The imperial designs of England and Spain emerged almost simultaneously during the sixteenth century. In 1541, only fifty years after Columbus founded on Hispaniola the first Spanish colony in the New World, Henry VIII took the decisive step of crowning himself King of Ireland. In *Language and Conquest in Early Modern Ireland: English Renaissance Literature and Elizabethan Imperial Expansion* (Cambridge: Cambridge University Press, 2001), Patricia Palmer addresses the similarities between the English and Spanish imperialist expansions, arguing that Castilian colonialism provided the ideological groundwork for the Tudor re-conquest of Ireland launched by Henry VIII and continued by Elizabeth I. In this sense, the English annexation of Ireland is, as Palmer claims, 'part of a much larger pattern of sixteenth-century colonial expansion' (p. 6).

75. Enda Duffy, *The Subaltern 'Ulysses'*, p. 4. On *Ulysses* as an anti-colonial text intended for an Irish audience, see C. L. Innes, 'Modernism, Ireland, and Empire: Yeats, Joyce and Their Implied Audiences', in *Modernism and Empire*, ed. by Howard J. Booth and Nigel Rigby (Manchester: Manchester University Press, 2000), pp. 137–55 (esp. pp. 148–54).

76. On the reception of Liberation Theology in Ireland, see Patrick F. McDevitt, 'Ireland, Latin America, and an Atlantic Liberation Theology', in *The Atlantic in Global History, 1500–2000*, ed. by Jorge Cañizares-Esguerra and Erik R. Seeman (Upper Saddle River, NJ: Prentice Hall, 2007), pp. 239–51.

CHAPTER 1

❖

Dissociations of Sensibility:
Cultural Decolonization and
Joyce's Reception in Spanish America

The Invention of Joyce's Modernism

In Chapter 5 of Joyce's *A Portrait of the Artist as a Young Man*, Stephen Dedalus explains his aesthetic theory to his fellow college student, Cranly. At a crucial point in his exposition, he makes a distinction between 'static' and 'kinetic' art: while the latter is 'improper' and incites feelings of 'desire or loathing', the former is the cause of the 'esthetic emotion' which arrests the mind and raises it above the squalid materiality of the external world.[1] After a complex elaboration of his quasi-scholastic approach to the artistic object, Stephen culminates his argument with his often-quoted description of the artist as the 'God of the creation, [who] remains within or behind or beyond or above his handiwork, invisible, refined out of existence, indifferent, paring his fingernails'. However, his carefully wrought argument is no sooner finished than it is gruffly deflated by another of his classmates, Lynch: 'What do you mean', he asks, 'by prating about beauty and the imagination in this miserable, Godforsaken island? No wonder the artist retired within or behind his handiwork after having perpetrated this country'.[2] With these remarks, it seems that Joyce is playing the aesthetic formalism of 'static art' against the social conditions of Ireland at the turn of the twentieth century. Early reviewers of Joyce's *A Portrait* and *Ulysses* were quick to identify Stephen's aesthetic views with those of Joyce and to oppose the structural complexity of his works to the Irish background of their contents.[3] As Joseph Brooker has noted, while some of these critics celebrated Joyce's narrative by focusing on its 'static' architectonics, others denigrated it on account of its 'kinetic' aspects.[4] The opinions of the first group, which included Ezra Pound and T. S. Eliot, constituted the critical foundation of Joyce's canonization as the epitome of 'high modernism'; the often enraged reactions of the second group eventually resulted in the notorious censorship of *Ulysses* in the United States and Great Britain until the 1930s.

Joseph Kelly has claimed that Pound and Eliot 'changed Joyce from an Irish writer into an avant-garde, cosmopolitan writer, shucking off his provincial husk'.[5] But how can one ignore the 'Irishness' of a writer whose entire *oeuvre* revolves around Dublin and the speech and customs of its people? For Pound and Eliot, the Irish content of Joyce's narrative was little more than the dull subject matter transfigured into art by the formal virtuosity of *A Portrait* and, most notably, *Ulysses*. This emphasis on the 'static' elements of Joyce's prose was a necessary critical step toward establishing his style and techniques as the remedy for the rapid dissolution of European cultural values after World War I. For instance, Pound affirmed that the 'realism' of *Ulysses* was the solution to the 'hell of contemporary Europe. The sense of style that Joyce's narrative represents would have saved America or Europe. The *mot juste* is of public utility'.[6] For the author of the *Cantos*, this stylistic precision was testimony to Joyce's detachment from the 'local stupidity' of his native Ireland and to his entrance 'into the modern world': 'He writes as a European, not as a provincial', Pound unambiguously stated in a piece entitled 'The Non-Existence of Ireland'.[7]

The 'modern' and 'European' characteristics of Joyce's *Ulysses* were also the main concern of Eliot in his well-known 1923 review '*Ulysses*, Order and Myth'. Eliot perceived in the mythical structure of *Ulysses* a paradigm of order fulfilling a function analogous to that which Pound assigned to Joyce's narrative precision, namely that of 'controlling, of ordering, of giving a shape and a significance to the immense panorama of futility and anarchy which is contemporary history'.[8] Though fragmentary, the post-Great War world of Eliot and Joyce could gain stability by association with the order of myth. Thus, what he called the 'mythical method' — the manipulation of 'a continuous parallel between contemporaneity and antiquity' — afforded the possibility of concentrating on the 'static' architecture of *Ulysses*, while ignoring its 'kinetic' contents. In this respect, A. Walton Litz maintained that 'Eliot was troubled from the start by the threat which Joyce's diverse and rambunctious prose might pose to the "classicist"', adding that, like 'a devoted but somewhat timid child, Eliot was trying to process Joyce's novel into a congenial world of "authority" and "tradition"'.[9] Therefore, the aesthetic principles of literary modernism as theorized and practised by Pound and Eliot found in Joyce's *Ulysses* a space for projection.

Indeed, Eliot the 'classicist' considered the 'static' order of *Ulysses* to be a remedy for the cultural fragmentation of the West, which he surely perceived as an extreme case of 'dissociation of sensibility'. Eliot introduced this concept in his essay 'The Metaphysical Poets' (1921), where he claimed that Donne, Chapman and other English poets of the early seventeenth century exemplified the perfect integration of lived experience and intellectual learning.[10] For these poets, feeling and thought were in perfect harmony, since their intellects were constantly pressing their experiences into systems or 'wholes'. Their minds were not assailed by the fragmentation that, according to Eliot, became increasingly frequent in English letters after the seventeenth century. Eliot must have noticed a strong parallel between this initial moment of 'dissociation of sensibility' in the English poetic tradition and the consequences for artistic expression that he attributed to the 'immense panorama of futility and anarchy' during the early decades of the twentieth century. In his review of *Ulysses* he sought an artistic frame to remedy the post-War 'dissociation of sensibility' in the interpretations of primitive myth elaborated by the emerging sciences of anthropology, ethnology and psychology:

Psychology (such as it is, and whether our reaction to it be comic or serious), ethnology, and *The Golden Bough* have concurred to make possible what was impossible only a few years ago. Instead of narrative method, we may now use the mythical method. It is, I seriously believe, a step toward making the modern world possible for art.[11]

What Eliot might have found appealing in these disciplines is their common goal to find in 'savage' cultures an organic and undivided mode of thought. Marc Manganaro has identified the French ethnologist Lucien Lévy-Bruhl as one of the central sources of Eliot's views in 'The Metaphysical Poets'. Manganaro argues that the unified sensibility that Eliot ascribed to these English poets closely resembles Lévy-Bruhl's notion of the *mentalité primitive*, a mentality that perceives physical objects and their spiritual value as 'un tout indécomposable' [a synthetic whole].[12] By linking *Ulysses* to the restorative potential of anthropological discourse, Eliot presents Joyce's novel as an effort to regain for art the mythical value of the *mentalité primitive* and as a remedy against the 'dissociation of sensibility' that affected the European psyche after World War I. In other words, for Eliot, the 'stasis' of the mythical structure informing Joyce's book emerges as a powerful and convincing illustration of how art can provide a redemptive space where the 'futility and anarchy' of contemporary life could be contained and controlled. Thus, the structural order of myth offers Eliot a space of representation where the unruliness of historical transformations and the external world could be successfully overcome. As Astradur Eysteinnson has noted, Eliot's aesthetic ideas in '*Ulysses*, Order and Myth' closely parallel those of Stephen in *A Portrait*, adding that their shared theory of art 'is frequently taken to constitute the center of the revolutionary *formal* awareness and emphasis that most critics detect in modernist works'.[13]

If the idea of a 'modernist' Joyce goes hand in hand with a formalist and cosmopolitan reading of his work, those who decried *Ulysses* as mere pornography emphasized, more often than not, the author's Irish 'backwardness'. As Kevin Dettmar has aptly noted, to say that a writer was 'Irish' during the first decades of the twentieth century 'was not simply to supply one's readers with information about the author's national origin; for whether consciously or unconsciously, the label "Irish" served to enmesh Joyce in a long history of British anti-Irish stereotypes'.[14] A case in point is H. G. Wells's 1917 review of *A Portrait*, where he interprets Joyce's 'cloacal obsession' and his anti-English feelings as the result of his 'limitations' as an Irishman. The 'kinetic' nature of Joyce's prose is perceived as a sign of underdevelopment with respect to England, whose modernity has successfully expunged the uncivilized features permeating *A Portrait*. Joyce, Wells writes, 'would bring back into the general picture of life aspects which modern drainage and modern decorum have taken out of ordinary intercourse and conversation'. To these remarks, he adds the revealing comment that 'We shall do Mr. Joyce an injustice if we attribute a normal sensory basis to him and then accuse him of deliberate offense'.[15] It appears that the cause of Joyce's impaired 'sensory basis' is, according to English novelist, his Irishness. Thus, where Pound and Eliot had to denationalize and 'modernize' Joyce to bring out the 'static' side of his work, Wells immediately links up his nationality and the 'kinetic' aspects of *A Portrait* to underscore the novel's 'backwardness'. Likewise, while Eliot saw in the 'order' of *Ulysses* a possible solution to the 'dissociation of sensibility' that plagued the modern world, Wells alerts us to the disrupting effects of *A Portrait* and Joyce's deficient sensorial perception.

Wells's notion of an Irish abnormal 'sensory basis' can be usefully connected to Kant's ideas on how aesthetic perception or 'taste' varies depending on race and nationality. For Kant, the right mode of aesthetic perception is that which can connect the purposiveness of nature to the cognitive structures of enlightened reason. Ethnic or national identity is a factor that affects this rapport between perception and cognition. In section four of his *Observations on the Feeling of the Beautiful and Sublime* (1764), Kant argues that 'finer feeling' or appropriate taste is to be associated mainly with Europeans, and specifically with the Germans: they have 'a fortunate combination of feeling, both in that of the sublime and in that of the beautiful'.[16] This 'fortunate combination of feeling', reminiscent of Wells's 'normal sensory basis', is denied to other nations and races in direct proportion to their geopolitical distance from Germany. The lowest end of this aesthetic spectrum is occupied by the 'Negroes of Africa' who 'have by nature no feeling that rises above the trifling'.[17] The racial difference between whites and blacks, the German philosopher believes, 'appears to be as great in regard to mental capacities as in color'.[18] It seems then that the racism behind colonial structures of power did not only find support in a 'denial of coevalness' between the colonizer and the colonized, as has been convincingly argued, but also in what we might call a 'denial of finer feeling'.[19]

Indeed, Wells's notion of what a 'normal sensory basis' should be might have been conditioned by his perception of the Irish not only as England's colonized 'other', but also as racially inferior. As Vincent Cheng has shown, 'the racial comparison most frequently and insistently made about the Irish during the latter half of the nineteenth century was with "negroes"'.[20] Wells's response to Joyce radically clashes with Eliot's and Pound's: far from being the champion of Western values, Wells sees Joyce as an intellectually deviant and anti-modern man, a man that, to borrow John Middleton Murry's words, 'would blow what remains of Europe into the sky [...] [due to his] rebellion against the lucidity and comprehensibility of civilized art'.[21]

This brief survey of Joyce's early reception in Europe illustrates the underlying connections between aesthetic theory, modernity and colonialism. These connections often determined and substantiated antithetical critical perceptions of *A Portrait*, and, most notably, *Ulysses*. Depending on the commentator, Joyce's prose was either 'static', 'cosmopolitan' and 'modern' or 'kinetic', 'Irish' and 'backwards'. It was the first Joyce who, until recently, dominated the critical tradition, which almost unanimously considered his work as the model of literary modernism.[22] Recently, critic Andrew Gibson has openly set out to recover the second Joyce, thus contributing to the ongoing 'Irishization' of the author started in the mid-1990s by Seamus Deane, Emer Nolan and Declan Kiberd, among others. Discussing Wells's review of *A Portrait*, Gibson claims that 'Joyce had introduced the sordid and obscene elements in the novel with malign or seditious intent. They were part of his Irish assault on England and English culture'.[23] Significantly, Gibson's emphasis on the relevance of Joyce's nationality for the reception of his work returns to the relationship among the kinetic, the Irish and the anti-colonial.

My argument for this chapter departs from that relationship: I believe that one effective way to unpack the anti-colonial dimension of Joyce's work is by stressing how the 'kinetic' aspects of his narrative frustrate the coherence and closure of stasis and form. So, for instance, if we try to provide a formalist analysis of 'Ithaca' (Chapter 17 of *Ulysses*), we will probably focus on how Joyce's religious catechism gives shape to a wealth of random materials. But an interpretation that stays alert to his ironic handling of all forms of authority would highlight the calculated ways in which the chapter exceeds and undermines the truth claims of science and religion. Leopold Bloom provides a provocative example of the collapse of disciplinary principles of coherence and cohesion when he gazes at the stars and muses about the permanent conflict between the boundless dimensions of the universe and the scientific laws devised to control, contain and systematize it. This conflict reminds Bloom of his futile efforts to calculate the quadrature of the circle, a mathematical exercise that involves reducing an infinite numeric series to a finite set of algebraic coefficients:

> [...] some years previously in 1886 when occupied with the problem of the quadrature of the circle he learned of the existence of a number computed to a relative degree of accuracy to be of such magnitude and of so many places, e.g. the 9th power of the 9th power of 9, that, the result having been obtained, 33 closely printed volumes of 1000 pages each of innumerable quires and reams of India paper would have to be requisitioned in order to contain the complete tale of its printer integers [...] the nebula of every digit of every series containing succinctly the potentiality of being raised to the utmost kinetic elaboration of any power of any of its powers. (*U* 15.1071–1082; emphasis added)[24]

The sprawling dimensions of these calculations signal the irreducibility of 'kinetic' reality to static laws, a point that informs 'Ithaca' as much as it informs the rest of the novel. The effect of Joyce's technique is, therefore, to expose (rather than remedy) the *failure* of abstract systems to bind and represent the material world. In 'Ithaca' this exposure becomes politically charged when we realize that, as Nicholas Whyte has amply demonstrated, scientific discourse in Ireland before independence remained the almost exclusive province of the colonial establishment, namely British officials and the Anglo-Irish Ascendancy.[25] Read in this way, *Ulysses* would incite rather than remedy the 'dissociation of sensibility' that, much to Eliot's chagrin, plagued European culture and civilization after the Great War. Due to the close links among aesthetics, modernity and colonialism that we have discussed above, it would be plausible to claim that exposing this 'dissociation of sensibility' amounts to a declaration of cultural independence, indeed to a decolonizing aesthetic move.

This way of reading Joyce, which has gained considerable ground in the Anglo-American academy in the last decade, was already in practice between the late 1940s and the 1970s among Spanish American writers and intellectuals, including some of those frequently associated with the 'boom'. By paying attention to how this critical approach to Joyce intersected with the experimental narrative of the period, we could call into question the equivalence between Anglo-American modernism and the *nueva novela*. Such approach can also reconnect the experimental literature of the period to the debate on decolonization that dominated cultural politics in Spanish America at the time. I am interested, therefore, in the possibilities that an historical recontextualization of Joycism in Spanish America might offer for an alternative literary history.

Reading Joyce in Spanish America

It is true that, as José Donoso wrote in his *Historia personal del 'boom'*, he and his contemporaries openly acknowledged the mastery of Kafka, Mann, Proust and Joyce over that of their native forefathers, D'Halmar, Gallegos, Alegría. Despite this declaration of literary preferences, it would be misleading to categorize the 'boom' writers as cosmopolitan aesthetes aloof to the history, culture and politics of Latin America. As Donoso argued, until the notorious Padilla affair the Cuban Revolution provided this group with a coherent ideological structure of continental scope.[26] In the words of the Chilean novelist: 'Creo que si en algo tuvo unidad casi completa el *boom* [...] fue en la fe primera en la causa de la Revolución Cubana' [I believe that if something provided the *boom* with unity [...] that was their initial faith in the cause of the Cuban Revolution].[27] By quoting these remarks, I do not want to imply that the new novelists constituted the literary wing of Fidel Castro's political project. My intention is rather to underscore that the new novel in Spanish America is not, as it has often been portrayed, a rootless type of narrative detached from the social and historical conditions of the region.

The 'boom' originated, Donoso argues, with the publication of Fuentes's *La región más transparente*, a novel which, for all its stylistic virtuosity, cannot be truly appreciated if one ignores its engagement with Mexico's history, culture and identity. For Donoso, *La región más transparente* belongs to a genealogy of profoundly Latin American books ('una estirpe de libros profundamente latinoamericana') that includes works so diverse as Ezequiel Martínez Estrada's *Radiografía de la pampa*, Mario Benedetti's *Montevideanos* and Leopoldo Marechal's *Adán Buenosayres*. This ethnic dimension did not pass unnoticed by Cortázar, who, in a letter to Fuentes dated 7 September 1958, complains that the novel's references to the peculiarities of Mexican life and culture are so detailed and specific that the non-Mexican reader often finds them hard to understand. However, these difficulties do not keep the author of *Rayuela* from perceiving in Fuentes's text problems and issues that also affected him as an Argentine. He writes: 'leyendo su novela, he subrayado centenares de pasajes, y he escrito al lado: *Argentina*. Me imagino que usted ha podido hacer lo mismo con algunos libros nuestros' [when I was reading your novel I underlined hundreds of passages, writing *Argentina* on the margin. I imagine that you could have done the same thing with our books]. Cortázar goes on to compare *La región* to Joyce's *Ulysses*, highlighting their close attention to local details. Although the Argentine novelist points out that Joyce's goals were more 'literary' than those of Fuentes, he recognizes in *Ulysses* the same dense local texture that he attributes to *La región*:

En suma: usted se ha despachado su *comedia humana* en un volumen sin pensar que contaba cosas ceñidamente locales, es decir muy difíciles para los no mexicanos [...] hasta llegar a una saturación no siempre comprensible. Por supuesto, Ulises [*sic*] no hace otra cosa; pero creo que Joyce perseguía más fines *literarios* que usted, ponía el acento en la técnica con un propósito de ruptura de moldes vetustos.[28]

[In sum: you have delivered your *human comedy* in one volume without thinking that the deeply local aspects you discuss are difficult to understand for non-Mexicans [...] you saturate the text with details that are sometimes barely comprehensible. Of course, Ulises [*sic*] did the same thing, but I believe that Joyce sought more *literary* goals than you, that he stressed the use of technique to break with old models.]

With this brief comment on the similarities between *Ulysses* and Fuentes's first novel, Cortázar is not only establishing Joyce's book as what would become a persistent point of reference for the aesthetics of the 'boom'; he is also crediting *Ulysses* with a local dimension that, as seen above, was conspicuously ignored by those that sought to transform Joyce into an iconic modernist. Cortázar's 'local' appreciation of Joyce was developed by some Spanish American critics and reviewers publishing between the mid-1940s and the 1960s. As César Salgado has noted, the 'interest in Joycean themes and narrative techniques paralleled a brief "boom" of critical studies and commentaries in Spanish on Joyce during the forties'.[29] He goes on to supply ample documentation to indicate that this was a period of active Joycean criticism in Spanish America: journals such as *Alfar*, *Contrapunto* and Lezama Lima's *Orígenes* featured translations of articles on Joyce by Valéry Larbaud, Edmund Wilson, Jacques Mercaton and Harry Levin; Herbert Gorman's biography, *James Joyce*, was published in translation in Buenos Aires; and Juan Jacobo Bajarlía's *Literatura de vanguardia del Ulises de Joyce y de las escuelas plásticas* was issued in 1946, a year after J. Salas Subirat's translation of *Ulysses* appeared. Salgado adds that, despite subsequent 'disfigurements' of established critical perspectives, the contribution to the Joycean debate by Hispanic critics constituted a case of paradigmatic dependence: 'All peninsular and Latin American approaches to *Ulysses* resort to "canonical" criticism, whether or not this operation is made explicit in the text'.[30] A substantial part of the Spanish American intelligentsia writing about Joyce during these years did echo received ideas from the Anglo-American academy and characterized Joyce's fiction as a cosmopolitan and modernizing aesthetic force. But this dependence is by no means typical of all the criticism on Joyce published in Spanish America at the time. Critics as prominent as Arturo Uslar Pietri expressed views that differed substantially — and in some cases flatly contradicted — the critical orthodoxy of Joycean studies. I believe that this 'heretical' line of criticism can open up an alternative context for the analysis of Joycean writing in Spanish America, a context that connects in meaningful ways the aesthetics of the new novel with the intense process of cultural decolonization of the period.

Before exploring these alternative contexts, it may be instructive to consider how the derivative Joyce scholarship that Salgado mentions inspired and informed a more general critical trend — pioneered by Emir Rodríguez Monegal and Carlos Fuentes — that came to categorize the *nueva novela* as a 'modernist' phenomenon.

To illustrate this point, I want to focus on a selection of articles about Joyce published between the 1940s and the 1960s in the prominent Buenos Aires journal *Sur*. Founded in 1931 by Victoria Ocampo, *Sur* and its associated press (Editorial Sur) published work that contributed to the journal's lofty mission, namely to find a cultural expression suitable for Argentina and South America by looking toward Europe.[31] Predictably, then, the journal and the press became major venues for the introduction of modernist aesthetics and continental philosophy in the region. As John King has noted, key figures of the boom (Cabrera Infante, Fuentes, Vargas Llosa, García Márquez) acknowledged that they first came in touch with the Anglo-American avant-garde through the pages of *Sur*.[32] Indeed, a perusal of *Sur*'s contents over the years is enough to get a sense of the prominent position that the editors accorded this kind of literature. For instance, a double issue on modern British literature published in 1947 featured translations of V. S. Pritchett, Stephen Spender, T. E. Lawrence, Virginia Woolf and T. S. Eliot, among many others. Four years later, on the occasion of the publication's twentieth anniversary, its secretary, Guillermo de Torre, celebrated the groundbreaking publishing efforts of *Sur*, which boasted the first Spanish translations of authors such as Huxley, Lawrence, Joyce, Woolf and philosophers such as Heidegger — whose 'What is Metaphysics?', de Torre reminds us, appeared in translation almost simultaneously with the original. As this list of names indicates, one of the main goals of the editorial board of *Sur* was to 'keep up' with the aesthetic and philosophical innovations from across the Atlantic.

As part of her efforts to create and maintain cultural ties between Europe and South America, Victoria Ocampo became acquainted with several relevant European literary figures, notably Virginia Woolf and T. S. Eliot. According to Woolf's personal diary, she meet Ocampo (or 'Okampo', as Woolf frequently spelled the name) in November 1934 at a photography exhibition in London. This initial encounter marked the beginning of a literary friendship that greatly influenced Ocampo's creative and critical writings. Years later, in a paper delivered at a meeting of an association of Argentine anglophiles, she referred to Woolf in highly idealized terms: 'Todo lo que esta mujer ha comprendido, sentido, pensado, se agrega en este momento a su belleza y la subraya. Se pregunta uno cómo se las ha arreglado para no pensar en nada vulgar, para no sentir nada bajo, pues ninguna vulgaridad, ninguna fealdad ha dejado marca en su rostro' [Everything that this woman has understood, felt, thought, adds to her beauty and enhances it. One wonders how she manages to avoid vulgar thoughts and low feelings, since no ugliness has left a mark on her face]. According to the Argentine writer, Woolf's physical appearance seemed to be a reflection of her writing style, which, despite its apparent disorder responds to inspired foresight, rigorous selection and discipline.[33]

Woolf held similar opinions about literary propriety, as becomes evident in her opinions about Joyce's *Ulysses*. Despite sharing technical similarities with her own work, she vehemently condemned the 'vulgar' features of Joyce's novel. As her diary entry for 16 August 1922 tells us, Woolf had read the first few chapters of the book with interest, but when she reached 'Aeolus', she quickly became 'puzzled, bored, irritated, and disillusioned' with a farrago of styles that seemed to be the work of 'a queasy undergraduate scratching his pimples'. Her final assessment is strongly reminiscent of Wells's critique of Joyce's 'cloacal obsession' in *A Portrait*: *Ulysses* is, she contends, the 'illiterate, underbred book [...] of a self taught working man' — of an 'egotistic, insistent, raw, striking, and ultimately nauseating' writer. This is no doubt a book that Woolf's refined literary network would certainly find unpalatable.[34] That Victoria Ocampo counted herself as part of such network, which included, among others, T. S. Eliot and Ezra Pound, was obvious. In fact, in light of Ocampo's laudatory comments on the order and discipline of Woolf's prose, it should come as no surprise that she also openly supported the type of elitist literature that T. S. Eliot promoted and practised. In a short editorial note in which Ocampo celebrates the Nobel Prize recently awarded to the British poet, she discusses the mission of Eliot's journal, *The Criterion*. That mission — to preserve the legacy of Western tradition and culture during times of social and political turmoil through highbrow, hermetic literature that is 'pocas veces inmediatamente popular' [rarely immediately popular] — was also embraced by Ocampo on behalf of her journal.[35] However, she stresses in an obviously self-depreciatory manner that there is an evident imbalance between England, 'un país de antiquísima tradición y cultura' [a country with a millenarian tradition and culture], and Argentina, 'un país de nivel cultural deficiente, con posibilidades literarias muy inferiores (amén de la inferioridad patente de su directora)' [a country with a clearly deficient cultural level, with inferior literary possibilities (let alone the obvious inferiority of the journal's director)].[36] For Ocampo the solution to this cultural lag is to build solid bridges between 'what Eliot stands for' (to use her own words) and journals such as *Sur*, which, she confesses, 'viven [...] y mueren' [live [...] and die] for the kind of literature championed by Eliot.

This brief discussion of Ocampo's literary alliances and how they determined the editorial choices of *Sur* offers useful points of reference to contextualize the critical treatment of Joyce in this journal. Given Ocampo's valorization of the rigor and order of Woolf's prose, and her defence of Eliot's Western elitism, it is understandable that the Joyce who found his way to the pages of *Sur*, far from being a dissonant anti-European voice, was one that bore a strong resemblance to the 'static', 'cosmopolitan' and 'modernist' Joyce of Pound and Eliot. The journal frequently featured translations of articles on Joyce by renowned English and American scholars, such as Stuart Gilbert and Joseph Prescott, who took decisive steps to institutionalize a 'modernist' interpretation of Joyce. In his popular *James Joyce's 'Ulysses'* (1930), Gilbert focuses on the Homeric parallels that provide the novel with structural consistency, thus developing Eliot's critical views in 'Ulysses, Order and Myth'. Using terms that remind us of Ocampo's description of Woolf's writing, Gilbert claims that Joyce subjects his work, 'for all its wild vitality and seeming disorder, to a rule of discipline as severe as those of the Greek dramatists'.[37] Since in this hyperclassical *Ulysses* 'we find the ideal silent stasis of the artist nearly realized, his personality almost impersonalized', one of Joyce's main achievements in the novel is 'to ban kinetic feelings from his readers' mind'.[38]

Only two years after the publication of Gilbert's guide to *Ulysses*, the book's main ideas were recast and summarized by Charles Duff in 'Ulises y otros trabajos de

James Joyce' [*Ulysses* and other works by James Joyce], a brief introduction to Joyce's life and work intended for the 'common reader' and published in the fifth issue of *Sur*. Here Duff recognizes an Irish dimension to Joyce's writing, but only to dismiss it as an abnormality. Relying on the stereotypical views on the Celt popularized in the late nineteenth century by Ernest Renan and Matthew Arnold, he claims that Joyce's typically Irish mind 'suffers from' ('padece') an effervescent imagination, a marked mysticism and a comic quality, all features that deviate from what Wells would call a 'normal sensory basis', but which inevitably permeate Joyce's texts.[39] However, these all too-Irish excesses are curtailed by Joyce's rigorous 'literary criterion', which as Duff tells us, is not Irish (nor English for that matter) but 'pan-European': 'Añádase al pan-europeísmo literario ese gigantismo de exuberancia irlandesa mencionado más arriba, y se tendrá noción aproximada de lo que podemos esperar de Joyce' [Add to this literary pan-Europeanism the gigantism of Irish exuberance mentioned above and you will get an approximate idea of what we can expect from Joyce].[40] With the precision of his style and the rigor of his formal methods, Joyce not only tempered his abnormal Irishness; he also succeeded in opening new paths for contemporary fiction by soaring above 'decadent kinetic art' ('el decadente arte kinético').[41] Therefore, Joyce's Irishness is conveniently pressed into shape by his pan-European outlook and his 'static' narrative techniques.

Gilbert himself further developed this formalistic approach to the Irish author's fiction by summarizing the main points of his *James Joyce's 'Ulysses'* in an article titled 'El fondo latino en el arte de James Joyce' [The Latin Background of James Joyce's Art], published in *Sur* in December 1944. After reading the first few pages we realize that 'Latin' stands for 'classical' and, more specifically, for 'classical order': 'Porque en *Ulises* — una de las obras maestras mejor ordenadas y más racionales que ha conocido el mundo — prevalece el espíritu latino y la lógica estricta de la antigua religión' [Because in *Ulysses* — one of the better organized and more rational masterpieces in the world — what prevails is the Latin spirit and the strict logic of the old religion].[42] According to Gilbert, it is from this 'old religion', Catholicism, and the teachings of Aquinas that Joyce inherited his ideal of 'static beauty'. Taking Stephen's theory of art in *A Portrait* as the author's own, Gilbert maintains that Joyce willingly shaped his work according to the 'static' order prescribed by scholasticism and embodied by Greek sculpture and literature, an order that he calls 'el ideal mediterráneo'. And it is only away from Ireland and in the heart of Paris, the city where he completed and eventually published *Ulysses*, that Joyce's genius could find the freedom it needed to fully blossom by being in touch with this ideal.[43] Thus Gilbert, like Duff, Eliot and Pound, found in the nuanced interaction between geopolitical location and aesthetics an effective dialectical tool to distance Joyce's *Ulysses* from its Irish background and place it firmly within the mainstream of the European literary tradition.

Gilbert's and Duff's critical views on Joyce established a solid foundation for subsequent analyses of the Irish author's work by Spanish American scholars publishing in *Sur*. Four years after the publication of Gilbert's 'El fondo latino en el arte de James Joyce', Emir Rodríguez Monegal, who was destined to become one of the main promoters of the 'boom', offered a panoramic appreciation of the twentieth-century novel in 'Aspectos de la novela en el siglo XX'. In this article he advances some views that would later become critical commonplaces in discussions of Joyce's work and literary modernism (including Spanish American 'modernism'). According to the Uruguayan critic, one of the defining aspects of the twentieth-century novel is what José Ortega y Gasset calls the 'dehumanization of art', that is, the elimination of realist or anecdotal material from the literary work, whose artistic value resides in its form and metaphorical language.[44] The tendency towards 'pure invention' uncontaminated by crude realist mimesis that Rodríguez Monegal perceives in authors such as Chesterton and Kafka is paradigmatically exemplified by the prose of James Joyce: 'La obra de James Joyce — toda la obra — puede ofrecer ejemplos de una transcendencia casi total de lo narrativo' [the works of James Joyce — all of them — can offer examples of an almost total transcendence of narrative details].[45] For Rodríguez Monegal, the real protagonist of Joyce's work is the experimental audacity of his language and style. He stresses that despite the apparent disorder that a superficial reading of *Ulysses* might suggest, the book possesses a rigorous and intentional structure untouched by 'improvisation' or 'chance'.[46] It is this strict order under the guise of disorder that this critic recognizes as the key feature of twentieth-century narrative. In order to render the richness of life in meaningful ways, 'el novelista necesita inventar hoy no sólo acciones significativas o conflictos absorbentes; debe inventar estructuras, multiplicar los ángulos, encerrar en la malla ubicua de la narración todo un universo' [contemporary novelists need to invent not only significant actions or absorbing conflicts; they should also invent structures, multiply the number of narrative points of view, capture in the ubiquitous net of the narrative a whole universe].[47] In 'Hacia una interpretación del hombre James Joyce' (*Sur*, 1959), Carlos Altschul supported Rodríguez Monegal's views as he also emphasized that the main goal of Joyce's intricate narrative architectures ('las intricadas arquitecturas de este novelista') was to create an 'autonomous' work of art. Of course, this autonomy required a detachment from the writer's cultural and national background. Joyce's interests were 'universal', and, therefore, Dublin should be regarded only as a frame, or even an excuse, for his linguistic monuments ('las construcciones monumentales como *Ulysses* y *Finnegans Wake*').[48]

It is not by chance that Rodríguez Monegal's treatment of Joyce and the twentieth-century novel overlaps in significant ways with his opinions about the 'boom'. As has been frequently noted, Rodriguez Monegal's edition of the controversial Paris-based journal *Mundo Nuevo* (1966–71) fostered the consolidation of a modernist approach to the *nueva novela* which was complicit with the strategic US cultural programme to support depoliticized abstract art and condemn realistic mimesis during the Cold War years.[49] A year after *Nuevo Mundo* was discontinued (partly because it was discovered that the periodical had been indirectly subsidized by the CIA through a front organization, the Congress for the Freedom of Culture), Rodríguez Monegal published *El boom de la novela latinoamericana* (1972), originally a series of articles in Octavio Paz's review *Plural*. *El boom* is, along with Fuentes's *La nueva narrativa hispanoamericana* (1969), one of the first systematic attempts to analyse the Spanish American new novel. In this critical study, Rodríguez Monegal underlines the boom's indebtedness to European modernism by establishing an explicit connection between the 'high modernist' Joyce — whose canonical authority he endorsed in 'Aspectos de la novela en el siglo XX' — and contemporary Spanish American authors such as Julio Cortázar, José Lezama Lima and Guillermo Cabrera Infante. The Uruguayan critic contends that the experimental writing of these artists gives shape to the literary phenomenon that he calls the 'novela del lenguaje', an experimental, self-reflective kind of text that derives directly from *Ulysses*. Novels such as *Rayuela*, *Paradiso* and *Tres tristes tigres* are all 'Joycean books' because their structure reveals 'una unidad de un sistema completo de significaciones' [the unity of a complete system of significations] which does not originate in the contents of the narration, but in its linguistic texture: 'No hay otra profundidad que la de la superficie, no hay significados sino significaciones, no hay otro compromiso que el de la escritura misma' [there is no more profundity than that of the surface, there are no meanings, only significations, there is no other compromise than that to writing itself].[50]

Rodríguez Monegal's Joyce, like the Joyce featured in *Sur*, emerges as a cipher of the modernist novel, a novel that is unambiguously celebrated for its dehumanized formal architectonics and not for the cultural specificity of its contents. The treatment of Joyce in *Sur* should not be isolated from the journal's mission, which, in Ocampo's words, was to uphold the kind of tradition and culture that T. S. Eliot defended and 'stood for'. Just as Ocampo tried to narrow the distance between the 'inferior' culture of South America and that of Europe, so most of the articles on Joyce published in her journal engaged in a thorough process of assimilation whereby the Irish writer's work was presented as 'static' and 'pan-European' rather than 'kinetic' and 'Irish'. The connections among Joyce's 'static' aesthetics, modernist narrative and the core of Western cultural values proved to be persistently long-lasting, since they created the critical context within which Fuentes articulated his ideas on Joyce and the new narrative (see Introduction to this book). In fact, one could trace a continuum between Rodríguez Monegal's 'modernist' characterization of Joyce's narrative, his views on the new novel and Fuentes's poststructuralist approach. Both Monegal and Fuentes ignore Joyce's Irish background to situate him within a purely linguistic realm. It is this idea of Joyce as a stylistic innovator — not as the author that Cortázar took as a point of reference for Fuentes's local specificity in *La región más transparente* — that predominates in recent scholarly discussions of Joycean narrative in Spanish America. But if it is true, as John King indicates, that the novelists of the boom first learned about Anglo-American modernism through the pages of *Sur*, I would also argue that the Joycean features of their fiction often clash with the 'static' and 'cosmopolitan' aesthetics often attributed to the author of *Ulysses* in the Buenos Aires publication. As we shall see in subsequent chapters, writers such as Jorge Luis Borges, Julio Cortázar, José Lezama Lima, Guillermo Cabrera Infante and Fernando del Paso can show us that Joyce's writing need not be read and rewritten exclusively in a modernist, cosmopolitan key; his fiction can also be taken as a point of departure to negotiate the position of the peripheral intellectual with regard to the culture of the metropolitan centres.

Anti-Colonial Joyce and The 'Emancipation of the Mind'

One can argue that this intellectual negotiation has been a constant concern for Spanish American intellectuals ever since political independence from Spain was achieved and Andrés Bello demanded the 'cultural autonomy of America'. As the Dominican literary critic Pedro Henríquez Ureña maintained in 1928, the literary history of Spanish America could be described as the history of the search for a specifically American mode of expression.[51] However, the historical period during which the critical assimilation of Joyce took place within the covers of *Sur* coincided with an intensification of this search for continental identity. This period witnessed the publication of Mariano Picón Salas' *De la Conquista a la Independencia* (1944), Pedro Henríquez Ureña's Harvard Lectures, *Literary Currents in Hispanic America* (1945), Leopoldo Zea's *La filosofía como compromiso y otros ensayos* (1951), Edmundo O'Gorman's *La invención de América: el universalismo de la cultura de Occidente* (1958); and Julieta Campos's translation of Frantz Fanon's *Los condenados de la tierra* (1965). It also coincided with the years of the triumph and consolidation of the Cuban Revolution and with the effervescent period of political decolonization of the nation states in Asia and Africa that formerly integrated the British and French Empires.

In 'Fanon y América', originally published in 1965 in *Casa de las Américas*, Roberto Fernández Retamar establishes valuable connections between revolutionary movements in Spanish America and the wider decolonizing world. The Cuban poet and critic maintains that even though the anti-colonial arguments of Fanon's *The Wretched of the Earth* were originally intended for the decolonizing African nations, they could be satisfactorily applied to Spanish America as well. As the concluding words of his essay state, 'Fanon tiene muchas cosas que enseñarnos a nosotros los latinoamericanos' [Fanon has many things to teach us Latin Americans].[52] In the Latin America of the 1950s and 1960s, the theories of the Algerian thinker inspired a vigorous struggle for what Leopoldo Zea felicitously called the 'emancipation of the mind', a phrase reminiscent of Ngugi wa Thiong'o's 'decolonization of the mind'.[53] Like Fernández Retamar, Zea presents the struggle for cultural self-determination as extending to the wider decolonizing world, which in his view includes Spanish America. Despite the historical fact that most South American republics attained political emancipation over a century before the nation states of Africa and Asia, Zea argued in a series of important publications that to overcome intellectual dependence, Spanish American artists and thinkers should adopt a philosophical perspective similar to that of the critical avant-garde that promoted the decolonization of the French and British empires. In general terms, this revolutionary attitude is at odds with the cultural supremacy of Europe, which T. S. Eliot, Pound and Ocampo acknowledged and upheld so fervently. Zea, Fernández Retamar and Fanon openly and actively supported the necessity of finding new ways of thinking that would radically depart from Western epistemological frames. Quoting Fanon, Zea expressed the urgent need to create a Latin American 'philosophy of liberation' in the following terms: 'Fanon [...] dice [que] si queremos hacer del mundo no occidental una copia del mundo occidental, dejemos que sean los occidentales los que se encarguen de hacerlo. Pero si queremos participar en la hechura de ese nuevo mundo, de ese hombre nuevo, sin que deje de ser hombre, entonces inventemos, descubramos' [Fanon says that if we want to turn the non-Western world into a copy of the Western world, then we should let the Western man carry out this task. But if we want to participate in the creation of this new world, of this new man, without preventing him from being human, then let us invent, let us discover].[54] This transcontinental emancipatory programme seeks a source of decolonizing force precisely in the differences between the margin and the centre, between American and Europe, which intellectuals like Ocampo arduously tried to overcome.

Eleven years after the first issue of *Sur* was released, *Cuadernos Americanos* was founded in Mexico, and in the third issue of the journal Zea published his groundbreaking essay, 'En torno a una filosofía americana', where he advocates a philosophical method tailored to the historical, cultural and social particularities of Spanish America. He maintains that to make a new beginning the most important problem that an emancipated Spanish American mind needs to address is the conflict between American experience and European ideas: 'El mal está en que queremos adaptar la circunstancia americana a una concepción del mundo que heredamos de Europa, y no adaptar esta concepción del mundo a la circunstancia americana' [the problem is that we want to assimilate American circumstances to a conception of the world inherited from Europe, not to assimilate that conception of the world to American circumstances].[55] Borrowing one of Eliot's most suggestive critical concepts, it may be reasonable to say that Zea's philosophical problem involves a 'dissociation of sensibility'. In fact, Eliot's phrase has been frequently used to talk about the self-estrangement felt by the colonized mind when confronted with the cultural norms of the metropolis. For instance, Declan Kiberd notes that turn-of-the-century Irish scholar Daniel Corkery articulated the conflict between the Irish child's schooling in the imperial culture and his emotional response to that culture as 'a reworked version of T. S. Eliot's notion of the dissociation of sensibility'.[56] More recently, Ngugi wa Thiong'o has made explicit use of Eliot's expression within an African context to make a point analogous to that of Corkery. He claims that the use of the colonial language for formal education in the British colonies in Africa 'resulted in the dissociation of sensibility [of children] from the natural and social environment, what we might call colonial alienation. The alienation became reinforced in the teaching of history, geography, music, where bourgeois Europe was always the centre of the universe'.[57] Zea's ideas find a meaningful context in this postcolonial theorization of the 'dissociation of sensibility', for he claims that the Latin American mind is constantly aware of a persistent mismatch between ideas and experience, between what is thought and what is felt.

Zea singles out this interstice between European knowledge and American reality as a truly Latin American site of philosophical and cultural production:

> El no haber podido ser europeos a pesar de nuestro gran empeño, permite que ahora tengamos una personalidad; permite que en este momento de crisis de la Cultura Europea sepamos que existe algo que nos es propio, y que por lo tanto puede servirnos de apoyo en esta hora de crisis. Qué sea este algo, es uno de los temas que debe plantearse una filosofía americana.[58]

[The fact that we could not become Europeans in spite of our great endeavours allows us to have a personality; it allows us to know that, at this moment of crisis of European Culture, there is something that belongs to us, and therefore can provide support in this time of crisis. What that something might be is one of the themes an American philosophy must posit.]

Contrary to what Ocampo proposed (namely, persisting in the attempt to become European or 'modern'), Zea regards the differences between Europeans and Latin Americans as the root of an authentic Latin American identity, an identity that should seek intellectual autonomy by refusing to simply receive and assimilate metropolitan knowledge. So rather than striving to palliate the 'dissociation of sensibility' that assails modern culture, the Mexican thinker suggests that the rupture created by such dissociation must be taken as a challenge to think beyond the bounds of European cultural referents and as an invitation to build a truly decolonized philosophy.

   Just as we can trace a continuum between Ocampo's Europeanist slant, the treatment of Joyce's aesthetics in *Sur*, and Rodríguez Monegal's and Fuentes's poststructuralist assessment of the new novel, so Zea's provocative arguments can be taken as an alternative paradigm against which to read the transcontinental dialogue between Joyce and Spanish American fiction. Arturo Uslar Pietri's 'La tentativa desesperada de James Joyce' (published in 1946 in *Cuadernos Americanos*) provides a suitable starting point for this enquiry. Uslar Pietri's article explores the 'kinetic' aesthetics of Joyce's *Ulysses* and its liberating potential. Unlike Eliot, Uslar does not interpret Joyce's novel as a recuperative effort to give shape to the crumbling monuments of European civilization. Joyce is neither concerned with creating an 'other' kind of literature nor with piecing together the fragments of a culture in crisis. This critic claims that the Irish novelist had to 'unlearn' the teachings and 'taboos' of European tradition and culture, forgetting 'todos los libros, todas las lecciones, todas las reglas' [every book, lesson and rule], before writing a novel that rediscovers the joy and exhilaration of seeing life in unprecedented ways. One of the 'taboos' that Joyce had to overcome was the denial of the body's artistic value. In Uslar's words: 'Todos nuestros órganos nos expresan. Nuestro sexo es como nuestros ojos o como nuestra inteligencia' [All our organs express us. Our sex is like our eyes or our intelligence].[59] *Ulysses* is an inspired example of this holistic view, for Joyce pays equal attention to the physical and spiritual dimensions of human experience. He charges the banal activities of a petite bourgeois with epic value instead of whittling down the unheroic and unsavoury aspects of existence to elevate life to mythical heights. According to the Venezuelan critic, the 'kinetic' details of *Ulysses* are not — as they were for Gilbert and others — raw materials subordinated to rigorous narrative techniques, but elements that provide a more accurate view of life and the self. If we only appreciate *Ulysses* for its structural reconstruction of the Homeric myth, Uslar contends, then the book is nothing more than an ostentatious archaeological boast ('un alarde arqueológico'). Instead, Joyce's *Ulysses* is a text that finds the mythical in the quotidian, offering the reader 'la odiseíca aventura presente del ser humano ante las mil formas de la circunstancia' [the Odyssean adventure of contemporary human beings facing the multiple forms of circumstance].

These 'human' (as opposed to purely formal) elements of *Ulysses* were celebrated by Hispanist Marcelino Peñuelas too, who in 'James Joyce tras el interrogante' (1957), also published in *Cuadernos Americanos*, dismisses the technical aspects and philological games of *Ulysses* that commanded so much attention among Anglo-American critics. Those formal and linguistic features, particularly the Homeric parallels, 'añaden muy poco a la obra, a su valor humano o literario' [add very little to the text, to its human or literary value].[60] Peñuelas also claims that the literary merit of Joyce's work is rooted in his suggestive treatment of 'human essence' — of issues such as the individual's struggle with the uncertainties of religious belief, the demands of national affiliation, or even the existential torment associated with idea of death. Notice the contrast between Uslar's and Peñuelas's emphasis on the multi-layered and ever-changing (kinetic) nature of human experience and Gilbert's classicist contention that *Ulysses* embodies the ideal silent stasis of the artist and that one of the main achievements of Joyce in the novel is 'to ban kinetic feelings from his readers' mind'.[61]

According to Uslar Pietri, Joyce's goal in *Ulysses* is to offer a fresh and full account of human life and experience that transcends the limitations (or 'taboos') of Western culture. Joyce's efforts to sidestep established constrictions and laws of 'method, logic, and expression' have 'magical' value. And his 'attempt' to 'torturar las formas y extraviar los sentidos' [torture the forms and displace the senses] is 'Baroque'.[62] Instead of appreciating *Ulysses* for its classical 'mythical method' or its static 'order', as T. S. Eliot and Stuart Gilbert did, Uslar attributes qualities to Joyce's narrative that he was to use elsewhere to differentiate Spanish American literature from the Western literary canon. In 'Lo criollo en la literatura' (1950), originally published in *Cuadernos Americanos*, Uslar sets out to outline the literary features that distinguish Spanish American letters from Spanish literature in particular and European literature in general.[63] Perhaps the most prominent of these features is the 'Baroque' tendency to express reality in convoluted ways. For the Spanish American mind, he maintains, life is not a balanced relation between intellectual forms and felt experience, but a tragic struggle that resists rational explanations — an intellectual predicament that recalls Eliot's 'dissociation of sensibility'. Reality is more 'felt' than 'thought' — the Spanish American is 'sentidor más que pensador' — given that European intellectual models tend to be considered as alien, imported and imposed. It is no coincidence that, as this critic points out, Spanish American literature is persistently 'impure', for it mixes and reshapes metropolitan literary trends and styles that in Europe remain separate. For instance, it is not uncommon to find classical and romantic features along with popular language and archaic expressions all mixed within the pages of the same Spanish American work. Uslar Pietri adds that the 'criollo' feeling of displacement caused by the disparity between thought and experience finds literary expression in a 'Baroque' and 'magical' language.

'Baroque' and 'magical'. That Uslar used the same terms to refer to both Joyce's *Ulysses* and the distinctive features of Spanish American literature suggests that he intuited a non-Western dimension in the Irishman's novel. The term 'magical' has been used and reused to exhaustion in discussions of contemporary Latin American narrative. Beyond the familiar combination of the 'real' and the 'fantastic', the 'mythical' and the 'historical', that popularly defines 'magical realism' (a term that has become shorthand for Third World exoticism), I want to further explore Uslar's combination of the 'magical' and the 'baroque' in a postcolonial key, emphasizing the shared potential of both concepts to define local experiences against hegemonic cultural formations. In this sense, the word 'magical' does not only refer to the colourful combination of pre-Hispanic myths and legends, a tropical setting, and supernatural events and motifs. It also refers to an alternative way of plumbing the depths of reality that opens up the possibility of other rationalities and other forms of expression.

Similarly, the 'Baroque' should not be simply understood as a historical or artistic period, but also as a decolonizing attitude connected with the disparity between ideas and reality that Zea considered to be a suitable starting point for a Latin American 'emancipation of the mind'. As Alejo Carpentier argued, the Baroque in Spanish America is not constrained to the seventeenth century, since it is 'a *spirit* and not a *historical style*'.[64] During the 1940s and the 1950s authors such as Carpentier, Lezama Lima and Uslar Pietri himself were proposing the Baroque as a category that could capture the essence of the Spanish American 'spirit' and its distance from the philosophical, cultural and literary traditions of Europe. As Monica Kaup has pointed out, 'the recovery of the Baroque' in Spanish American intellectual circles during this period 'is linked to the crisis of the Enlightenment and instrumental reason. The twentieth century crisis of Enlightenment rationality opens the way for the rediscovery of an earlier, alternate rationality'.[65] This early theorization of the Baroque among Spanish American scholars would later (in the 1960s and 1970s) crystallize into what has come to be known as the 'Neobaroque', whose main literary practitioners included Carpentier, Lezama Lima and Severo Sarduy.[66]

Lois Parkinson Zamora has recently claimed that the 'kinetic energy of Baroque space' in Spanish America, along with its 'impulse to expand and displace', is an 'instrument of postcolonial self-definition'.[67] It is her conviction that the Baroque sensibility is 'countermodern, not postmodern', meaning that it contests modernity not by simply deconstructing its ideological principles, but also by actively looking for alternative artistic and philosophical forms.[68] Zamora is therefore drawing a useful distinction between the internal development of Western rationality and the intellectual production of the periphery.[69] Certainly, the European Baroque has been recodified in Spanish America throughout history, from the seventeenth-centuries poems of Sor Juana Inés de la Cruz and the exuberant ornamentation of the Rosary Chapel in Puebla to the twentieth-century novels of Alejo Carpentier and José Lezama Lima. This redefinition of a prominent artistic trend has provided Spanish Americans with a means of intellectual, artistic and political self-determination. As Walter Mignolo maintains, since the 'Baroque of the Indies' should be understood as a decolonizing 'ethos' 'at the level of the state and the civil society', it 'cannot therefore be placed together as one more chapter of the European Baroque'.[70] Thus, the Spanish American redeployment of the complex visual and verbal forms of the Baroque becomes a self-conscious celebration of contradiction, disparity, heterogeneity — of the sense of fragmentation and dislocation that imbues the displaced mind of the 'criollo'. In other words, the Baroque 'sensibility' in Spanish America revels in excess, chaos, discordance, or, to put it in Eliot's terms, in the 'dissociation' it experiences when facing the conflict between colonial structures of power and knowledge and a multifaceted experience that resists and transcends those structures. It might be argued, then, that what this postcolonial use of the Baroque ultimately throws into relief is (to paraphrase Zea again) the rift between 'American circumstances' and a 'conception of the world inherited from Europe'.

Whereas Eliot lamented the failure 'to find the verbal equivalent for states of mind and feeling' associated with the 'dissociation of sensibility', Spanish American intellectuals and artists turned such disparity into a strategy of cultural decolonization. Eliot celebrated the capacity of the poet's mind to 'amalgamate disparate experience' so that 'the noise of the typewriter or the smell of cooking [...] are always forming new wholes'.[71] The Spanish American 'Baroque' sensibility also assimilates and recycles disparate elements, but it eschews the solidity of closed systems (or 'wholes'), thriving instead on contradiction, difference, openness. These contrasting approaches to literary representation are closely paralleled by the conflicting interpretations of Joyce's *Ulysses* found in '*Ulysses*, Order and Myth' and 'La tentativa desesperada de James Joyce'. Unlike Eliot's 'modernist' Joyce, who stands as a champion of the European tradition, Uslar Pietri's 'Baroque' Joyce actively devises ways to 'unlearn' the teachings of such tradition. Where Eliot sees a monumental attempt to create a 'new whole' out of the fragments of a rapidly disintegrating civilization, Uslar Pietri perceives a reflection of the Spanish American 'criollo' mind and the 'magical' and 'Baroque' literature it generates. Indeed, in 'La tentativa desesperada de James Joyce', the Venezuelan critic telescopes Joyce's kinetic aesthetics and his 'countermodernity' (to use Zamora's term) to suggest a transatlantic connection between Spanish American literature and Joyce's narrative beyond Anglo-American modernism. This implied connection takes place against the backdrop of the intense debate on cultural decolonization that permeated literary criticism, philosophy and political thought in Spanish America after World War II — during the years that witnessed Leopoldo Zea's call for the 'emancipation' of the Spanish American mind and the formulation of an 'American' philosophy', Uslar Pietri's and Carpentier's theories of the Baroque, and Frantz Fanon's articulation of his powerful anti-colonial discourse in *Peau noire, masques blancs* (1951), *L'An V de la revolution algérienne* (1959) and *Les Damnés de la terre* (1961). Examined within this context, the overlapping and crisscrossing between Joyce's work and Spanish American literature and criticism exceeds the scope of the Western canon, suggesting an alternative transnational literary geography that connects peripheral, postcolonial sites beyond the bounds of the European literary tradition.

Notes to Chapter 1

1. James Joyce, *A Portrait of the Artist as a Young Man*, p. 205.
2. Ibid., p. 215.
3. On Joyce's views on aesthetics, see William T. Noon, *Joyce and Aquinas* (Hamden, CT: Archon, 1970); Umberto Eco, *The Aesthetics of Chaosmos: The Middle Ages of James Joyce*, trans. by Ellen

Esrock (Tulsa,OK: University of Tulsa Press, 1982); and Jacques Aubert, *The Aesthetics of James Joyce* (Baltimore, MD: Johns Hopkins University Press, 1992). Noon's classic study explores the influence of scholastic philosophy on Joyce. Eco also emphasizes the Irish writer's indebtedness to Thomism and the persistence of scholasticism and allegorical structures in his fiction, especially *Ulysses*. Aubert's well-documented book focuses on Joyce's aesthetic theory as it developed in his critical writings. For an insightful and well-documented study on the conceptualization of Joyce's 'Irishness' in the early reception of his work, see Kevin Dettmar, 'Joyce/ "Irishness"/ Modernism', in *Irishness and (Post)Modernism*, ed. by John S. Rickard (Lewisburg, PA: Bucknell University Press, 1994), pp. 103–58.

4. Joseph Brooker, *Joyce's Critics: Transitions in Reading and Culture* (Madison: University of Wisconsin Press, 2004), p. 21.

5. Joseph Kelly, *Our Joyce: From Outcast to Icon* (Austin: University of Texas Press, 1998), p. 9.

6. Ezra Pound, *Pound/Joyce: The Letters of Ezra Pound to James Joyce, with Pound's Essays on Joyce*, ed. by Forrest Read (New York: New Directions, 1967), p. 93.

7. Ibid., pp. 32–33.

8. T. S. Eliot, '*Ulysses*, Order and Myth', in *James Joyce: The Critical Heritage*, ed. by R. H. Deming, 2 vols (New York: Routledge and Kegan Paul, 1970), I, 268–71 (p. 270).

9. A. Walton Litz, 'Pound and Eliot on *Ulysses*: The Critical Tradition', in *'Ulysses': Fifty Years*, ed. by Thomas F. Staley (Bloomington: Indiana University Press, 1974), pp. 5–18 (p. 15).

10. T. S. Eliot, 'The Metaphysical Poets', in *'The Waste Land' and Other Writings* (New York: Random House, 2002), pp. 224–34.

11. Eliot, '*Ulysses*, Order and Myth', p. 270.

12. Marc Manganaro, 'Dissociation in "Dead Land": The Primitive Mind in the Early Poetry of T. S. Eliot', *Journal of Modern Literature*, 13 (1986), 97–110. That Eliot knew the work of Lévy-Bruhl in substantial depth is an amply documented fact. On T. S. Eliot and Lévy-Bruhl, see David Spurr, 'Myths of Anthropology: Eliot, Joyce, Lévy-Bruhl', *PMLA*, 109, 2 (1994), 266–80.

13. Astradur Eysteinsson, *The Concept of Modernism* (Ithaca, NY: Cornell University Press, 1990), p. 10.

14. Dettmar, 'Joyce/'Irishness'/Modernism', p. 105.

15. H. G. Wells, 'James Joyce', in *James Joyce: The Critical Heritage*, I, 86–88 (pp. 86–87).

16. Immanuel Kant, *Observations on the Feeling of the Beautiful and the Sublime*, trans. by John T. Goldthwait (Berkeley: University of California Press, 1960), p. 104.

17. Ibid., 110.

18. Ibid., 111.

19. The phrase 'denial of coevalness' is due to Johannes Fabian, who argues in *Time and the Other: How Anthropology Makes Its Object* (New York: Columbia University Press, 1983) that a foundational mechanism for the Eurocentric constructions of 'otherness' consists of the articulation of the cultural hegemony of the metropolitan culture as temporal norm. Dominated cultures would then be 'primitive deviations' which permanently lag 'behind' that norm. Notice, in this regard, the irony involved in the modernist appropriation and transformation of the 'primitive' as raw material for 'new' artistic forms that could salvage the integrity of Western culture.

20. Cheng, *Joyce, Race, and Empire*, p. 27.

21. John Middleton Murry, '*Ulysses*', in *James Joyce: The Critical Heritage*, I, 195–98 (p. 196).

22. On the continuities among Pound, Eliot, and the canonical image of a modernist Joyce supported by the New Criticism, see Jeffrey Segall, *Joyce in America: Cultural Politics and the Trials of 'Ulysses'* (Berkeley: University of California Press, 1993), pp. 115–36.

23. Andrew Gibson, *Joyce's Revenge: History, Politics, and Aesthetics in 'Ulysses'* (Oxford: Oxford University Press, 2002), p. 2.

24. References to *Ulysses* will be made parenthetically in the text to the Hans Gabler edition: James Joyce, *Ulysses: A Critical and Synoptic Edition*, ed. by Hans Walter Gabler (London: Routledge, 1984), abbreviated as *U* and followed by the chapter and line numbers.

25. Nicholas Whyte, *Science, Colonialism and Ireland* (Cork: Cork University Press, 1999).

26. Cuban poet Heberto Padilla, initially a supporter of Castro's revolution, was placed under house arrest after the publication of his collection of poems, *Fuera de juego* (1968), which was considered subversive of the regime. Many writers that had supported Castro until then,

including Cortázar, Fuentes and García Márquez, expressed great dissatisfaction with this act of repression.

27. José Donoso, *Historia personal del 'boom'* (Madrid: Alfaguara, 1999), p. 60–61.
28. Julio Cortázar, 'Carta de Julio Cortázar', in *La región más transparente*, by Carlos Fuentes (Madrid: Alfaguara, 1994), pp. 525–29 (pp. 526–27).
29. Salgado, *From Modernism to Neobaroque*, p. 89.
30. Ibid., 91.
31. For David Viñas this attitude of cultural dependence crystallized in what he called 'the trip to Europe', a trip that symbolizes the abandonment of the materiality or the 'body' of American reality in order to attain the 'spirit' of Europe. According to Viñas, *Sur* embodied this trend by promoting the figure of the disengaged, individualistic and bourgeois writer. See David Viñas, *De Sarmiento a Cortázar* (Buenos Aires: Siglo Veinte, 1971). On 'the trip to Europe', see Viñas, *De Sarmiento a Cortázar*, pp. 141–214; and his *Literatura argentina y realidad política* (Buenos Aires: Siglo Veinte, 1971), pp. 3–80.
32. John King, *'Sur': A Study of the Argentine Literary Journal and its Role in the Development of a Culture* (Cambridge: Cambridge University Press, 1986).
33. Victoria Ocampo, *Testimonios* (Buenos Aires, Editorial Sudamericana, 1946), pp. 93, 97.
34. Virginia Woolf, *A Writer's Diary* (New York: Harcourt Brace Jovanovich, 2003), p. 46.
35. Michael H. Levenson has argued in *A Genealogy of Modernism: A Study of English Literary Doctrine, 1908–1922* (Cambridge: Cambridge University Press, 1984) that the founding of the *Criterion* is the 'mark of modernism's coming of age [...] because it exemplifies the institutionalization of the movement, the accession to cultural legitimacy' (p. 213).
36. Victoria Ocampo, 'T. S. Eliot', *Sur*, 159 (1948), 7–10 (pp. 7–8).
37. Stuart Gilbert, *James Joyce's 'Ulysses'* (New York: A. A. Knopf, 1930), p. 40.
38. Ibid., pp. 30–31.
39. On the Victorian tradition of the romanticized Celt and its contribution to racist discourse in England, see Lewis Perry Curtis, *Anglo-Saxons and Celts: A Study of Anti-Irish Prejudice in Victorian England* (New York: New York University Press, 1968) and *Apes and Angels: The Irishman in Victorian Caricature* (Washington, DC: Smithsonian Institution Press, 1971); and Luke Gibbons, 'Race Against Time: Racial Discourse and Irish History', *Oxford Literary Review*, 13, 1/2 (1991), 95–117.
40. Charles Duff, "*Ulises* y otros trabajos de James Joyce", *Sur*, 5 (1932), 86–127 (p. 95).
41. Ibid., p. 98.
42. Stuart Gilbert, 'El fondo latino en el arte de James Joyce', *Sur*, 122 (1944), 11–24 (p. 15).
43. Ibid., p. 11.
44. See José Ortega y Gasset, *La deshumanización del arte y otros ensayos de estética* (Madrid: Alianza, 1981). For Ortega, the vulgarity of the contents of an artistic object can never be the source of refined aesthetic experience. Only a select few ('una minoría especialmente dotada') can perceive the complexity of the purely formal elements that give shape to a work of art.
45. Emir Rodríguez Monegal, 'Aspectos de la novela en el siglo XX', *Sur*, 159 (1948), 86–96 (p. 94).
46. Ibid., p. 94.
47. Ibid., p. 96.
48. Carlos Altschul, 'Hacia una interpretación del hombre James Joyce', *Sur*, 260 (1959), 24–36 (p. 25).
49. See Lawrence Schwartz, *Creating Faulkner's Reputation: The Politics of Modern Literary Criticism* (Knoxville: University of Tennessee Press, 1988) for a discussion of the canonization of Faulkner as a cosmopolitan, modernist author, as part of the US Cold War cultural project to depoliticize art. Deborah Cohn has traced the influence of this project in the translation and promotion of contemporary Spanish American writers in the US, focusing on Alejo Carpentier, in 'Retracing *The Lost Steps*: The Cuban Revolution, the Cold War, and Publishing Alejo Carpentier in the United States', *CR: The New Centennial Review*, 3, 1 (2003), 81–108.
50. Rodríguez Monegal, *El boom de la novela latinoamericana*, p. 89.
51. Pedro Henríquez Ureña, *Seis ensayos en busca de nuestra expresión* (Managua: Nueva Nicaragua, 1986), p. 39.

52. Roberto Fernández Retamar, 'Fanon y América Latina', in *Algunos usos de civilización y barbarie* (Havana: Letras Cubanas, 2003), pp. 225–35 (p. 234).
53. Leopoldo Zea, *La filosofía como compromiso y otros ensayos* (Mexico: Tezontle, 1952), p. 57.
54. Leopoldo Zea, *Dependencia y liberación en la cultura latinoamericana* (Mexico: Joaquín Mortiz, 1974), p. 47. On the philosophical exchange between Fanon and Zea, see Robin Fiddian, 'Latin America and Beyond: Transcontinental Dialogue in the Work of Leopoldo Zea', *Interventions*, 5, 1 (2003), 113–24.
55. Leopoldo Zea, 'En torno a una filosofía americana', *Cuadernos Americanos*, 3 (1942), 63–78.
56. Declan Kiberd, 'Modern Ireland: Postcolonial or European?', in *Not on Any Map: Essays on Coloniality and Cultural Nationalism*, ed. by Stuart Murray (Exeter: University of Exeter Press, 1997), pp. 81–100 (p. 90).
57. Ngugi wa Thiong'o, *Decolonising the Mind: The Politics of Language in African Literature* (Portsmouth, NH: Heinemann, 1986), p. 18.
58. Zea, 'En torno a una filosofía americana', p. 68.
59. Arturo Uslar Pietri, 'La tentativa desesperada de James Joyce', *Cuadernos Americanos*, 27 (1946), 256–65 (p. 261).
60. Marcelino C. Peñuelas, 'James Joyce tras el interrogante', *Cuadernos Americanos*, 91 (1957), 183–200.
61. Gilbert, *James Joyce's 'Ulysses'*, pp. 30–31.
62. Uslar Pietri, 'La tentativa desesperada de James Joyce', p. 260.
63. Arturo Uslar Pietri, 'Lo criollo en la literatura', in *Veinticinco ensayos: antología* (Caracas: Monte Ávila, 1969), pp. 39–50.
64. Alejo Carpentier, 'The Baroque and the Marvelous Real', *Magical Realism: Theory, History, Community*, ed. by Lois Parkinson Zamora and Wendy B. Faris (Durham, NC: Duke University Press, 1995), pp. 89–108 (p. 95).
65. Monica Kaup, 'Becoming-Baroque: Folding European Forms into the New World Baroque with Alejo Carpentier', *CR: The New Centennial Review*, 5, 2 (2005), 107–49 (p. 108).
66. On the Neobaroque and its relation to (post-)modernity, see Irlemar Chiampi, *Barroco y modernidad* (Mexico: Fondo de Cultura Económica, 2000), especially pp. 17–41.
67. Lois Parkinson Zamora, *The Inordinate Eye: New World Baroque and Latin American Fiction* (Chicago: University of Chicago Press, 2006), pp. xvi–xvii.
68. Zamora, *The Inordinate Eye*, pp. 294–95.
69. It is important to note, however, that the postcolonial and the postmodern/poststructuralist merge in some instances, thus confusing the distinct geopolitical genealogies that Zamora is careful to keep separate. See, for instance, Severo Sarduy's essay, 'El barroco y el neobarroco', in *América Latina en su literatura*, ed. by César Fernández Moreno (México: Siglo Veintiuno, 1974), pp. 167–84, where he discusses the 'Neobaroque' using terms and concepts borrowed from poststructuralist theory. See also Severo Sarduy, *Barroco* (Buenos Aires: Editorial Sudamericana, 1974).
70. Mignolo, *The Idea of Latin America*, p. 62.
71. Eliot, 'The Metaphysical Poets', p. 232.

CHAPTER 2

The Limits of Parody: Allusion and Cosmopolitanism in Jorge Luis Borges

In *La nueva novela hispanoamericana* (1969), Carlos Fuentes boldly claims that without Borges the 'new novel' in Spanish America would not have existed. It was Borges's accomplishment, Fuentes contends, to have created a truly Latin American language — a playful language that reacts against a calcified and derivative literary tradition dominated by primitive forms and parochial topics. But the Mexican writer adds that this new language also renovates (or 'replenishes', to use John Barth's often-quoted term) Western literary forms in a postmodern age of lost certainties: 'lo que debe indicarse en seguida es que este signo de apertura que se impone al mundo cerrado de la tradición y el poder latinoamericanos coincide con la única posibilidad de la literatura occidental cuando ésta se vuelve consciente de haber perdido la universalidad' [what should be immediately noted is that the sign of openness that transforms the closed world of Latin American tradition and power is also the only value Western literature can embrace after losing its universality].[1] Such 'sign of openness' provides the grounds for a common measure of periodization that overcomes the cultural divide between Europe and Latin America. The liberating creativity of the Latin American writer merges with the metropolitan response to the loss of absolute values, thus configuring a new cultural geography which, despite shifting, dislocating and mixing centres and peripheries, still manages to provide a single unified picture of the world.

Although Borges's foundational role for the new novel is an almost undeniable fact, it would be a mistake to overlook his resistance to totalizing designs, even if those designs thrive on indeterminacy and 'openness'. It would be hard to find an author whose range of literary, cultural and philosophical reference is broader than Borges's. And yet, those references are deployed to make the attentive reader conspicuously aware of an inherent displacement, of what Cortázar termed *sentimiento de no estar del todo*. In this chapter I would like to concentrate on the ways in which Borges's literary allusions signal that displacement. Thus, rather than reading Borges as a rootless cosmopolitan artist, or even as a precursor of literary postmodernism on both sides of the Atlantic, I want to look at how his use of parody establishes a particular relationship with European culture and civilization that exceeds the bounds of authoritative canons, taxonomies and paradigms. In other words, I am interested in showing how Borges borrows and recycles a wide variety of cultural elements from the most disparate sources, including Homer's epics, Shakespeare's plays and Eliot's poems, but always refuses to assemble them into a single system, concept or idea.

As is so often the case, one can gain useful insights into Borges's convictions about literature and culture by analysing his nuanced treatment of other artists. James Joyce is a case in point. Emir Rodríguez Monegal argued that Borges's 'ficciones', the direct precursors of the Spanish American new novel, could be read as 'scale reductions' of *Ulysses*. Like Rodríguez Monegal, I wish to connect the interaction between Borges and Joyce with the roots of contemporary fiction in Spanish America. But by comparing Joyce and Borges I set out to contest and reverse the persistent assumption that these two peripheral writers wrote as Europeans. Joyce's critical reception in the Anglo-American academy closely parallels that of Borges. Borges, like Joyce, was accepted into the mainstream of the Western tradition only after he had been cleansed of his nationality and turned into a cosmopolitan literary icon, into a 'modern master', as Paul de Man called him. This cleansing of local residues has often allowed literary critics and theorists to claim their fiction as points of departure for postmodern and poststructuralist critiques of modernity.[2]

As social analysts Ernesto Laclau and Chantal Mouffe have shown, textual indeterminacy can be interpreted as an ideological nomadism of sorts: as a liberating critique of modernity and its foundational inconsistencies.[3] In a similar fashion, my discussion will draw attention to how Borges's fiction, particularly his use of parody, eschews the authority of the Western literary tradition and challenges its means of periodization. But rather than analysing his iconoclastic handling of the canon through the lens of deconstruction, I will tease out his ability to generate alternate literary genealogies. Whereas Fuentes invokes textual and linguistic indeterminacy to suggest a cultural synthesis between the centre and the periphery, I concentrate on how Borges prevents such synthesis by articulating his displaced status through quotations and parodies of texts belonging to the core of Western literature. Following Beatriz Sarlo, I should like to read Borges as an author 'who is at once cosmopolitan and national' — an author whose writing is not governed by the dictates of cultural nationalism and yet is imbued by a local and marginal perspective.[4]

Historically, Borges's 'cosmopolitanism on the edge', to use Sarlo's felicitous phrase, may be interpreted as an attempt to resolve the debate between the 'nationalists' and the 'cosmopolitans' that dominated Argentine society since the late nineteenth century. Those who advocated linguistic and racial purity as the essential cornerstone for a strong Argentine nation dreaded the 'degeneration' of the Spanish language and perceived the massive influx of immigrants as a dangerous social threat. A reaction to this 'nationalist' perspective came from a group of intellectuals, including Domingo Faustino Sarmiento and Juan Bautista Alberdi, who embraced immigration and the 'Europeanization' of culture as the foundation of a truly cosmopolitan and 'civilized' society. The value of Borges's intervention in this debate is to demonstrate its fallacious nature by showing that both alternatives remain deeply entrenched within a colonial mentality. In his essay 'Las alarmas del doctor Américo Castro', for instance, Borges disarticulates with merciless lucidity historian Américo Castro's complaints about the 'corruption' of the Spanish language in South America, underlining the absurdity of Castro's defence of the equally 'impure' and 'corrupt' Peninsular Spanish as the linguistic norm for the Hispanic world. More nuanced is Borges's critique of the cosmopolitanism embraced by Sarmiento and Alberdi, who flatly rejected ethnic essentialism to imitate metropolitan cultural and intellectual fashions (mainly French and English). The fabulist's mature fiction, particularly *Ficciones* and *El Aleph* — written during the period that witnessed the spectacular rise of the staunch populist nationalism of Juan Domingo Perón — might seem to defend a cosmopolitan stance beyond all local attachments. However, Borges's achievement is to have articulated his marginality — his 'Argentinness' — without renouncing to incorporating in his fiction the most diverse foreign materials.

In this sense, his 'cosmopolitanism on the edge' constitutes a relevant example of the phenomenon that James Clifford has labelled 'discrepant cosmopolitanism' — that is, a conception of cosmopolitanism imagined from the displaced perspective of colonial histories and peripheral spaces within modernity. Such transnational affiliations produce 'wordly, productive sites of crossing; complex, unfinished paths between local and global attachments' and not a single picture of the world regulated by universalistic systems of power and knowledge.[5] Along these lines and grounding his argument on a conception of modernity as always already colonial — the modern/colonial world system — Walter Mignolo has differentiated the totalizing and globalizing projects emerging from modernity (Christianity, the Enlightenment, Marxism) from 'critical cosmopolitanism', which like Borges's 'cosmopolitanism on the edge' and Clifford's 'discrepant cosmopolitanism' stems from the repressed underside of modernity.[6]

Allusion beyond Tradition

In order to elucidate how Borges articulates this kind of cosmopolitanism, I find it useful to discuss his use of parody and allusion in light of his critical treatment of Joyce's work. In my view, these two aspects highlight the Argentine writer's peripheral status within the modern/colonial world system, allowing us to interpret his narrative as a 'wordly, productive site of crossing' where allusions to the Western literary tradition and beyond are deployed to articulate 'complex, unfinished paths between global and local attachments'. As we shall see, this type of reading may be applied to Borges's use of parody as accurately as to his nuanced response to Joyce.

Borges's well-documented interest in Joyce spanned several decades, from his 1925 review of *Ulysses* and his partial translation of the novel's last page, which he published in the Buenos Aires periodical *Proa*, to his attendance at the centennial Joyce symposium held in Dublin in 1982. My intention here, however, is not to provide an exhaustive catalogue of the literary parallels and contrasts between these two authors. Partial attempts to carry out this task have been completed with variable success and bear witness to the fruitful interaction between the Irishman and the Argentine.[7] Here I want to focus on a very particular aspect of that interaction, namely Borges's critical response to Joyce's use of parody and literary allusions. His assessment of Joyce can be interpreted as an illuminating 'meta-commentary' on his own method of allusion and its relevance for the configuration of a 'cosmopolitanism on the edge'.

Borges's 'El acercamiento a Almotásim' provides a convenient starting point for our discussion. This early fictional piece is particularly relevant for our concerns because it includes an explicit reference to Joyce's *Ulysses* and to its Homeric parallels as an allusive technique. This text includes a review of an imaginary book, Mir Bahadur Alí's *The Approach to Al-Mu'tasim*. The plot summary refers to the quest of a young law student from Bombay who embarks on a mystical journey to find Almotásim, a man who irradiates intellectual clarity to the rest of humankind. The narrative finishes, we are told, right when the protagonist is about see Almotásim's face. The short critical commentary that follows the summary dismisses the scholarship devoted to the search for original sources, an opinion that appears to contradict the theme and structure of *The Approach*, a book that revolves around an unwavering quest for an origin. This contradiction might be explained to some extent if we interpret the story as an allegorical dramatization of Borges's agonistic relationship with the European literary tradition. Just as the student's pilgrimage toward a source of universal knowledge described in *The Approach* is abruptly suspended in the end, so Borges seeks, revisits, recycles, transforms but ultimately recoils from authoritative sources of literary value, refusing to tether his writing to canonical models originating overseas. From the estranged perspective of the Argentine writer, the literary order dictated by the Western tradition — its genres, its period terms, its pantheon of classics — is as alien, chaotic and confusing as the circuitous itinerary that the young student follows in *The Approach* — or as elusive as Almotásim himself. Read in this way, the errant, erratic and eventually unfulfilled search that shapes the plot of *The Approach* metaphorically undoes the literary logic that privileges originals over copies as well as the authority of the classics enshrined by tradition. It is in this context that we should understand Borges's disapproval of the search for Homeric parallels (or sources) in Joyce's *Ulysses*: 'Los repetidos pero insignificantes contactos del *Ulises* de Joyce con la Odisea homérica siguen escuchando — nunca sabré porqué — la atolondrada admiración de la crítica' [the repeated though insignificant contacts between Joyce's *Ulysses* and Homer's *Odyssey* keep attracting — I will never know why — the foolish admiration of the critics].[8]

That Borges did not read *Ulysses* as a literary monument firmly rooted in the Western literary tradition — as a modern rewriting of the Homeric classic — becomes apparent in his scattered critical notes on the novel. In a 1937 biographical sketch of Joyce, he argues that *Ulysses* is chaotic at first sight. In order to perceive its 'occult and strict laws', the reader is referred to Stuart Gilbert's *James Joyce's 'Ulysses'* (1930), a classic study that epitomizes the sort of criticism censured in 'El acercamiento a Almotásim'.[9] Four years later, in 'Fragmento sobre Joyce', written shortly after the Irish writer's death, Borges again describes *Ulysses* as an 'indecipherably chaotic' novel. Although published in *Sur*, this note offers an appreciation of *Ulysses* that subtly undermines the critical orthodoxy associated with Eliot's order of myth and Gilbert's emphasis on Joyce's indebtedness to Homer. 'Fragmento sobre Joyce' openly dismisses the Homeric parallels that Stuart Gilbert made the object of his book and Eliot took as the foundation of his 'mythical method', referring to them as '*tics* voluntarios'. Indeed, Borges might have agreed with the critic Hugh Kenner's observation that the object reading of *Ulysses* 'is not to reconstruct the schema, any more than one eats a dinner to reconstruct the recipes'.[10] For the Argentine writer, the revered 'severa construcción y la disciplina clásica de la obra' [strict construction and the classical discipline of the work] is simply 'insignificante'.[11]

In 'Vindicación de *Bouvard et Pécuchet*', Borges claims that *Ulysses* represents the death of the novel as a genre. In this, he coincided with T. S. Eliot, who also saw in *Ulysses* the beginning of a new genre. The novel, Eliot argued, 'ended with Flaubert and with James', while Joyce inaugurated a more ambitious and 'orderly' form with his book.[12] T. S. Eliot's ostensible critical goal in '*Ulysses*, Order and Myth' was to refute Richard Aldington's assessment of Joyce's novel as 'an invitation to chaos', but his larger theoretical motivation was to offer a normative interpretation of the Irishman's chaotic narrative by selectively reading its 'mythical' side as a paradigm of order.[13] Instead of emphasizing the restorative value of the book's classical structure and 'order', Borges focuses on the chaotic features of *Ulysses* to typify the new post-novelistic genre. In 'El arte narrativo y la magia', the Argentine writer argues that novels should reproduce the haphazard disorder of life through a contrived set of correspondences, presenting determinism as coincidence and chaos under the guise of order. This arrangement would emphasize the mutual interrelation of the transient, fleeting and contingent aspects of experience without specific reference to an overarching structural framework. According to Borges, *Ulysses* is the most accurate illustration of this kind of text, for it creates an 'autonomous world' ('orbe autónomo') 'de corroboraciones, de presagios, de monumentos' [of corroborations, of auguries, of monuments].[14] What Borges perceives in *Ulysses* is, therefore, neither a paradigm of 'order' nor an avatar of a classical text in modern garb. He suggests that despite its implicit Homeric subtext, the allusive texture of *Ulysses* is not mainly intended to anchor the contents of the book to a pre-existent literary model. On the contrary, this texture is envisioned as a mosaic of intratextual parallels and cross-references that provides the book with a kind of coherence which, like the elusive logic of superstition and magic, resists the imposition of general explanatory principles. Indeed, *Ulysses* abounds in apparently trivial details and references that weave an internal network of signposts and correspondences holding the text together. For instance, Stephen's recollection of his dream about a 'street of harlots', a man holding a melon against his face and a 'red carpet' becomes indeed a prophetic 'augury' of his encounter with Bloom later in the day (U 3.365–69). Together they will wander around Dublin's red district, a 'street of harlots', and afterwards Bloom, the worshipper of his wife's melon-shaped buttocks ('He kissed the plump mellow yellow smellow melons of her rump, on each plump melonous hemisphere' [U 17.2241–42]) will offer the artist his friendship and give him 'red carpet' treatment, inviting him to come to his home and share a cup of cocoa.

For Borges, this type of internal allusion provides *Ulysses* with a structural coherence that is not rooted in the imitation of classical models. The liberating power of this system of echoes contrasts with the function of parody in Eliot's 'mythical method'. As Linda Hutcheon has claimed, what distinguishes parody from other kinds of allusion is its critical edge, a critical edge that Eliot perceived in Joyce's rewriting of the *Odyssey*. As the British poet contends, *Ulysses* not only offers a mimetic rendering of Homer's epic, but also stresses that the cultural values embodied by the classical text were at risk and had to be reactivated. Hutcheon affirms that 'Eliot could be said to use parody in order to capitalize on its doubleness, to harmonize within art the schisms within culture'.[15] The textual mechanics of parody parallel in significant ways the complex relationship between his well-known notions of 'tradition' and 'individual talent'. One can certainly argue that Hutcheon's concise definition of parody as an 'authorized transgression' also describes the role of 'the individual talent' within 'tradition'.[16] In his familiar piece, 'Tradition and the Individual Talent' (1919), Eliot asserts that individual originality depends heavily on what has been inherited from literary predecessors, declaring that 'the past should be altered by the present as much as the present is directed by the past'.[17] Literary value derives from the lessons imparted by past poets, a conviction that he supports with his proposal of 'an impersonal theory of poetry'.[18] Thereby, poetry is an 'escape from personality' and individual feelings, a move that is underscored by making ultimate appeal to the ancients. In order to find a true poetic voice, he points out, the artist should write 'with a feeling that the whole of the literature of Europe from Homer and within it the whole of the literature of his own country has a simultaneous existence and composes a simultaneous order'.[19] The rewritings of a previous model carried out by parody and the individual talent are ultimately re-inscribed within the pervasive sameness of tradition. This is not to say that this sameness overrules difference: no one would dispute that Virgil's *Aeneid* and Dante's *Divine Comedy* are 'different' from the Homeric poems that inspired them. But that difference always remains within the bounds of a unitary literary tradition — after all, Virgil begins his epic poem where Homer's *Iliad* leaves off (the fall of Troy) and Dante's guide in the *Inferno* is no other than Virgil. Tradition is therefore a space of undisputed sameness that controls and regulates the measure of difference allowed to literary change.

Parody has been frequently considered a constitutive element of literary modernism. Fredric Jameson notes that 'parody found a fertile area in the idiosyncrasies of the moderns and their "inimitable" styles'. These styles deviate from a norm 'which then reasserts itself', thus maintaining the order and coherence of the cultural fabric while registering historical and social change in aesthetic terms.[20] But the sameness that parody refuses to obliterate is not only aesthetic, but also epistemological. Douwe W. Fokkema characterized modernism as the attempt of the artist to provide 'a valid, authentic, though strictly personal view of the world in which he lived', adding that modernist writers 'tried to climb on the empty throne of God in order to spread the gospel of their private semantic universe'.[21] Modernists believed that the artwork could provide a new symbolic transcendence which could palliate the devastating effects of war, colonialism and existential nihilism that plagued Europe at the turn of the twentieth century. In the face of social squalor, the 'high modernists' retreated to an aesthetic realm where Western values could be healed and reactivated.

If as Fokkema argues modernist art sought to replace religious beliefs, it would not be completely inaccurate to suggest that Eliot's tradition and the impersonality it demands constitute an ideological framework akin to religion. This connection was actually suggested by Eliot himself, who in *Religion and Literature* (1934) declared that literary criticism 'should be completed by criticism from a definite ethical and theological standpoint' and added that the '"greatness" of literature cannot be determined solely by literary standards'.[22] Ethical and mythical principles and values seem to be interchangeable as dogmatic touchstones for literary worth. As Timothy Materer has put it, 'the terms "Tradition and the Individual", or "Classic and Romantic", are drastically narrowed down when they are transformed, in *After Strange Gods*, into "Orthodoxy and Heresy"'.[23] Just as the individual conscience must follow the dictates of religious dogma, individual talent must express emotion by referring to canonical literature. Eliot's reliance on tradition was accompanied by a marked distrust of the poetic value of everyday experience. As he put it in 'Tradition and the Individual Talent': 'It is not in his personal emotions, the emotions provoked by particular events in his life, that the poet is in any way remarkable or interesting'.[24] He therefore suggests that one should not look for artistic materials in the sordidness of the real world but rather in the lines of the *Aeneid* or *Paradise Lost*.

Borges exceeds the bounds of Eliot's tradition through his strategy of allusion, which becomes an effective instrument to subvert the creed of artistic impersonality. The Argentine writer does not use parody to imitate a pre-existing model within a closed literary system, but rather to dismantle the idea of system itself. His fiction revises, reshapes and reconceives canonical texts, but ultimately undermines their universal merit and permanence. This practice of borrowing freely from a literary system without reasserting its ultimate authority involves a gesture of 'transgressive imitation' rather than 'authorized transgression', to quote again Hutcheon's definition of parody.

In order to sharpen our understanding of Borges's iconoclastic method of allusion I wish to return to his opinions about *Ulysses* in 'El arte narrativo y la magia'. I find it intriguing that within the same sentence, he can define *Ulysses* as both 'predestined' and 'autonomous': 'el *predestinado Ulises* de Joyce' is the best illustration of 'un orbe *autónomo* de corroboraciones, de presagios, de monumentos'.[25] Even though this novel may be described as a modernist parody of a Homeric original, its abrogation of logical causality undoes its derivative quality. Put differently: whereas the Homeric subtext makes *Ulysses* a 'predestined' work, the 'magical' logic governing the interrelation of its narrative elements endows it with 'autonomy'. This is not autonomy from a previous literary model, but from a cause-and-effect logic which filters out randomness and fits disparate events into coherent structures. These structures, which at a textual level might be called plots or fables, parallel the order demanded and perpetuated by Eliot's tradition. Indeed, what Borges calls 'natural' causality organizes experience through calculated and abstract operations, reducing the richness of life to an idea, a formula, an argument or a philosophical system. This is also the type of causality that governs the parodic relation between originals (causes) and imitations (effects) and, by extension, the connection between tradition and the individual talent.[26] This logic ensures that newness is always inserted within the confines of an established literary paradigm, forming a link in a single chain of interlocking texts. By contrast, the 'magical' arrangements that Borges perceives in *Ulysses* dismantles this hierarchy by refusing to press experience into a set of authorized models sanctioned by tradition. The 'autonomy' of Joyce's book derives from a 'precise and frantic' logic that exceeds and interrupts the parodic revisions and inversions that sustain the closed and stable limits of tradition. It is this kind of autonomy that I want to relate to Borges's peripheral position as an Argentine writer. No doubt Borges must have felt deeply the contradiction involved in asserting his creative independence or 'autonomy' through a language and a tradition that he was somehow 'predestined' to inhabit. Like the young lawyer in 'El acercamiento a Almotásim', or even like Zeno in the famous paradox so dear to Borges, the author of *Ficciones* is always at one remove from the canon and the language that nonetheless determine his creation.

The paradoxical combination of adjectives — 'predestined' and 'autonomous' — that Borges used to describe *Ulysses* is also apt to address the relation of the Argentine writer to the Western tradition. In 'El escritor argentino y la tradición' (1932), an essay that recalls Eliot's 'Tradition and the Individual Talent' in its main points, Borges, like Eliot, posits an unavoidable ('predestined') link between tradition and individual expression. However, he goes against the grain of a unified and totalizing literary tradition as advocated by Eliot. Borges affirms that the Argentine writer can claim as his own 'toda la cultura occidental' [all Western culture], but that he establishes a critical distance from it due to his marginal status. He goes on to relativize the demands of tradition as a matter of arbitrary choices, stating that what Argentines write will always be considered part of the Argentine tradition, regardless of what the past prefigured: 'Todo lo que hagamos con felicidad los escritores argentinos pertenecerá a la tradición argentina' [Anything we Argentine writers can do successfully will belong to the Argentine tradition].[27] With this assertion, he leads us to think that tradition does not follow a cause-and-effect, 'natural' logic. It is the effect rather than the cause that leads to an interpretation of the latter as such; whatever individual Argentine writers create — not what the past determines — will constitute Argentine tradition. In this sense, the 'autonomy' of personal individuality takes precedence over (and disrupts) 'predestined' literary change.

In 'Kafka y sus precursores', a recasting of Borges's ideas on influence, authorship and tradition, he reuses the argument of 'El escritor argentino y la tradición' to further destabilize the influence of tradition upon artistic creation defended by Eliot. Borges maintains that Kafka's writing creates its own literary antecedents and not the other way around. Echoing T. S. Eliot with an ironic intent, Borges writes that 'cada escritor *crea* a sus precursores. Su labor modifica nuestra concepción del pasado, como ha de modificar el futuro' [each writer *creates* his precursors. His work modifies our conception of the past just as it will modify the future].[28] This last sentence, to which a footnote citing T. S. Eliot's *Points of View* (1941) is appended, supports the British writer's critical views, but its contextual significance reverses them. The reference is to pages 25 to 26, which correspond to Eliot's 'Tradition and the Individual Talent', precisely to the part where he claims that no poet 'has complete meaning alone. His significance, his appreciation, is the appreciation of his relation to the dead poets and artists'.[29] Nevertheless, Borges dislocates the direction of influence posited by Eliot as he makes the emergence of literary lineages contingent on individual talent. Therefore, according to Borges, influence responds to a backward-forward — or 'magical' — dynamic instead of depending on the canonical authority of the dead poets.

Borges's critique of Eliot's idea of tradition is further developed in his short essay 'La eternidad y T. S. Eliot', originally published in 1933. In this piece he makes explicit the connection between 'predestination' and 'tradition' as he relates Eliot's tradition to the Christian notion of eternity. Borges notes that the eternal dimension of the Holy Trinity elevates it out of historical time: the triangular relationship between the Father, the Son and the Holy Ghost is forever happening and it pervades and predetermines the past, the present and the future. Eliot's 'Tradition and the Individual Talent', the Argentine writer points out, postulates an aesthetic eternity akin to that of Christianity. In Eliot's scheme, the European literary tradition since Homer occupies a place analogous to that of the Holy Trinity in the Christian paradigm. Within this tradition, the literary pantheon of the classics creates a totality from which there is no escape, forcing the new artist to submit to the authority of the past and its eternal rules of taste. Borges is quick to react against Eliot's doctrine, which, like its Christian version, leaves no room for radical dissent. The British critic's hypothesis is 'inept', for as Borges demonstrates, it involves a fundamental absurdity: the dogmatic rigidity that canonizes the classics denies the possibility of variations of taste over time.[30] No matter what the future might bring and no matter what one's personal preferences and ethnic background are, one should always assume that the 'illiterate' *Odyssey* or *El Quijote*, an 'unsophisticated novel' ('una novela popular'), are invested with universal and unchanging literary value.

In light of Borges's instructive comparison between the Holy Trinity and Eliot's 'tradition', we could argue that if dissension from tradition ever came to happen, it should be condemned as an aberrant heresy. Borges's short story 'Los teólogos' elaborates on this implication. Set in the sixth century in Europe, this story revolves around the intellectual rivalry between theologians Aureliano and Juan de Panonia. Although they are both church doctors who set out to condemn the same heresies to construct a universal Christian orthodoxy, Aureliano feels compelled to rebut Juan's arguments out of personal pride. 'Los teólogos' thus stages the drama of two opposed sensibilities trapped within the same religious and philosophical tradition. Aureliano's commitment to outwit his enemy in argument and style indicates the individual's quest for originality against the backdrop of a set of shared beliefs. Paradoxically, however, he defeats Juan only after he misquotes him and reveals that one of his refutations of a heresy is itself heretical (thus condemning him to the stake). Aureliano's strategy of misquotation not only turns orthodoxy into heresy, but also allows him to attain personal glory and intellectual distinction. Without indulging in a Romantic reverence of the 'I', Borges vindicates the autonomy of the individual talent, suggesting that even though the weight of tradition may be ineluctable, it can be modified and challenged in unsuspected ways. That Juan and Aureliano become the same person in the omniscient eyes of God after they die does not diminish the value of heretical transgression to articulate new meanings. The message of the story might be that religious orthodoxy, like literary tradition, is not an immutable monolith, but rather the result of the conflict between conservative forces and the innovative power of heresy.[31]

Allusion as Labyrinth

Borges's 'El Inmortal', a short story originally published in *El Aleph* (1949), can be read as a more extended though not less inspired dramatization of this conflict between tradition and personal creativity. My analysis of the text will focus on how Borges's use of parody intertwines with his subtle subversion of Eliot's classicism and his treatment of *Ulysses*. For Eliot, the main aspects to be admired and imitated in Joyce's masterpiece are the parallels between the wanderings of an average man around the streets of Dublin and the mythical journey of Odysseus. These parallels, the basis of the 'mythical method', endow the novel with 'universal value' and a distinguished place within tradition. Superficially, Borges's 'El Inmortal' appears to be a precise application of Eliot's 'method'. The story tells about a common Roman soldier, Marco Flaminio Rufo, who attains eternal life after drinking from the River of Immortality. He becomes Homer, inexplicably quoting from the Greek text of the *Iliad* upon tasting the magical waters, but also Ulysses, a fact reinforced not only by the eventful journey on which he embarks, but also because he claims to be 'Nobody' (Greek *Outis*), using the name the hero assumes when confronted by Cyclops Polyphemus in the *Odyssey*. The narrative of Flaminio Rufo's pilgrimage around the globe and across the centuries is indeed a condensed replica of Homer's epic, a miniature *Odyssey* that also echoes other works of Western literature and philosophy. Besides Homer, we find references to Pliny, Descartes, Thomas de Quincey and Vico, among others.[32] This dense fabric of literary and historical references is highlighted in the postscript to the story, where the narrator mentions a fictional commentary that discusses the main interpolations found in the main text. Nahum Cordovero, the author of this study, attributes the text to Joseph Cartaphilus, the bookseller who possesses the mysterious manuscript containing the captivating autobiography of the Immortal that Borges transcribes for us. This puzzling detail leads us to conclude that the narrative of Rufo-Homer-Ulysses might have been penned by Cartaphilus himself, in which case he would merge with those three personas and become one more avatar of the Immortal. Therefore, the Roman soldier turns into Homer after he drinks the sacred waters of the immortal river, but he also reincarnates the legendary Wandering Jew, one of whose names is no other than Joseph Cartaphilus.

This conflation of Homer and the Wandering Jew connects Borges's text and Joyce's *Ulysses*. *Ulysses* is also the story of a wandering Jew, Leopold Bloom, whose actions acquire mythical proportions through association with Ulysses's trials. However, if we interpret 'El Inmortal' as an extended commentary on Eliot's ideas on *Ulysses* and the 'mythical method', we are led to conclude that instead of emphasizing the redemptive powers of myth and tradition, the story underlines the devastating effects that those powers have on originality and personality. The grip of immortality, tradition and poetic impersonality, Borges suggests, is deadening rather than liberating. As he responds to Eliot's method from his Argentine perspective, he finds in Joyce not the mythical order that the British writer celebrates, but a labyrinthine worldview close to his own. His comment about the differences between the Europeans and the South Americans are worth remembering at this point: 'el mundo, para el europeo, es un cosmos, en el que cada cual íntimamente corresponde a la función que ejerce; para el argentino es un caos' [the world for the European is a cosmos where everybody is linked intimately to his own function; for the Argentine, it is a chaos].[33]

In 'El Inmortal', this chaotic perspective emanates not only from the narrator's specular personality but also from the allusive texture of the story. The labyrinth of literary references underlying the text is suggested by a dream that Flaminio Rufo has after he envisions the towers of the City of the Immortals: 'Insoportablemente soñé con un exiguo y nítido laberinto: en el centro había un cántaro; mis manos casi lo tocaban, mis ojos lo veían, pero tan intrincadas y perplejas eran las curvas que yo sabía que iba a morir antes de alcanzarlo' [Unbearably, I dreamed about an exiguous and clear labyrinth: there was a jar in its centre; my hands could almost touch it, my eyes could see it, but the curves were so intricate and perplexing, that I knew I was going to die before reaching it].[34] Michael Evans has related the textual universe evoked by this vivid dream to the evanescent figure of Homer: 'Homer is the name which stands for the source of all writing: a source which, like the water jar in Rufus's dream, remains eternally out of reach'.[35] References to Homer and his works permeate the allusive fabric of 'El Inmortal'. But these allusions are used to dismantle rather than to endorse the value that imbues literary classics. Besides being one of the protagonist's personas, Homer also appears in the story as a troglodyte, a member of the tribe of speechless immortals who live in the inhospitable waste land that surrounds the city. Rufo interprets his silence as a sign of savagery, and sets out to teach him a few words, including the name he gives him, 'Argos', which is also the name of Ulysses's dog in the *Odyssey*. Homer, the literary patriarch whose unchanging authority constitutes the pillars of tradition and the mythical method, here assumes the role of a father indoctrinated by his son, of the teacher who learns his lesson from a student, of the master whose literary meaning is created and preserved by his predecessor. As the poet himself confesses, the number of lines he remembers from the *Odyssey* is less than what the poorest rhapsodist would be able to recite. In 'El Inmortal', Homer becomes a void to be filled, an author that comes into being by virtue of what his predecessors or translators make of him. Similarly, his immortality ceases to have foundational value for Western literature, an aspect which can be read as an ironic critique of Eliot's contention in 'Tradition and the Individual Talent' that the best part of a poet's work is that 'in which the dead poets, his ancestors, assert their immortality most vigorously'. In 'El Inmortal' Homer's immortality, far from being the vigorous inspiration of new literary creation, is the cause of decadence and silence. The Greek poet's authority as a foundational figure is therefore endlessly deferred and the reader is sent on an endless search for an elusive, perhaps non-existent, source of literary meaning. Instead of leading to an original model, the allusions embedded in the text provoke a sense of estrangement and dislocation that calls to mind the young lawyer's truncated search in 'El acercamiento a Almotásim' as well as the 'magical' order that Borges associated with *Ulysses*.

The links between Borges's allusive method and his views on *Ulysses* become more evident when we compare the symbolic implications of the city in 'El Inmortal' and *The Waste Land*.[36] The city in *The Waste Land* is the material representation of Eliot's negative conception of contemporary life, of its endemic corruption and decadence. London is presented as an 'Unreal City' that evokes Dante's *Inferno*. It also merges with urban centres past and present to conjure up the sense of chaos, destruction, fragmentation and sterility that runs through the poem:

> What is the city over the mountains
> Cracks and reforms and bursts in the violet air
> Falling towers
> Jerusalem Athens Alexandria
> Vienna London
> Unreal.[37]

The modern city is thus associated with the threat of disorder. Confronted with this bleak scenery, the poet wonders: 'Shall I at least set my lands in order?' And the answer is, we might venture, yes. To undertake this enterprise, he is only left with 'These fragments I have shored against my ruins'.[38] Those fragments, fragments from a better past, correspond, in literary terms, to the lessons of the dead poets and tradition, which are the only adequate means to symbolically buttress the chaos that the city represents. Desmond Harding has characterized the post-Great War, industrial city as 'a menacing force beyond the capacity of human experience to control or even sometimes comprehend', offering Eliot's poem as a paradigmatic negative response to such destructive force.[39] The threat of the modern city elicits from Eliot a similar response as the unruly aspects of Joyce's prose in *Ulysses* that he strove to fit into an organized, mythical pattern.

It is in this light that we have to read the scholarly notes appended to *The Waste Land*. These notes detailing the literary sources of several lines scattered throughout the poem might have stemmed from Eliot's compulsion to order what he called the 'immense panorama of futility and anarchy which is contemporary history'.[40] Acknowledging the material borrowed from past poets can effectively arrest and control the fragmented images that populate the poem. Thus, *The Waste Land* evokes disorder only to re-inscribe it into an authoritative frame that signifies order. Eliot's allusive method is, then, designed to underwrite his idea of tradition as firm artistic grounding. Within this context, the metaphor of the modern city as chaos gains special significance when contrasted with the image of the 'monument', which he used to refer to the work of the 'dead poets' who preside over the realm of tradition. In his own words, the 'existing monuments form an ideal order among themselves'.[41]

Significantly, Ronald Bush has pointed out that '*Ulysses*, Order and Myth', often invoked to identify the techniques lying behind the construction of *The Waste Land*, 'belongs to the period when Eliot was reshaping, not composing, his poem', when he was adding, among other things, the notes.[42] He wrote the first version of the poem while suffering from severe bouts of depression and anxiety, completing its last two sections in a sanatorium in Lausanne. When the writer recovered, he was horrified at what he characterized as a 'sprawling, chaotic poem'.[43] Therefore, the notes become part of a strategy to regain control over personal and literary turmoil, eventually leading to the re-inscription of order, authority and tradition. They are a critical move to turn ruins into monuments.

Eliot's method of literary reconstruction enters into conflict with Borges's transgressive approach to tradition and the classics. Specifically, *A Coat of Many Colours*, the scholarly study by the fictional doctor Nahum Cordovero mentioned in the postscript to 'El Inmortal', can be read as a devastatingly ironic reversal of the endnotes in *The Waste Land*.[44] Like Eliot, Cordovero draws the reader's attention to the borrowings from previous sources embedded in the text. But instead of re-establishing order with this identification of sources, Cordovero becomes one more mirror reflection of an unreachable original author-figure. As noted above, his attribution of the manuscript to Joseph Cartaphilus closely connects the Jewish antiquarian with Flaminio Rufo and Homer. Cordovero's Jewish name also relates him to Cartaphilus, and, by extension, to Homer, to the Wandering Jew and, ultimately, to everyone and 'No one', the name that the protagonist assumes eventually. As Ronald J. Christ observes, both 'the title, *A Coat of Many Colours*, and the author's name, Nahum Cordovero, [...] disclose an artifice within artifice which is the hallmark of Borges'.[45] The title of his book is reminiscent of the biblical Joseph and his 'coat of many colours'. This coat is, etymologically, a *cento*, which is Latin for 'patchwork quilt'. This etymology establishes a specular relationship between Cordovero's study and its subject matter, the autobiography of the Immortal, which is indeed a richly textured patchwork of literary and historical allusions. The uncanny similarities between the text and the study convert the critic into the author and the character of the text he analyses. Therefore, whereas Eliot's endnotes acknowledge the value and stability of canonical authority, Borges's postscript fictionalizes and ultimately dissolves such authority through an endless game of mirror reflections.

As happens in *The Waste Land*, the motif of the city in 'El Inmortal' proves a valid illustration of Borges's citational method. Flaminio Rufo describes the entrance to the City of the Immortals as a dark, underground maze consisting of an indefinite number of geometrically regular chambers with doors endlessly leading from chamber to chamber. When he eventually emerges from this symmetric chaos, Rufo finds himself in the middle of a fascinating city of great antiquity. The Roman officer describes its enigmatic buildings as a labyrinth in which order and symmetry coexist with chaos and purposelessness. The City can be interpreted not only as a symbolic projection of Borgesian allusion as suggested by Rufo's unsettling dream about the water jug, but also of Joyce's *Ulysses* as read by Borges. *Ulysses* as described in 'El arte narrativo y la magia' is, like the City of the Immortals, a labyrinth of symmetries that lacks any overarching structure and purpose: it is an enigmatic conflation of order and disorder, of 'predestination' and 'autonomy'. The similarities between the city and the book are strengthened by the fact that the urban setting traversed by Rufo is a replica of the original City of the Immortals, just as *Ulysses* is a modern rewriting of Homer's *Odyssey*. The immortals endeavoured to reconstruct a new city from the ruins of an old one, but instead of recapturing the harmony of the old monuments, they could only build a place described as a 'parodia o reverso' [parody or reverse] of the original place. However, this urban parody does not reinforce the value of its model. Instead it becomes a terminal point, an inhospitable space that forces the immortals, including Homer, to leave its confines.

The reconstruction of the City parallels the narrative composition of *Ulysses*, as they both produce ordered chaos from fragments of a previous model. In an interview, Roberto Alifano asked Borges whether he thought that Joyce used Homeric symbolism to provide a complete and ordered vision of human experience. He answered that such vision is never fully integral, arguing that after finishing *Ulysses* the reader is left with a 'sensación de caos'. He claimed, however, that the work abounds in symmetries, and that its chaos is really a cosmos, but a secret one ('ese caos es más bien un cosmos, pero un cosmos secreto').[46] This 'secret cosmos', which does not depend on the archetypal authority of the Homeric model but on a mysterious code generated by the text itself, might be the most accurate description of Borges's peripheral status and his critical distance from the Western tradition, of his 'cosmopolitanism on the edge'. Like the perplexing architecture of the City of the Immortals, the 'secret' and 'magical' logic that he attributes to *Ulysses* stresses the eccentricity of the novel, its labyrinthine texture. It might not be a coincidence that Borges's laudatory 'Invocación a Joyce' referred to the Irishman's works as 'arduos laberintos, / infinitesimales e infinitos' [arduous labyrinths / infinitesimal and infinite].[47]

If we agree with Claudio Guillén's contention that 'a cultural whole or a literary system could be visualized, metaphorically speaking, as the verbal and imaginary equivalent of an ancient yet living, persistent yet profoundly changing *city*', then we would be compelled to claim that, in light of the foregoing analysis, Eliot inhabits the monumental surface of this *civitas verbi*, while Borges, like Flaminio Rufo, wanders through its labyrinthine underside.[48] As Malcolm Bowie put it in memorable terms, 'Borges inhabits literature as one might inhabit a great city — surprised by its curiosities, pausing at its crossroads, crossing and recrossing its thoroughfares endlessly, switching from its surface to its underground routes, and never wanting it to be a single portentous thing'.[49] A similar conclusion could be drawn from Borges's treatment of *Ulysses* and Eliot's 'mythical method'. Where the Argentine writer perceives an 'other' ('magical') order, the British poet sees a portentous enterprise to restore and preserve the monolithic foundations of the 'monuments' of tradition. Borges reads Joyce like he inhabits tradition: from a perspective which dislocates Western civilization and culture by punctuating literary discourse with the *situatedness* of the peripheral writer.

Although Borges frequently argued that individuality is merely a mirage, that all men are really one man, and all books one book written by avatars of the same author, he envisioned this cultural commonality or cosmopolitanism from the a process of nation formation. The cultural nationalism that the name 'Fergus Kilpatrick' evokes is indeed a parody of the imperial system, but a parody that re-inscribes difference within the sameness of such system. As Partha Chatterjee has aptly put it:

> Nationalism denied the alleged inferiority of the colonized people; it also asserted that a backward nation could 'modernize' itself while retaining its cultural identity. It thus produced a discourse in which, even as it challenged the colonial claim to political domination, it also accepted the very intellectual premises of 'modernity' on which colonial domination was based.[55]

Read in this light, Ryan's 'revival' of his Gaelic grandfather reinforces the cultural homogeneity that sustains the colonial system. Cleansing the figure of Fergus Kilpatrick of his act of treason implicitly sustains the binary opposition that separates the colonizer from the colonized and positions them in a hierarchical relationship. Borges exposes the limitations of Ryan's wholehearted celebration of the hero by showing that it is precisely Nolan's translation and Kilpatrick's act of treason that ultimately spark the revolution. The creator of national consciousness is not a hero, but a traitor or a translator. Nolan, like Borges himself, resorts to the colonial culture to assert the independence of his nation, but in doing so, he does not reinforce the authority of such culture. Instead, Nolan's creative mistranslation disrupts the binary oppositions that sustains the colonial order, since it demonstrates that the oppressed can appropriate the culture of the oppressor without producing servile imitations. Far from constituting a tribute to the metropolitan culture, Nolan's parody of Shakespeare becomes a fissure that literally turns into political resistance.

Brazilian theorist Roberto Schwarz claims that 'in countries where the culture is imported, parody is almost a natural form of criticism'.[56] But as we have seen, parody can either re-inscribe within sameness the transgression it involves, or it can generate an excess of meaning that cannot be assimilated to a unified cultural, literary or political system. In Derrida's words: 'to use parody or the simulacrum as a weapon in the service of truth or castration would be in fact to reconstitute religion';[57] but parody can also be a radical force that, like Borges's 'laughter' as described by Foucault in *The Order of Things*, 'shatters' the 'familiar landmarks' of Western culture and thought, 'breaking up all the ordered surfaces and all the planes with which we are accustomed to tame the wild profusion of existing things, and continuing long afterwards to disturb and threaten with collapse our age-old distinction between the Same and the Other'.[58] The first use of parody fails to transcend the closed limits of the system within which it operates, ultimately upholding its stability. This parodic mechanism underlies what Homi Bhabha calls 'hybridity' or 'mimicry'. As Bhabha argues, 'hybridity' is concerned with unsettling 'the mimetic or narcissistic demands of colonial power' by turning 'the gaze of the discriminated back upon the eye of power'.[59] This backward glance has the unnerving effect of revealing that the colonizer depends on the construction of an 'other' for self-definition. The relationship between colonizer and the colonized is, according to Bhabha, a game of masks that conceals an ultimate lack of stable identities. But hybridity, one could argue, still ties up the cultural and political destiny of the colonial 'other' to the metropolis, this time not because of the demands of a project of imperial expansion, but owing to a shared lack of ontological points of reference. The hybrid subject is still compelled to use metropolitan forms to voice his resistance to hegemonic authority, and his anti-colonial resistance can only emerge as a constant deconstruction (or parody) of the colonial model. In contrast, Nolan's translation and staging of Shakespeare's plays move beyond this act of deconstruction, for they embody the revolutionary sort of parody that Foucault associated with Borges. We should not forget that the Nolan's parody of the English playwright is not merely a playful act of transgression, for it ultimately results in a revolution that seeks to build a new sense of community and a liberated culture. In this sense, the Irish writer illustrates Walter Benjamin's contention (expressed in a somewhat different context) that 'it is the task of the translator to release in his own language that pure language which is under the spell of another, to liberate the language imprisoned in a work in his recreation of that work'.[60]

A possible critique of this utopian reading might be that Nolan's translation results not only in revolution, but also in death. And it could also be argued that Kilpatrick's death is the ultimate act of nationalist fervour, its disinterestedness being the arresting emblem of the nationalist martyr. In dying for his 'patria', Kilpatrick is literally staging the ultimate sacrifice of personality that the collective realm of the nation demands from its citizens. But his death is the result of loyalty as much as it is the consequence of his act of treason. Viewed in this way, Kilpatrick's death might also function as a reminder that the monolithic cultural nationalism that his name evokes is indeed an absence, a lack that, very much like Homer in 'El Inmortal', can turn into radical agency only when it becomes the site of translation/treason. The hero's death also links his condition to that of Borges's Immortal himself, for whom individuality and freedom could only be attained after regaining the gift of death. As the Immortal puts it:

> La muerte (o su alusión) hace preciosos y patéticos a los hombres [...]. Todo, entre los mortales, tiene el valor de lo irrecuperable y de lo azaroso. Entre los Inmortales, en cambio, cada acto (y cada pensamiento) es el eco de otros que en el pasado lo antecedieron, sin principio visible, o el fiel presagio de otros que en el futuro lo repetirán hasta el vertigo.[61]

> [Death (or its allusion) makes men precious and pathetic [...]. Everything among mortals has an irretrievable and perilous value. Among the Immortals, on the other hand, every act (and every thought) is the echo of others that preceded it, without a visible origin, or the faithful premonition of others that will repeat it to oblivion in the future.]

While death symbolizes the ultimate act of personal abnegation for the integrity of the nation, Borges's short story incites us to read this motif as an interruption of the circular relationship between the self and abstract ideas about collective identity, between individual personality and the accumulation of 'actos' and 'pensamientos' that give shape to a culture, perpetuating its image as in an endless gallery of mirrors. Death might rubricate patriotic sacrifice and ensure the continuity of the traditional values that define an 'imagined community', but it also marks the precise moment at which the identification between citizen and nation comes to an abrupt involvement with Irish folklore. Although Mulligan unveils the artificiality of imperial forms of interpellation, repeatedly mocking the Englishman's interest in Irish culture and presenting revivalist art as satisfying the demands of the occupier, he is unable to transcend hegemonic structures and strictures, subverting them but never threatening to collapse the colonizer–colonized distinction. As what V. S. Naipul called a 'mimic man', Mulligan appropriates the language of authority, but only to reinsert it within the colonial imagery. It is as if the local culture, even in its most cosmopolitan or 'Hellenic' guise, existed only for the sake of a centre, to fulfil its colonial fantasies of control and domination. It is this subservient act of compliance with the occupier that Stephen deems proper of 'a jester at the court of his master, indulged and disesteemed, winning a clement master's praise' (U 2.43–44).[65]

By contrast, Joyce's transgressive use of parody becomes an effective strategy to rethink the role of artistic creation in postcolonial settings. His repudiation of the cultural revival that dominated the Irish cultural and political scene during his lifetime has been traditionally interpreted as a refusal to seriously engage in political matters.[66] This aloofness to the revivalist tendencies of his time, along with his choice to live in exile, was also taken as proof of his staunch 'cosmopolitan' alliances. However, reading Joyce's Ulysses from the vantage point afforded by Borges's 'Tema del traidor y del héroe' detaches it from a reductive national-vs.-cosmopolitan deadlock and illuminates its value as a renovated form of post-imperial writing. Like Borges's Nolan, Joyce exposes the shortcomings of cultural nationalism and Mulligan's mimicry by showing that they are still deeply entrenched in the master-and-servant logic that they set out to expose. For the Irish writer, 'parody is no merely temporary transgression, but a gesture that precedes a radical break' that will clear the ground for new forms of interaction between individuals, culture and politics.[67]

Borges's evocative description of the City of the Immortals and its subterranean 'stone network' can help us visualize these alternative ensembles of social and cultural relations. The underground labyrinth lacks a fixed origin, a centre, but it is not a chaotic space, for it is organized according to a strict geometrical structure. This precise yet puzzling order (reminiscent of the 'magical' patterns that Borges notes behind the construction of Ulysses) also characterizes the purposeless buildings of the city: as in an Escher drawing, its dead-end corridors, its inverted stairways, its doors leading to dark cells lack any finality, but they still give shape to an urban geography described as a 'kind of parody or inversion' of the original city. The bewildering architecture of the city and the convoluted form of the labyrinth project in spatial terms a sense of wonder, estrangement and displacement akin to the marginal status of the colonized that inhabits the culture of the colonizer. At the same time, however, Borges's city also suggests new and audacious designs, designs that do not radiate from a centre or derive from an original blueprint. As a novel architectural rearrangement unforeseen by the original builders of the City of the Immortals, the parodic city provides a visual equivalent of what Frantz Fanon defined as the post-nationalistic stage in anti-colonial struggles. In The Wretched of the Earth, the Martinican thinker charts a tripartite scheme toward decolonization: occupation, nationalism, liberation. The third stage marks the utopian moment at which the colonized turns away from the imperial model — from the forms and ideas sanctioned by the occupier — to forge a new culture whose authenticity depends neither on a return to a pre-colonial native source nor on the imitation of the inherited culture, a culture that the fully emancipated mind can now remodel without being dominated by it. It is after this final stage is completed that the colonized allows himself to speak freely, liberated from the desires of an alien authority.[68] As we have shown, the forward-looking articulation of such liberated mode of expression in the writings of Joyce and Borges heavily relies on the ability of parody to dismantle the hierarchical relationship between models and copies, between originals and imitations, that underpins the Western canon.

Borges's disavowal of a unified historical and literary world picture regulated by metropolitan designs is emphasized not only by the contents but also by the narrative structure of his short story, 'Tema del traidor y del héroe'. His choice to call it 'theme' and not 'story' highlights the text's lack of closure and its provisional shape. We are told that the story is a draft describing a political situation that could be equally true in a number of countries or regions, all of which have been 'oppressed and tenacious' and share a colonial past: Poland, Ireland, Venice, or any South American or Balkan state. This openness registers at a rhetorical level the political transformations required by anti-colonial liberation, since it is implied that if the histories of these countries were fictional plots, they would lack closure, thus remaining open to utopian endings yet unwritten. According to Fanon, the 'immobility to which the colonized is condemned can be challenged only if he decides to put an end to the history of colonization and the history of despoliation in order to bring to life the history of the nation, the history of decolonization'.[69] 'Liberation' is not only antagonistic to teleological master-plots originating in the metropolis, but also to their narrative articulation — to their mode of storytelling — as Borges's text implies. Otherwise, liberation would simply amount to inventing a tradition modelled on the *schemas* of the hegemonic culture. 'Tema del traidor y del héroe' complements Fanon's observations by configuring a malleable narrative form where the histories of colonized groups from 'oppressed and tenacious' regions are neither assimilated to metropolitan designs nor doomed to silence, but instead cross and recross, enacting encounters 'in the periphery' and moving beyond the history of Western civilization, which is also 'the history of colonization'. This innovative form thus gives narrative shape to a 'cosmopolitanism on the edge' that does not stem from the repudiation of local particularism, but which is rooted in an act of shared irreverence and mutual recognition on the margins.

These cosmopolitan affiliations, originally enabled by the 'history of colonization' and yet resistant to hegemonic grids of reference, provide a suitable frame to approach the literary dialogue between Joyce and Borges as an encounter on the margins, or the underside, of the Western canon. Borges's reading and rewriting of Joyce distances the Irish writer from the conception of modernism institutionalized by Eliot's criticism and poetics. That is, their interrelation underscores the chasms and gulfs between Europe and its decolonizing periphery, knitting together a transnational literary tapestry whose various multicoloured threads do not constitute a single image, but rather create unforeseen entanglements, partial figures and designs that expose what Borges in the poem 'Cosas' calls 'el reves del prolijo mapamundi' [the other side of the detailed world map] and 'el otro lado del tapiz' [the other side of the tapestry].[70] Read in this way, Borges's 'scale reduction' of Joyce's fiction is pivotal in the development of Spanish American literature, not because it directs the course of the region's narrative towards the innovations of Anglo-American (post-)modernism, but rather because it effects a decolonizing shift away from aesthetic modernity as defined by Eurocentric canons and literary histories.

Notes to Chapter 2

1. Fuentes, *La nueva novela hispanoamericana*, p. 32.
2. On Borges and continental theory, see Emir Rodríguez Monegal, 'Borges and La Nouvelle Critique', *Diacritics*, 2, 2 (1972), 27–34 and Carlos J. Alonso, 'Borges y la teoría', *Modern Language Notes*, 120, 2 (2005), 437–56. On Joyce and theory see Geert Lernout, *The French Joyce* (Ann Arbor: University of Michigan Press, 1990) and Alan Roughley, *James Joyce and Critical Theory: An Introduction* (Ann Arbor: University of Michigan Press, 1991).
3. Ernesto Laclau and Chantal Mouffe, *Hegemony and Socialist Strategy: Towards a Radical Democratic Politics*, trans. by Winston Moore and Paul Cammack (London: Verso, 1985).
4. Beatriz Sarlo, *Jorge Luis Borges: A Writer on the Edge*, ed. by John King (London: Verso, 1993), p. 4. Other works that have delved into the relevance of Borges's 'Argentinness' in his literary work are Sylvia Molloy, *Signs of Borges*, trans. by Óscar Montero (Durham, NC: Duke University Press, 1994) and 'Lost in Translation: Borges, the Western Tradition and Fictions of Latin America', in *Borges and Europe Revisited*, ed. by Evelyn Fishburn (London: Institute of Latin American Studies, 1998), pp. 8–20 and Daniel Balderston, 'Borges: The Argentine Writer and the "Western" Tradition', in Fishburn, ed., *Borges and Europe Revisited*, pp. 37–48.
5. James Clifford, 'Mixed Feelings', in *Cosmopolitics: Thinking and Feeling beyond the Nation*, ed. by Pheng Cheah and Bruce Robbins (Minneapolis: University of Minnesota Press, 1998), pp. 362–70.
6. Walter D. Mignolo, 'The Many Faces of Cosmo-Polis: Border Thinking and Critical Cosmopolitanism', *Public Culture*, 12, 3 (2000), 721–48. 'Cosmopolitanism' as a theoretical category has attracted a notable amount of critical attention in recent years. On 'cosmopolitanism' within a Latin American context, see Noël Salomon, 'Cosmopolitanism and Internationalism in the History of Ideas in Latin America', *Cultures*, 6, 1 (1979), 83–108 and Jacqueline Loss, *Cosmopolitanisms and Latin America: Against the Destiny of Place* (New York: Palgrave Macmillan, 2005), especially pp. 1–42. On the intersection between literary modernism and a 'critical' version of cosmopolitanism defined by 'an aversion to heroic tones of appropriation and progress, and a suspicion of epistemological privilege, views from above or from the center' (p. 2), see Rebecca Walkowitz, *Cosmopolitan Style: Modernism Beyond the Nation* (New York: Columbia University Press, 2006).
7. There is a substantial number of studies that focus on the literary ties between Borges and Joyce. Louis A. Murillo, in *The Cyclical Night: Irony in James Joyce and Jorge Luis Borges* (Cambridge, MA: Harvard University Press, 1968) studies the presence of irony in both authors, though in separate chapters and rarely establishing connections between them. Andrés Sánchez Robayna, in 'Borges y Joyce', *Ínsula*, 437, 1 (1983), 1, 12, offers an appraisal of Borges's reception of Joyce's work in his critical writings. Along the same lines, Antonio Ballesteros in 'Controversias, exilios, palabras y cegueras: Joyce en Borges', in *James Joyce: Límites de lo diáfano*, ed. by Carmelo Medina and others (Jaén: Universidad de Jaén, 1998), pp. 61–71, and Suzanne Jill Levine in 'Notes on Borges's Notes on Joyce: Infinite Affinities', *Comparative Literature*, 49, 4 (1997), 344–59, focus on Borges's explicit references to Joyce and Joyce's work as well as on the biographical parallels between the authors. In 'Barroco Joyce: Jorge Luis Borges's and José Lezama Lima's Antagonistic Readings', in *Transcultural Joyce*, ed. by Karen Lawrence (Cambridge: Cambridge University Press, 1998), pp. 63–93, César A. Salgado delves into Borges's ambivalent relationship with Joyce's aesthetics.

Beatriz Vegh's 'A Meeting in the Western Canon: Borges's Conversation with Joyce', *European Joyce Studies*, 14, 1 (2002), 85–97, remarks Borges's and Joyce's shared 'semicolonial' status and focuses on Borges's 1925 article and partial translation of *Ulysses* in *Proa*. Sergio Gabriel Waisman also assesses this Borgesian translation in 'Borges Reads Joyce: The Role of Translation in the Creation of Texts', *Variaciones Borges*, 9 (2000), 59–73. Thomas Rice offers insightful connections between the two authors in 'Subtle Reflections on/upon Joyce in/by Borges', *Journal of Modern Literature*, 24, 1 (2000), 47–62. Andrés Pérez Simón, 'Borges' Writings on Joyce: From a Mythical Translation to a Polemical Defence of Censorship', *Papers on Joyce*, 7/8 (2001/02), 121–37, documents Borges's references to Joyce in his critical writings.

8. Borges, *Obras completas*, I, 417–18.

9. Borges, *Obras completas*, IV, 251.

10. Hugh Kenner, *Dublin's Joyce* (Bloomington: Indiana University Press, 1956), p. 225.

11. Jorge Luis Borges, 'Fragmento sobre Joyce', in *Borges en "Sur", 1931–1980* (Buenos Aires: Emecé, 1999), pp. 167–69 (p. 168).

12. Eliot, '*Ulysses*, Order and Myth', p. 270.

13. Ibid., p. 269.

14. Borges, *Obras completas*, I, 222.

15. Linda Hutcheon, *A Theory of Parody: The Teachings of Twentieth-Century Art Forms* (Urbana and Chicago: University of Illinois Press, 2000), p. 99.

16. Ibid., p. xii.

17. T. S. Eliot, 'Tradition and the Individual Talent', in *'The Waste Land' and Other Writings* (New York: Random House, 2002), pp. 99–108 (p. 101).

18. Ibid., p. 104.

19. Ibid., p. 100.

20. Fredric Jameson, *Postmodernism, or, The Cultural Logic of Late Capitalism* (Durham, NC: Duke University Press, 1991), p. 16.

21. Fokkema, *Literary History, Modernism, and Postmodernism*, pp. 40–41.

22. T. S. Eliot, *Points of View* (London: Faber and Faber, 1941), p. 145.

23. Timothy Materer, 'T. S. Eliot's Critical Program', in *The Cambridge Companion to T. S. Eliot*, ed. by David Moody (New York: Cambridge University Press), pp. 48–59 (p. 58).

24. Eliot, 'Tradition and the Individual Talent', p. 106.

25. Borges, *Obras completas*, I, 244; emphasis added.

26. Ibid., p. 245.

27. Ibid., p. 273.

28. Borges, *Obras completas*, II, 90.

29. Eliot, *Points of View*, p. 25.

30. Jorge Luis Borges, *Textos recobrados, 1931–1955* (Buenos Aires: Emecé, 2001), p. 51.

31. On heresy in Borges's fiction, see Ted Lyons and Pjers Hangrow, 'Heresy as Motif in the Short Stories of Borges', *Latin American Literary Review*, 3, 5 (1975), 23–35.

32. For a detailed commentary on the literary sources of 'El Inmortal', see Ronald J. Christ, *The Narrow Act: Borges's Art of Allusion* (New York: New York University Press, 1969), especially the last chapter.

33. Borges, *Obras completas*, II, 37.

34. Ibid., I, 573.

35. Michael Evans, 'Intertextual Labyrinth: "El Inmortal" by Borges', *Forum for Modern Language Studies*, 23, 3 (1984), 275–81 (p. 280).

36. The critical studies that compare these two texts focus on their similarities rather than their differences. Ronald J. Christ argues in *The Narrow Act* that *The Waste Land* provides 'not only an analogous form but parallel content as well. In a word, both *The Waste Land* and "El Inmortal" are centos which come to pretty much the same conclusion' (p. 214), namely a shared sense of fragmentation. He goes on to offer a list of parallels that is expanded and complemented by Joseph Rosenblum's study of the themes and symbols common to both texts, '"The Inmortal": Jorge Luis Borges's Rendition of T. S. Eliot's *The Waste Land*', *Studies in Short Fiction*, 18, 2 (1981), 183–86. Rosenblum does not problematize the relationship between the texts either, presenting it as a matter of dependence or influence.

37. T. S. Eliot, 'The Waste Land', in *'The Waste Land' and Other Writings*, pp. 38–56 (pp. 49–50).
38. Ibid., p. 51.
39. Desmond Harding, *Writing the City: Urban Visions and Literary Modernism* (London: Routledge, 2003), p. 13.
40. Eliot, '*Ulysses*, Order and Myth', p. 270.
41. Eliot, 'Tradition and the Individual Talent', p. 101.
42. Ronald Bush, *T. S. Eliot: A Study in Character and Style* (New York: Oxford University Press, 1984), p. 71.
43. Ibid., p. 70.
44. Borges, *Obras completas*, I, 544.
45. Christ, *The Narrow Act*, p. 212.
46. Roberto Alifano, *Conversaciones con Borges* (Madrid: Debate, 1986), p. 114.
47. Borges, *Obras completas*, II, 409.
48. Claudio Guillén, *Literature as System* (Princeton, NJ: Princeton University Press, 1971), p. 12.
49. Malcolm Bowie, 'Borges and the Art of Allusion', in Fishburn, ed., *Borges and Europe Revisited*, pp. 124–28 (p. 126).
50. On Borges's ideas about collective identity and national culture see Silvia Rosman, *Dislocaciones culturales: nación, sujeto y comunidad en América Latina* (Rosario: Beatriz Viterbo, 2003), especially pp. 109–33. On Borges's critique of cultural nationalism, see also William Rowe, 'How European Is It?', in Fishburn, ed., *Borges and Europe Revisited*, pp. 21–36 and Gabriel Riera, '"The One Does Not Exist": Borges and Modernity's Predicament', *Romance Studies*, 24, 1 (2006), 55–66.
51. On Borges and translation, see Efraín Kristal, *Invisible Work: Borges and Translation* (Nashville, TN: Vanderbilt University Press, 2002) and Sergio Gabriel Waisman, *Borges and Translation: The Irreverence of the Periphery* (Lewisburg, PA: Bucknell University Press, 2005).
52. Douglas Hyde, 'The Necessity of De-Anglicizing Ireland', in *The Revival of Irish Literature*, ed. by Charles Duffy and others (London: T. Fisher Unwin, 1894), pp. 115–61 (p. 160–61).
53. Lloyd, *Anomalous States*, p. 103.
54. Kiberd, *Inventing Ireland*, p. 151.
55. Partha Chatterjee, *Nationalist Thought and the Colonial World: A Derivative Discourse* (Minneapolis: University of Minnesota Press, 1993), p. 30.
56. Roberto Schwarz, *Misplaced Ideas: Essays on Brazilian Culture*, ed. by John Gledson (London: Verso, 1992), p. 40. See also Roberto Ferro's 'Introduction' to the collective volume *La parodia en la literatura latinoamericana*, ed. by Roberto Ferro (Buenos Aires: Universidad de Buenos Aires, 1993), where he claims that parody is the discursive mode through which Latin America has historically questioned hierarchies of authority and paradigms of centre/periphery, model/copy and original/translation (pp. 7–9). On parody and Latin American culture, see also Else Viera, 'Ig/noble Barbarians: Revisiting Latin American Modernisms', in *Postcolonial Perspectives on the Cultures of Latin America and Lusophone Africa*, ed. by Robin Fiddian (Liverpool: Liverpool University Press, 2000), pp. 70–102.
57. Jacques Derrida, *Spurs: Nietzsche's Style / Eperons: Les Styles de Nietzsche*, trans. by Barbara Harlow (Chicago: University of Chicago Press, 1981), p. 99.
58. Michel Foucault, *The Order of Things: An Archaeology of the Human Sciences* (London and New York: Routledge, 2002), p. xvi.
59. Homi Bhabha, *The Location of Culture* (London: Routledge, 2004), pp. 159–60.
60. Walter Benjamin, *Illuminations: Essays and Reflections* (New York: Schocken, 1969), p. 80.
61. Borges, *Obras completas*, I, 580.
62. On Borges's interest in Giordano Bruno, see Robert Carroll, 'Borges and Bruno: The Geometry of Infinity in "La muerte y la brújula"', *Modern Language Notes*, 94, 2 (1979), 321–42.
63. Kiberd, *Irish Classics*, p. 474.
64. Borges, *Obras completas*, I, 482.
65. On Joyce's critique of Mulligan's role as 'native informant' see Cheng, *Joyce, Race, and Empire*, pp. 151–84. On Mulligan and mimicry, see Eric D. Smith, 'The Mimetic "Spirit of Denial": Buck Mulligan and the Cultural Limits of Mockery', *Papers on Joyce*, 9 (2003), 19–33.
66. This 'apolitical' portrayal of Joyce has been challenged in a number of publications. See

Dominic Mangianello, *Joyce's Politics* (London: Routledge, 1980) and Christy Burns, *Gestural Politics: Stereotype and Parody in Joyce* (Albany: State University of New York Press, 2000).

67. Kiberd, *Inventing Ireland*, p. 342.
68. Frantz Fanon, *The Wretched of the Earth*, trans. by Richard Philcox (New York: Grove, 2004).
69. Ibid., p. 15.
70. Borges, *Obras completas*, II, 513–14.

CHAPTER 3

❖

Double Consciousness and Counter-Myth in Julio Cortázar's *Rayuela*

The question is: can one do something different, set out in another direction? Beyond logic, beyond Kantian categories, beyond the whole apparatus of Western thought — for instance, looking at the world as if it weren't an expression of Euclidian geometry — is it possible to push across a new border, to take a leap into something more authentic?

JULIO CORTÁZAR, Interview with Luis Harss and Barbara Dohmann

...la hotelera, irlandesa y por lo tanto no euclidiana, comprendería sin esfuerzo que donde cabían dos cabían tres. [...the hotelkeeper, who was Irish and therefore non-Euclidian, would easily understand that where two fit three would fit too.]

JULIO CORTÁZAR, *62. Modelo para armar*

In *Dialectic of Enlightenment* (1944) Theodor Adorno and Max Horkheimer interpret the voyage of Ulysses in the Homeric epic as a metaphor for the birth of modernity. Ulysses's resistance to the seductive yet deadly allure of Circe and the Sirens indicates the triumph of reason over myth, of the superior capacities of calculation and 'cunning' over ritualistic and magical powers. Similarly, the hero's eventual return to his homeland, Ithaca, signals the consolidation of bourgeois rationality after leaving behind the threats of pre-rational forces. Although Ulysses's successful homecoming establishes secular rationality as the privileged structure of thought, the episodic narrative of his voyage reveals the exclusions on which the legitimacy of the Enlightenment is founded, thus exposing rationality's duplicity as universal 'Spirit' and nihilistic 'anti-life force'.[1] Adorno and Horkheimer claim that due to this constitutive duplicity the Enlightenment never fully effaces what it buries, and is therefore always haunted by its dialectical opposite: myth.

This neat dialectic between reason and myth, thesis and antithesis, home and abroad, can be dismantled with particular force when the symbolic significance of the Ulyssean journey is imagined and re-enacted by those for whom modernity is an imposed discourse. In colonial situations where the subordinated elites set out to achieve political emancipation, embracing the authority of modernity often led to the embarrassing contradiction of articulating one's act of rebellion with the rhetorical strategies of the dominant power. Ever since independence from Spain was achieved during the nineteenth century, this paradox has characterized Spanish American cultural and literary discourse in a persistent manner.[2] Either in metaphorical or thematic terms — as a means of psychological characterization or as a plot-structuring device — the narrative of the journey has been frequently deployed in Spanish American letters to delve into the vexed relationship between the New World and Europe.[3] Authors concerned with the articulation of an American (as opposed to European) identity often faced the uncomfortable historical fact that what they were striving to conceptualize as 'home' was actually the 'abroad' of European modernity, for America was, since its 'invention' (to use Edmundo O'Gorman's apposite term) a mythical space destined to project and fulfil the utopian longings of European rationality and history.[4]

Deliberately or not, foundational texts of the Spanish American canon such as José Eustasio Rivera's *La vorágine*, Rómulo Gallegos's *Doña Barbara*, Alejo Carpentier's *Los pasos perdidos* and Ernesto Sábato's *El túnel* expose the inconsistencies of modernity's historical narrative. Caught on the cusp between the redemptive rhetoric of European modernity and the mythic space of the American continent, these texts posit a metaphorical voyage of homecoming and discovery 'in reverse' as they document the incompatibility between European knowledge and a geographical space that resists assimilation to such knowledge. Some of the most representative fiction of Julio Cortázar could be added to this list. His first novel, *Los premios* (1960), revolves around the trials of a group of Argentines who, after winning a lottery prize, embark on a European cruise liner whose destination remains a mystery. Soon the cruise passengers become painfully aware of the absurdity of their existence on board and engage in a persistent search for a 'centre' (indeed, a 'home') that could endow their lives with transcendental meaning. Similarly, *62. Modelo para armar* (1968) presents an interconnected web of characters without psychological consistency or vital purposes who remain in constant transit around evanescent spaces simply called the 'city' and the 'zone'.

But perhaps the most complete exploration of the symbolic possibilities of the Ulyssean voyage to articulate the discontinuities between Spanish America and Europe is found in Cortázar's most celebrated work, *Rayuela* (1963). The protagonist, Horacio Oliveira (who is explicitly characterized as a 'Hodious Hodysseus' in the novel) is an Argentine intellectual who embarks on a search for transcendental meaning beyond what he considers the alienating structures of reason and civilization. Joining Oliveira in his journey towards the 'other side' of convention and habit, I would like to discuss Cortázar's critique of modernity and how it intersects with his deployment of myth in *Rayuela*. Contrary to what criticism attuned to postmodernist theories of the text has generally suggested, I will not contend that Cortázar's fiction simply stages the dissolution of the binarism between rationality and myth. Roberto González Echevarría, for instance, has claimed that Cortázar's 'mythology of writing', his aesthetic grammar, revolves around 'a hegemonic struggle' between myth and reason 'for the center, which resolves itself in a mutual cancellation and in the superimposition of beginnings and ends'.[5] Without trying to discredit this sort of interpretation, I argue that rather than merely engaging in a deconstruction of the dialectic of Enlightenment, Cortázar finds in the constitutive contradictions of such dialectic fertile ground to imagine an alternative counter-myth to the totalizing myth of modernity. This counter-myth is not an Archimedean 'elsewhere' or 'kibbutz of desire', as Oliveira would like to think. Nor is it a definite point of arrival, an alternative Ithaca that simply reverses Ulysses's voyage and redirects it towards the shores of irrationality and myth. Instead, Cortázar's transgressive use of myth thrives on the double consciousness afforded by the experience of modernity on the margins.

In order to conceptualize this counter-mythical creativity, I should like to compare and contrast it with modernist aesthetics, given that the experimental form and language of *Rayuela* have been customarily associated with literary modernism. In *Journeys through the Labyrinth*, Gerald Martin points out that this novel stands as the epitome of 'Spanish American Modernism' and that its publication in 1963 marked 'the precise moment at which "Joycism" appeared to assume the main thrust of Spanish American fiction'.[6] According to Martin, *Rayuela* constitutes a nodal point that connects Joycean modernist poetics (or what he calls the 'Ulyssean novel' referring to *Ulysses*) and the Spanish American novel. This association has been more recently discussed to emphasize the dated quality of *Rayuela*, as well as its lack of 'authenticity', when read from a contemporary, postmodern perspective that exposes the reductive ethnocentrism of literary modernism. For instance, Neil Larsen claims that Cortázar's 'modernism' has been perceived as politically inauthentic ever since 'a global shift within what we might call the ideology of reading' has affected Latin American literature. This critic contends that the recent attention to 'testimonial' works has exposed the limitations of Cortázar's avant-gardism to engage culturally and politically with Latin American reality.[7] I agree that reading *Rayuela* in a modernist or postmodernist key, as 'the Latin American *Ulysses*', as Larsen puts it, disables the novel's capacity to generate inventive alternatives to modernity that could go beyond a politically sterile exposure of its inescapable contradictions. I also agree that interpreting the nexus between Joyce and Cortázar against the background of modernism ignores their aesthetic and cultural marginality, transforming them into canonical figures of a transnational avant-garde placed above local attachments. However, I contend that one could forcefully dispel Cortázar's political 'inauthenticity' by taking his reception of Joyce's work as an apt starting point to discuss what I have called his creative counter-myth, that is, his narrative response to the decolonizing struggles that took place in Latin America in the 1950s and 1960s. I will use this counter-mythical attitude as a frame to rethink the ties between Joyce and Cortázar beyond the bounds of Anglo-American modernism.

That the Argentine writer admired Joyce's artistic achievement in *Ulysses* is a well-documented fact.[8] This admiration finds its most obvious expression in an interview with Evelyn Picón-Garfield, who asked Cortázar to name five books that he would save from a bonfire which would consume all the books in the world. He could only mention *Ulysses*, a volume which, he believed, summarizes universal literature.[9] He also considered Joyce's novel to be a model for his own artistic endeavours in *Rayuela*. Shortly after the novel was released, Juan Carlos Ghiano published a scathing review in the Argentine newspaper *La Nación*. In his rejoinder, Cortázar retorted that the reviewer had failed to see the radical novelty of his work just as (Cortázar imagined) contemporary reviewers censured Joyce for failing to adopt the conventional 'language of the tribe' and the realistic style of Thomas Hardy or John Galsworthy.[10] It seems obvious that the Argentine novelist perceived in Joyce's prose the irreverence toward canonical culture which he identified with his literary preferences, which he discussed in an interview with Luis Harss and Barbara Dohmann. Cortázar admitted that as a young man he was drawn to the poetry of Valéry, Eliot and Ezra Pound, that is, to what he called 'the Goethian tradition' in obvious reference to the classicism of these authors. But this is a tradition he distanced himself from as a mature writer because 'it's entirely circumscribed within the mainstream of the Western tradition'. Instead, he became more interested in what he called a 'literature of exception', since exceptions offer 'an opening or a fracture and also, in a sense, a hope'.[11]

In Chapter 79 of *Rayuela* we find what is perhaps the most concise and illuminating formulation of what Cortázar understood as a 'literature of exception'. The chapter consists of a collection of fragmentary and seemingly unconnected theoretical notes where the novelist and critic Morelli (arguably Cortázar's alter ego) describes the characteristics of a new genre, the *roman comique*. The main aim of the *roman comique* is to overcome the *schemas* and constraints of Western knowledge by exploring new ways ('otros rumbos') of characterization, textual organization and authorial presence. This new narrative form recoils from the coherence of 'closed orders' and invites the reader to develop a personal relationship with the text and to freely explore possible meanings and messages unforeseen by the author or other readers. The *roman comique* embodies the 'fracture' that Cortázar associates with the 'literature of exception', for, unlike the novel, which as a 'creature of choice in the Western world' is content 'con un orden cerrado' [with a closed order], it seeks 'la apertura y para eso cortar de raíz toda construcción sistemática de caracteres y situaciones' [an opening by cutting the roots of all systematic construction of characters and situations].[12] Morelli affirms that the method to achieve this narrative revolution is irony and constant self-criticism ('la autocrítica incesante') and that the example to follow is set by Joyce's *Ulysses*. On a superficial level, it might seem that he is simply describing the most salient textual features of *Rayuela* and then establishing a close correspondence between those features (notably self-reflexivity and irony) and the aesthetics of modernism via Joyce. However, the implied similarities between Morelli's narrative theory and literary modernism begin to dissolve if we focus on the contrasting implications of irony and self-criticism for Cortázar and for modernist discourse. If irony for Cortázar–Morelli means an interruption of coherence, a 'fracture' opening up new literary dimensions unregulated by a bankrupt rationality, it could be argued that modernist irony functions as a mechanism of epistemological restitution.

To distinguish the irony of Cortázar's *roman comique* from that found in Euro-American modernism, let me first return to the dialectic between myth and rationality. In *Literature, Modernism and Myth*, Phillip Bell explains that modernist literature is characterized by 'mythopoeia', which he defines as a mode of expression that consciously presents rationality as myth. This imbrication of the mythical and the rational generates a sense of ironic distance that manages to preserve the universal legitimacy of modernity in a time of cultural crisis. According to Bell, philosophical works published in Europe during the first two decades of the twentieth century widely reflected the crisis of representation associated with the loss of faith in Europe's cultural superiority. Referring to Heidegger's notion of the 'age of the world picture', this critic asserts that one of the defining features of modern thought is that it is aware of its own relativity.[13] This awareness generates the 'double consciousness of living a world view *as* a world view [...] of recognizing a world view as such while living it as conviction'.[14] The rational is thus self-consciously lived as mythical. From this perspective, the relationship between myth and rationality ceases to be dialectical and becomes supplemental or symbiotic, thus configuring a symbolic space that palliates and restores the representational capacity of reason under the sign of irony.

In 'A Note on Modernism' (in *Culture and Imperialism*), Edward Said is more precise about the historical determinations that shaped the development of European modernism and relates the ironic distance that Bell attributes to 'modernist mythopoeia' to the growing familiarity that turn-of-the-century Parisians or Londoners had with colonial cultures. The looming awareness of exotic civilizations overseas seeped into the core of the metropolis and became the source of discomforting anxiety for the European imagination, as shown by characters such as Marlowe in Conrad's *The Heart of Darkness* or Aschenbach in Mann's *Death in Venice*. If Marlowe reports Kurtz's African horror back in London, on the quiet waters of the River Thames, Aschenbach dies from an Asian plague in one of the most splendid centres of European culture, Venice. This disturbing sense of unrest, Said argues, also conditions and shapes the formal innovations of modernist narrative. The realist faith in mimetic representation, as well as the triumphalist rhetoric of the literature of Empire (e.g. Kipling), was undercut by the disquieting realization that Western Europe is only one among many other cultures. This conviction, along with the Spenglerian sense of decline that accompanied it, changed the way in which culture in the metropolis reflected upon itself; it could no longer take itself seriously, only ironically. In modernist literature, irony manifests itself as 'a desperate attempt at a new inclusiveness'. According to Said, the encyclopaedic form of Joyce's *Ulysses* and Proust's *In Search of Lost Time*, or the self-conscious juxtaposition of cultural fragments drawn from diverse cultures found in *The Waste Land*, are elements that can be read as a 'response to the external pressures on the culture from the *imperium*'.[15] Thus, modernist irony and the double consciousness that it creates are part of an aesthetic strategy that tries to solve the crisis of representation plaguing the West: 'the irony of a form that draws attention to itself', Said contends, is a means of 'substituting art and its creations for the once-possible synthesis of the world empires'.[16]

Cortázar's apparent association with modernism breaks down when interpreted in light of his political discourse. Nothing could be further from his purpose than upholding an aesthetic *Ersatz* that could reactivate in literary terms the global reach of world empires. Although the case for a 'postcolonial modernism' can be built on a purely formalistic basis (fiction written by authors from the British ex-colonies, such as Salman Rushdie or Arundhati Roy, frequently displays experimental features traditionally related to Anglo-American modernism and postmodernism), the critical validity of such label diminishes if we concentrate on the ideological and political implications of modernist aesthetics. In 'El compromiso del escritor', Cortázar underlined the contradictions of using metropolitan forms to express revolutionary impulses and acknowledged that anti-totalitarian gestures might be inescapably doomed to resort to the language of power. However, he offered one possibility to escape from the panoptic purview of this language: a 'revolución constantemente inventiva' [constantly inventive revolution]; a revolution that does not rely on the promise of a utopian future or a transcendental truth, nor on the restorative powers that Bell and Said attribute to literary modernism.[17] Instead, this revolution recombines life and culture in unconventional and unsuspected ways, achieving autonomy from reified laws by reshuffling, recycling and rearranging the elements that such laws convert into 'closed orders' and normative discourses. Although commonly associated with the anti-imperialism of the sixties in Latin America, Cortázar's 'revolutionary inventiveness' moves beyond abstract ideologies and monolithic party lines as it intersects more broadly with the rhetoric of irony and self-criticism that characterizes the *roman comique*.

Therefore, I do not intend to frame Cortázar's critique of hegemonic structures of power and knowledge within the leftist ideology that revamped the anti-colonial movements of the 1960s. The Argentine writer's unfaltering refusal to subtract artistic freedom from political engagement should discourage us from reducing his idea of 'invention' to the rigid mechanics of capital, labour and class struggle. As Santiago Colás points out, Cortázar repeatedly criticized the kind of revolutionary attitude that followed ideological dogmas blindly. Instead, the Argentine writer challenges his readers to reconceive reality by always turning it into something new: 'the way poets have always made something new of the elements at hand, the way life makes something by combining what is lying around, the way the stargazer makes something out of a group of gleaming pins stuck in the cool cushion of the night sky'.[18] Thus, I will not link Cortázar's 'revolución constantemente inventiva' to the schemes of Marxist materialism, but to the 'double consciousness' that arises from relentlessly imagining the surging contours of novel cultural and historical configurations against the backdrop of established interpretations of the world. Instead of repairing the fault lines of rationality through what Bell calls 'modernist mythopoeia', Cortázar's double consciousness engages with life's contradictions without ever offering permanent solutions. It involves a split perspective which does not unite myth and rationality into a conciliatory synthesis; instead it opens up an imaginative space — a space of 'invention' — by perpetually recoiling from all types of final closure. This revolutionary dimension offers common ground to discuss Cortázar's notion of 'literature of exception' and its nuanced connection with Joyce's fiction.

The challenges of what I take to be Cortázar's double consciousness are best exemplified by the trials and tribulations of Horacio Oliveira in *Rayuela*. Argentine by birth, Oliveira emigrates to Paris for reasons that are never clearly stated, and once there he becomes emotionally involved with a Uruguayan woman known as 'La Maga'. To a large extent, the relationship between Oliveira and La Maga parallels that between Ulysses and the pre-rational, mythical forces that he finds during his voyage back to Ithaca (note that Circe was a 'maga' or sorceress, and that her name in Spanish is frequently preceded by that word in the common expression *La maga Circe*). Oliveira's hyperintellectual mind sharply contrasts with La Maga's natural and untutored intuition, which he interprets as the cure for his metaphysical anxiety: 'Hay ríos metafísicos, ella los nada como esa golondrina está nadando en el aire, girando alucinada en torno al campanario [...]. Yo describo y defino y deseo esos ríos, ella los nada. Yo los busco, los encuentro, los miro desde el puente, ella los nada' [There are metaphysical rivers, she swims them just like that swallow is swimming in the air, spinning around the bell tower [...]. I describe and define and desire those rivers, she swims them. I search them, find them and look at them from the bridge, she swims them].[19] Judging from these lines, it seems obvious that Oliveira sees La Maga as the endpoint of his existential quest. It is no coincidence that the opening words of *Rayuela* are '¿Encontrará a La Maga? [Will he find La Maga?].[20] This quest, like Ulysses' voyage as read by Adorno–Horkheimer, stems from an original duplicity that ought to be overcome after one side of such duplicity controls the other.

Oliveira is painfully aware that there is something tragically wrong with reason, civilization and culture. Referring to the Cartesian *cogito*, he affirms: 'en mi caso el *ergo* de la frasecita no era tan ergo ni cosa parecida' [in my case, the *ergo* in the little phrase was not so *ergo* or anything like it].[21] To escape from the strictures of rationality, he seeks a vague transcendental realm which he designates with a variety of labels ('kibbutz of desire', 'paradise lost', 'mandala') and identifies with La Maga. The most obvious difference between Oliveira's search and the Ulyssean journey (as interpreted by Adorno–Horkheimer) is that they advance toward opposite ports of call. If Homer's hero strays from the corrupting allure of Circe the sorceress, Oliveira — staging what might be interpreted as a dialectics in reverse — longs to embrace the raw vitality of La Maga. In either case, however, the dialectic nature of the process is left unchallenged as the double consciousness that it involves is perceived as an obstacle or intermediate phase prior to a revelatory moment of resolution: either Ulysses's homecoming and the triumph of reason or Oliveira's abandonment of the regulations of culture and the attainment of a mystical state of communion with the untapped pre-rational forces he thinks La Maga embodies.

Contrary to what happens in modernist discourse, the irony that permeates *Rayuela* is not intended as a strategy to overcome the double consciousness provoked by the underlying duplicity of the Enlightenment. Cortázar shows that by pursuing a transcendental 'oneness' Horacio is simply repeating the structures that he anxiously tries to escape from. In doing so, the Argentine novelist makes the powerful point that to 'take a leap' beyond the bounds of reason one must rupture the closure achieved through the dynamics of thesis–antithesis–synthesis. His ironic treatment of Oliveira's grand metaphysical designs is perceived throughout the novel. Perhaps the most obvious example involves the fact that La Maga's supposedly genuine and untutored experience of reality does not really stand as a static antithesis to Oliveira's rationality. Just as he strives to see through La Maga's eyes, she is committed to acquire the kind of bookish learning that Oliveira perceives as an obstacle to a fuller form of existence. As La Maga tells Oliveira: 'Vos buscás algo que no sabés lo que es. Yo también y tampoco sé lo que es. Pero son dos cosas diferentes' [You look for something and you don't know what it is. I do too, and I don't know what it is either. But they are two different things].[22] This chiasmic crossing of intellectual destinies implies that the pristine space that Oliveira looks for and La Maga is supposed to embody is always already the site of culture. The irony of this detail, if still deriving from the interplay between myth and rationality, exposes rather than supports the modernist transformation of myth into a supplement that restores the harmony of a *ratio* in crisis.

That there is no utopian 'other' side beyond what Oliveira perceives as alienating intellectual structures is further underscored by Cortázar's division of the novel into two main parts: 'Del lado de allá' [From the Other Side] and 'Del lado de acá' [From This Side], corresponding respectively to the chapters about the protagonist's time in Paris and to those narrating his return to Buenos Aires. The division of the novel, like the intellectual interplay between Oliveira and La Maga, deceptively suggests a play of opposites between self and other, culture and nature, Europe and America. One of the most memorable passages in the novel, the climactic plank episode in Chapter 41, provides a nuanced illustration of how these pairs of opposites do not stand in dialectical opposition, but are rather mirror reflections of each other. This chapter, the first that Cortázar drafted for the novel, invites a metaphorical interpretation of the unusual event that it narrates. The opening scene shows us Oliveira trying to straighten up bent nails with a hammer. This task, whose purpose is never explained, requires extreme care and skill, since striking the nail beyond what is necessary can bend it too much in the opposite direction and not only render the task useless, but also hurt Oliveira. That he ends up with his hands covered in blood and bruises prepares us for the message of the chapter as a whole, that is, that his philosophical pursuits end up simply reversing the metaphysical problems he seeks to resolve and transcend.

Frustrated by his failure to straighten the nails, Oliveira decides to ask his friends and next-door neighbours, Manuel Traveler and his wife, Talita, for some more nails (as well as some *mate* weed). Before fully developing the implications of this episode, I would like to pause and show how Cortázar's characterization of Traveler and Talita is another indication that the dualism that informs the protagonist's thinking is as much of a mirage as the synthetic unity that he pursues. Oliveira, a contemporary avatar of Ulysses (albeit a frustrated one), returns from Paris to Buenos Aires and reunites with his *Doppelganger*, Traveler, a man who, despite what his name might indicate, has never left Argentina. He uncannily embodies all the aspects that Oliveira tries to evade, particularly the tawdry and sedentary bourgeois mentality which he vehemently opposes but can never overcome. At forty, Traveler 'seguía adherido a la calle Cachimayo, y el hecho de trabajar como gestor y un poco de todo en el circo "Las Estrellas" no le daba la menor esperanza de recorrer los caminos del mundo *more* Barnum' [was still stuck on Cachimayo Street, and the fact that he worked as a manager and jack-of-all-trades for a circus called 'Las Estrellas' gave him no hope of travelling around the world like Barnum].[23] Oliveira sees him as an accomplished Ulysses that never had to embark on a perilous journey to embody 'la rendición' and 'la vuelta a casa y al orden' [surrender, homecoming and the return to order].[24]

However, these differences paradoxically reveal their profound similarities. As Oliveira cryptically puts it, 'la diferencia entre Manú y yo es que somos casi iguales' [the difference between Manú and myself is that we are almost identical].[25] One important similarity relates to how they both fail to achieve their goals: just as Traveler faces and eventually comes to terms with the conviction that he might never leave Buenos Aires, so Oliveira becomes gradually and painfully aware that there might be no final destination for his spiritual journey, no metaphysical unity that would overcome his doubts and uncertainties: 'A Oliveira le iba a doler siempre no poder hacerse ni siquiera una noción de esa unidad que otras veces llamaba centro' [It was always going to hurt Oliveira that he could not even get an idea of that unity that he sometimes called centre].[26] The irony of Traveler's name could also apply to the futility of Oliveira's 'search'. If Traveler's name stresses the distance between his goals and his actual condition and actions, Oliveira's failed attempts to reach metaphysical harmony expose the shortcomings of his dialectical method. Ironically, he does not return 'home' to Buenos Aires to find La Maga, as he had originally intended, but only to come across the dreaded 'order' that he perceives in his *Doppelganger*.

Let me now return to the episode of the plank to further illustrate Oliveira's failure to move from this side to the other side. Since the Travelers live right across from Oliveira and their windows face each other, he devises a plan to avoid going down the stairs and then up again to the their apartment. He decides to build a bridge between the two facing windows using planks so that Talita could cross and deliver the nails he needs. This episode can be taken as a scale reduction of *Rayuela* as a whole. In one of his drafts for the novel, Cortázar wrote that the scene is intended to symbolize 'el paso de un mundo a otro' [the passage from one world to another], a comment followed by the annotation 'BA [Buenos Aires] → Paris'.[27] In this particular episode, as well as throughout the Buenos Aires chapters, Talita doubles as La Maga. Oliveira sees in her what he saw in La Maga: an unmediated mythical recess than can cure his metaphysical ailments and help him with his 'passage' from one side to the other. To achieve this goal, he tries to extricate the mythical force represented by Talita from the reified rationality of Traveler, thus finding a passageway toward intellectual fullness. However, Oliveira's effort to move beyond the teachings of culture and civilization proves as fruitless as his attempt to use the plank to bridge the gap between the two windows.

Talita eventually fails to cross from one side to the other and goes back to Traveler, showing how Oliveira's aspirations to find an 'elsewhere', a transcendental 'home', trap him in an endless spiral that repeats the structures he intends to destroy. She is not the escape route that Oliveira thinks she is, but a replica of the alienating habits and norms he desperately tries to shake off. Like La Maga, she deceptively appears to be the solution to his existential dilemmas, but functions as just another, perhaps even more ironic reminder that liberating the mind from the grip of reason is a fantasy, a mirage, an unreachable utopia. After all, Talita is first characterized as a 'reader of encyclopaedias' with an anthropological interest in 'los pueblos nómadas y las culturas transhumantes' [nomadic tribes and itinerant cultures].[28] Her job as a pharmacist also involves organizing, classifying and labelling, activities that evoke the rational operations of the mind instead of the untamed life force of primitive myth. It is Oliveira himself who, in one of his moments of insight, reveals her true role in the novel: 'Es un hecho que vos [Talita] te sumás de alguna manera a nosotros dos [Traveler y Oliveira] para aumentar el parecido, y por lo tanto la diferencia' [It is a fact that when you (Talita) join us (Traveler and Oliveira) you accentuate our similarities, and therefore our differences].[29]

By stressing Oliveira's inability to attain a non-dualistic form of thinking and being, Cortázar revises what Adorno and Horkheimer term the constitutive 'cunning' of modernity, archetypically represented by Ulysses in the *Odyssey*. Oliveira's failed quest emphasizes that the forces of pre-rational myth that the Homeric hero's 'cunning' suppresses are ultimately a mirage, a projection devoid of actual content. Cortázar's message is that there is no real dialectic because there is no real antithesis to the thesis of modern rationality. If we reconsider, for instance, the episode of the Sirens in Homer's *Odyssey* from the vantage point afforded by *Rayuela*, it could be argued that when Ulysses's ship steers past the island of the Sirens, the hero, tied rigidly to the mast with his ears unplugged, would have been unable to distinguish the deadly and alluring song of the nymphs from utter silence. For Cortázar that deafening silence is absolute, just as the mythical power of the Sirens — which is supposedly controlled and contained by the 'cunning' and self-restraint of bourgeois mentality (allegorized in Homer's poem by the hero's decision to have his seamen tie him up) — is simply a wishful projection of reason. Ulysses's hypothetical inability to hear the ravishing chant of the Sirens would symbolize the incapacity of the mind to move towards an elusive and imaginary 'other side', a symbolic space that *Rayuela* constantly and teasingly evokes only to demonstrate that it does not really exist.

But if we assume that there is no 'other side' beyond modernity, how can we speak of 'double consciousness' in Cortázar's text? Through our discussion of Oliveira's frustrated search, we have already established that such 'double consciousness' does not stem from the synthesis of myth and rationality observed in 'modernist mythopoeia', since Cortázar presents myth as a 'utopia' in its most negative sense, that is, as a 'non-space' that can be summoned neither as an antithesis to reason nor as its supplement. In a powerfully humbling gesture, he confronts reason with one of its most embarrassing contradictions, namely its lack of a dialectical dimension. The 'double consciousness' that I recognize in *Rayuela* involves an interruption of the self-effacing duality of consciousness that Hegel presented as the motor of the Western 'Spirit'. As Hegel explains in *Phenomenology of Spirit*:

> There exists for Self-Consciousness another self-consciousness; Self-Consciousness has come *out* from *itself*. This has the following double signification: Self-Consciousness has lost itself, since it finds itself as *another* being; thereby it has superseded the other, since it also does not view this other as a being, but sees *itself* in the other. Self-Consciousness must supersede *this* otherness (which is its *own* otherness).[30]

However, when the intermediate step of projecting otherness fails to materialize, the evolving process of self-conscious transformation of the same is interrupted. It is this denial of otherness that allows Cortázar to both impede the Hegelian synthesis and to articulate a strategic position from which to expose the constitutive contra-dictions of the humanist idea of man, of individual autonomy and self-knowledge.

From a transcultural, postcolonial perspective, this particular place of transgression and difference takes shape when the 'other' of Western civilization claims autonomy from the relationship with the 'self' that generates Hegel's 'self-consciousness'. W. E. B. Du Bois, who attended the University of Berlin during the 1890s while the institution was in the midst of a 'Hegelian revival', expressed the 'other's' sense of alienation from the purview of Western universals in his famous formulation of the Afro-American 'double consciousness': 'It is a peculiar sensation, this double consciousness, this sense of always looking at one's self through the eyes of others, of measuring one's soul by the tape of a world that looks on in amused contempt and pity. One ever feels his twoness, — an American, a Negro; two souls, two thoughts, two unreconciled strivings'.[31] Cortázar refers to a similar sensation when he discusses what he calls the *sentimiento de no estar del todo* [feeling of not being all there], a sense of displacement from 'cualquiera de las estructuras, de las telas que arma la vida y en que somos a la vez araña y mosca' [any of the structures, of the webs that life spins and in which we are both the spider and the fly].[32] According to Cortázar, this *sentimiento* is the driving principle of his fiction and his life, both of which, he argues, can be placed under 'el signo de excentricidad' [the sign of eccentricity]. Just as Du Bois's 'double consciousness' emanates from his racial difference and from his vindication of humanity for the African-American community, so Cortázar's *sentimiento* derives, we might argue, from his marginal status as a Spanish American intellectual and his efforts to create a form of expression liberated from the strictures of traditional literary culture, that is, a 'literature of exception' that cannot be assimilated to 'the mainstream of the Western tradition'. Both Du Bois and Cortázar fully embrace their eccentric condition, refusing to get caught in the ebb and flow of dialectical thinking. Their act of resistance involves the affirmation of a recalcitrant 'otherness' that can never become the object of desire of the hegemonic culture.

Argentine philosopher Enrique Dussel has theorized this otherness from a Latin American perspective in a series of influential publications. Dussel, drawing on the philosophy of Emmanuel Levinas, attempts to articulate a space of radical alterity through his proposal for a Latin American 'philosophy of liberation'. His intellectual programme intersects in meaningful ways with the philosophical implications of Cortázar's writing. In *Filosofía de la liberación*, first published fourteen years after *Rayuela*, Dussel stresses the relevance of location in the global economy of philosophical production and consumption. He contends that it is from the peripheral location occupied by those that consume rather than produce 'legitimate' knowledge that an emancipating dissociation from Western rationality can take place: 'Distant thinkers, those who had a perspective of the center from the periphery [...] these are the ones who have a clear mind for pondering reality'.[33] This perspective should not be conceived as a utopian 'elsewhere' beyond the totalizing scope of reason — that is, as a 'mythical' or pre-rational mode of thinking uncontaminated by the language and structures of modern philosophy. For Dussel, a fully liberated Latin American thought stems from 'non-Being, nothingness, otherness, exteriority, the mystery of no-sense' — from a space that remains within the boundaries of modernity, but proves to be recalcitrant to the syntheses of modern epistemology.[34] This space of exteriority shifts our attention from a dialectic of universality and particularity, of self and other — whereby the latter is progressively assimilated to the former — to a tactical affirmation of difference and positionality that amounts to an interruption of such dialectic.

But how does one speak from this locus? What sort of speech is uttered from this space of 'exteriority'? Of course, as Oliveira's experience has taught us, this exteriority cannot be reached through dialectical means. Although he is resolved to abandon the culture of Europe as a legitimate philosophical referent, refusing to accept reason as a valid analytical tool, he is still caught within the dualistic mindset that underpins the culture he tries to escape from. Cortázar's central message in *Rayuela* might be that we can only achieve true 'otherness' and break out of the rhetoric of self and other, reason and myth, home and abroad, by positioning ourselves on 'This Side' (Buenos Aires) to look at 'That Side' (Paris), by inventing ways of looking at the world that are not sanctioned by the categories and mental structures of the metropolis. This refocused perspective can send Oliveira, but also us readers, on an inverted voyage of discovery, revealing what Dussel calls 'a clear mind for pondering reality', for looking at 'the center from the periphery' and ploughing new paths that can help us set out in a different direction, 'beyond logic, beyond Kantian categories, beyond the whole apparatus of Western thought', to paraphrase Cortázar's words in the epigraph to this chapter.

In the chapters grouped under the title 'De otros lados (capítulos prescindibles)' [From Diverse Sides (expendable chapters)] we find illuminating proposals to help us think about these alternative philosophical pathways. Mainly composed of quotations and excerpts from a wide variety of sources, this section contains brief notes by Oliveira's favourite novelist, Morelli, where he elaborates on the main philosophical issues introduced in the other two sections. In Chapter 71, Morelli addresses the driving concerns of Oliveira's quest. His opening question tries to find a definition of the protagonist's elusive spiritual goal: '¿Qué es en el fondo esa historia de encontrar un reino milenario, un edén, un otro mundo?' [What is, after all, that story about finding a millenary kingdom, a paradise, an other world?]. Morelli's contention, like Dussel's, is that this utopian realm does not exist unless we imagine it, for it lacks a stable form or a given content. 'Ese mundo no existe, hay que crearlo como el fénix' [That world does not exist, it must be created like the phoenix]. He suggests that to radically undermine the stale habits and structures of rationality and language we must cease to think in linear and hierarchical terms. An exteriority from the unfolding development of modernity cannot be reached '[h]asta no quitarle al tiempo su látigo de historia, hasta no acabar con la hinchazón de tantos *hasta*' [until we take away from time the whip of history, until we prick the blister caused by so many *untils*].[35] Morelli implies that this rebellious act cannot be performed unless we abandon a teleological conception of history: 'Error de postular un tiempo histórico absoluto: Hay tiempos diferentes *aunque* paralelos' [It is a mistake to postulate an absolute historical time: there are different, *albeit* parallel, times].[36]

The fundamental difference between the multi-layered historical terrain that Morelli describes and the linear logic informing modernity may be evoked through the contrast between Ulysses's homecoming in Homer's poem and Morelli's compelling image of the phoenix. While the hero's voyage embodies a relentless and calculated progression toward a closed order, the unexpected shapes of the phoenix symbolize unpredictable pathways that veer off established itineraries. Dussel's notion of the 'analectic', which he opposes to Hegelian dialectics, can help us clarify the meaning of Morelli's phoenix-like approach. The 'analectic' moment occurs when the 'other' constitutes itself as an autonomous entity, and not as a projected antithesis to be later assimilated by the sameness of rationality and the currents of history. To put it in Cortázar's evocative terms, the 'analectic' takes place when one breaks away from 'el cangrejo de lo idéntico' [the crab of identity] to acquire the 'simultaneous porosity of the sponge', or, we might add, the protean nature of the phoenix.[37]

Morelli relates this porosity to the central concept of *figura*: 'Digamos que el mundo es una figura, hay que leerla. Por leerla entendamos generarla' [Let's say that the world is a figure: we have to read it. By reading it I mean generating it]. The term *figura* has been traditionally associated with the allegorical interpretation of biblical texts. In his classic definition, Eric Auerbach explained that *figura* involves 'the interpretation of one worldly event through another; the first signifies the second, the second fulfils the first. Both remain historical events; yet both, looked at in this way, have something provisional and incomplete about them; they point to one another and both point to something in the future, something still to come, which will be the actual, real, and definitive event'.[38] What Morelli captures from this biblical concept is not the promise of an 'actual, real, and definitive event', but the phoenix-like, provisional and incomplete permutations among the elements of a *figura*. The writing and reading practice that these *figuras* inspire challenges Oliveira's thirst for unity and, on a larger scale, the grand narratives of history and modernity imagined by the Western mind. The relationship between Traveler and Oliveira could be seen as one of the central *figuras* in the text, for, as discussed above, they complement each other in a non-dialectical manner, thus perpetuating their tension without ever reaching an 'actual, real, and definitive' moment of conciliation or resolution. This 'figural' interaction, which also applies to Oliveira and La Maga-Talita, displaces habitual assumptions about psychological coherence and invites us to read 'from the interstices'. As Cortázar wrote in his essay, 'Del sentimiento de no estar del todo': 'Escribo por falencia, por descolocación; y como escribo desde un intersticio, estoy siempre invitando a que otros busquen los suyos y miren por ellos el jardín donde los árboles tienen frutos que son, por supuesto, piedras preciosas' [I write because of a lack, because of a sense of dislocation; and since I write from an interstice, I am always inviting others to look for their own interstices and to look at the garden where the trees bear fruits that are, of course, precious stones].[39]

The practice of reading and writing 'from the interstices' further defines the differences between Cortázar's narrative method and the aesthetics of literary modernism. The endless 'interstitial' creation suggested by Morelli's conception of *figura* could be usefully connected to the 'constantly inventive revolution' that Cortázar viewed as the driving principle behind creative innovation.[40] The mechanics of *figura* and the 'inventive revolution' are at odds with what Bell calls 'modernist mythopoeia'. In what could be called a typically homeopathic operation, the modernist text places myth at the core of representation to palliate its constitutive fault lines, to control, order and give 'a shape and a significance to the immense panorama of futility and anarchy which is contemporary history', quoting yet again Eliot's words in '*Ulysses*, Order and Myth'. By contrast, Cortázar seeks to interrupt that operation, imagining and articulating 'other' meanings beyond the 'closed orders' of reason and civilization. If the modernists envision modernity as myth, Cortázar articulates counter-myths that open up the field of representation to the diverse subjectivities that have 'a perspective of the center from the periphery' (Dussel). Putting it differently: the modernists react to the unsettling awareness that modernity is after all a myth, a fiction and not the embodiment of universal truth, by striving to preserve its integrity and coherence through irony; in contrast, Cortázar reacts to such realization from the vantage point afforded by his critical distance from the norms of modernity — that is, from the differential perspective afforded by 'double consciousness' in the Du Boisian sense.

In order to further elucidate the differences between literary modernism and Cortázar's writing, let me take a brief detour from our discussion of *Rayuela* to look at Roland Barthes's reflections on myth. In *Mythologies*, Barthes writes that 'myth' can be understood as the mechanism of making things look 'falsely obvious'. More specifically, a 'myth' for Barthes is a historical system of signification that acquires universally legitimacy by transforming 'History' into 'Nature'. Myth is based on 'a robbery by colonization', for it involves a totalizing act of interpretation that sweeps away all potential challenges to its authenticity.[41] The French critic adds that there are three different ways to interpret a myth. The first way is adopted by the 'the producer of myths', who wholeheartedly believes that myth provides an accurate picture of the world. The second way stems from the realization that there is nothing 'natural' about the way myths organize and create meaning. This is the type of approach adopted by the 'mythologist', who 'deciphers the myth [and] understands the distortion' involved in turning 'History' into 'Nature', but refuses to question the truth of mythical paradigms. Finally, the third approach 'is dynamic, it consumes the myth according to the very ends built into its structure: the reader lives the myth as a story at once true and unreal'.[42] This hermeneutical position resonates with the implications of 'modernist mythopoeia', for it understands that myth involves a fundamental lie, but salvages it as a viable means of representation.

Significantly, Barthes's three approaches leave the representational powers of myth intact; whether convinced of its authenticity or aware of its falsity, the positions outlined above remain *within* the semantic and ideological realm created by myth. The example that the French thinker provides to illustrate his three approaches might be useful to consider the possibility of a fourth approach that we could link to Cortázar's 'double consciousness'. Barthes's example is the magazine picture of a black French soldier saluting the French flag. The first approach is manifested by the journalist who presents this image as a particular embodiment of the abstract concept 'French imperiality'. The second approach is taken by the perceptive observer who realizes that the saluting soldier is an 'alibi of coloniality' and that the myth of imperiality is based on an act of repression and appropriation.[43] The third approach is taken by the critical thinker who deeply reflects about that act of repression and understands that imperiality itself is a fiction and not a historical necessity. In all three cases, the voice that we fail to hear is that of the black French soldier. To be sure, the soldier is fully entitled to take any of the approaches above. But he can choose a fourth option, namely becoming fully aware of his otherness and articulating the double consciousness that, as Du Bois put it, stems from the 'sense of always looking at oneself through the eyes of others, of measuring one's soul by the tape of a world that looks on in amused contempt and pity'. This fourth approach abandons the limits of myth and assumes a position of exteriority or eccentricity.

As our discussion of *Rayuela* suggests, Cortázar's text persistently evokes such a position and in doing so it deviates from modernist aesthetics. Modernist mythopoeia can hardly be credited with the potential to transcend the limits of the myth of modernity and 'imperiality'. Barthes himself eschews the possibility of ever 'vanquish[ing] the myth from the inside: for the very effort one makes in order to escape its stronghold becomes in its turn the prey of myth'. But he insinuates a possible way out of this circularity, which prefigures the form that the fourth approach to myth might take: 'Truth to tell, the best way against myth is perhaps to mythify it in its turn, and to produce an *artificial myth*: and this reconstructed myth will in fact be a mythology'. He adds that the power of this counter-myth is that it gives the myth it 'mythifies' 'its basis as a naivety which is looked at'.[44]

Once again, focusing on Barthes's examples will advance my argument, finally bringing it to address the issue that originally prompted our discussion: the literary interaction between Joyce and Cortázar. According to Barthes, Flaubert's *Bouvard et Pécuchet* constitutes the best example of what he considers a 'second-degree' myth or 'artificial' myth, that is, a myth that questions the legitimacy of a prevailing and preceding myth and superimposes on it a further layer of signification derived though independent from it. Such myth resembles Morelli's *figura* because it recycles, reshuffles and rearranges the cultural blocks of established myths in unprecedented ways. In the French semiotician's view, the ludicrous intellectual pursuits of Flaubert's eccentric characters are not only a demystification of Western culture; this demystification becomes in turn a new myth, a new form to organize reality that belies the universality of the original myth in a more radical manner than a deconstructive critique could allow. In Barthes's words, 'the rhetoric of Bouvard et Pécuchet becomes the form of the new system', not simply the deconstruction of the old one.[45] In less technical though no less sophisticated terms, Borges anticipated the French philosopher's insights in his note, 'Vindicación de *Bouvard et Pécuchet*', where he argues that the 'idiocy' of Flaubert's characters should be separated from the ideas they ridicule: 'Inferir de los percances de estos payasos la vanidad de las religiones, de las ciencias y de las artes, no es otra cosa que un sofisma insolente o que una falacia grosera. Los fracasos de Pécuchet no comportan un fracaso de Newton' [To infer from the trials of these clowns the vanity of religions, the sciences and the arts, is an insolent sophism or a gross fallacy. Pécuchet's failures do not involve Newton's failure].[46] While this statement could be easily read as a vindication of Western knowledge and an indictment of Flaubert's characters and their parodic distortions, the title that Borges chooses for his article suggests otherwise.

Indeed, Borges might have perceived in the actions of Flaubert's characters a dramatization of the irreverence and eccentricity that he attributed to the South Americans, the Jews and the Irish in 'El escritor argentino y la tradición'. The preposterous actions of Bouvard and Pécuchet, who copied thousands of treatises on a wide variety of disciplines without fully understanding them, but eventually perceiving their absurdity, bear a certain resemblance to Borges's critical distance from Western culture and literature, or even with what Dussel called a 'perspective of the center from the periphery'. Taking this connection to its logical conclusion, one could argue that the counter-mythical imagination of Flaubert's characters projects a frame liberated, though derived, from the portentous myths of Western culture; that is, Bouvard and Pécuchet's function is to belie the universality of reason and culture, but in doing so they are not restricted to merely dismantling the truth of established disciplines of knowledge. They also rearrange the cultural blocks they have taken apart into new configuration, indeed into new myths.

This counter-mythical optic offers the possibility of rethinking the literary conversation between Joyce and Cortázar beyond the scope of Anglo-American modernism. Borges himself related Bouvard and Pécuchet's distortions of science and philosophy to Flaubert's anti-realistic transformations of the novel, transformations that Joyce's *Ulysses* came to epitomize: '¿No es el *Ulises*, con sus planos y horarios y precisiones, la esplendida agonía de un género?' [Isn't *Ulysses*, with its maps and schedules and precisions the splendid agony of a genre?].[47] Borges implies here that we should see the meticulous construction of *Ulysses* as an exercise analogous to Flaubert's transformations of novelistic discourse and, by extension, to Bouvard and Pécuchet's painstaking distortions of a whole body of 'legitimate' knowledge. We could argue that for Borges the value of Joyce's book resides in revising and reshaping the habits and norms of literature and culture, in creating a novel form of writing that makes readers abandon the comforts of plot and shared logic. In 'El arte narrativo y la magia', for instance, the Argentine writer describes *Ulysses* as the best example of a narrative causality that, like magic, escapes rigid, univocal and linear concatenations of causes and effects. What remains after sidestepping the strictures of logic and shared sense is a system of 'vigilancias, ecos y afinidades' [alerts, echoes and affinities] among the novel's numerous episodes that creates 'un orbe *autónomo* de corroboraciones, de presagios, de monumentos' [an *autonomous* orb of corroborations, of presages, of monuments].[48]

In one of the short sketches included in 'De otros lados', Oliveira imagines a universe that, like Joyce's *Ulysses* as read by Borges, escapes from the constraints of rational order — a magical space that bursts open rigid structures and then rearranges the pieces left in new and imaginative ways. He observes, we are told, 'un universo cambiante, lleno de maravilloso azar, un cielo elástico, un sol que de pronto falta o se queda fijo o cambia de forma. Ansié la dispersión de las duras constelaciones, esa sucia propaganda luminosa del Trust Divino Relojero' [a changing universe, full of marvellous chance, an elastic sky, a sun that suddenly disappears, or stands still, or changes its shape. I longed for the dispersion of the hard constellations, of that filthy and luminous propaganda of the Divine Watchmaker Trust].[49] The logic, disciplines and categories of the allegorical 'watchmaker' (mythmaker?) constitutes the common ground from which the following possibilities depart, all facets of the same rebellious attitude that seeks 'an opening or a fracture and also, in a sense, a hope' : a) Du Bois's 'double consciousness'; b) the 'counter-myth' or 'second-degree' myth that Barthes illustrates with Flaubert's *Bouvard et Pécuchet*; c) the 'magical' narrative organization that Borges perceived in the 'orbe autonomo' of *Ulysses*; d) Morelli's phoenix-like *figuras* (incidentally, Morelli is compared to Bouvard and Pécuchet in chapter 66 of *Rayuela*: 'Facetas de Morelli, su lado Bouvard et Pécuchet, su lado compilador de almanaque literario' [Facets of Morelli, his Bouvard et Pécuchet side, his side as the compiler of literary almanacs]).[50] With this insight, we can now retrace our steps and reconsider the relationship between Joyce and Cortázar. *Ulysses* serves as the model for Morelli's *roman comique*, but it also overlaps with Cortázar's commitment to a 'constantly inventive revolution' in literature. I suggest that this overlapping takes place in a counter-mythical space that finds interconnecting projections in Du Bois's 'double consciousness', Borges's narrative 'magic', Morelli's *figura* and Dussel's 'exteriority'. Although this space is non-historical in the sense that it remains as a formless *possibility* open to a plurality of voices and political and cultural projects, it does enable a fully historicized reconsideration of the relationship between James Joyce and Cortázar. Of course, there exists the possibility of comparing *Ulysses* and *Rayuela* on the basis of stylistic similarities, to claim that both works represent the type of narrative widely associated with modernism and characterized by spatial form, multiple temporalities and linguistic experimentation. But this formalistic approach does not acknowledge the geopolitical eccentricity of these works nor the social and political contexts that conditioned their composition.

A historicist analysis of the intersection of *Ulysses* and *Rayuela* was first proposed by Roberto Fernández Retamar. He compared the two novels by looking at Oliveira's and Stephen Dedalus's parallel responses to the cultural landscapes of Argentina in the 1950s and 1960s and Ireland at the turn of the twentieth century, respectively (see the Introduction to this study). Commenting on Oliveira's existential predicament, he writes: 'En cierta forma ese ahogo, esa opacidad de la sociedad argentina actual, y de casi todas las sociedades de la América Latina, se expresan en Oliveira en forma similar a aquel ahogo de la sociedad irlandesa que se manifiesta en Esteban' [In a way, the stifling opacity of contemporary Argentine society (and of almost all societies in Latin America) is expressed by Oliveira in a way that recalls the oppression of Irish society experienced by Stephen].[51] Read from this perspective, *Ulysses* and *Rayuela* are analogous not only because they share a certain number of formal characteristics, but also because they engage with similar historical circumstances. Though separated by more than forty years, these two novels were conceived and written when major social transformations were taking place in Ireland and Spanish America. These transformations occurred against a shared background of cultural and political decolonization. 1922, the year *Ulysses* was published in Paris, was also the year when the independent Irish Free State was created, an event that many saw as the culmination of an intense process of cultural and political emancipation from British colonial domination. This decolonizing struggle prefigured the massive wave of Third World liberation movements in the 1950s and the 1960s. The Irish campaign for Home Rule led by the legendary Charles Stuart Parnell and the cultural revivalism promoted by the Gaelic League and the Irish Literary Renaissance provided a compelling anti-colonial model for the wider postcolonial world. For instance, the resistance shared by Ireland and India was noted by Jawaharlal Nehru, the first Prime Minister of the independent Indian state. In a letter to his daughter, he highlighted the common colonial legacies and political destinies of both nations, observing that 'oppressed and struggling countries, all those who are dissatisfied and have little joy in the present, have a way of looking back to the past and searching for consolation in it'.[52] In Spanish America, the utopian longings that infused the initial years of the Cuban Revolution also intersected with the anti-colonial movements in the former British and French empires. That a Leopoldo Zea or a Roberto Fernández Retamar made frequent references to the work of thinkers such as Frantz Fanon indicates that the Latin American struggles for self-determination during the fifties and the sixties were imagined as being part of the wider project of Third World liberation. As Diana Sorensen has pointed out, the revolutionary stirrings of the period and the dreams of 'a different sense of community' were often accompanied by feelings of solidarity with other subjugated areas such as Algeria, Congo, Vietnam and Palestine.[53]

Within this common context, Joyce and Cortázar coincided in their resistance to framing decolonizing impulses within narrow nationalistic doctrines and party politics. It is not by chance that Cortázar described the defence of self-sufficient ethnic identities with the same metaphor that Adorno and Horkheimer used to illustrate the birth and consolidation of modernity: the Ulyssean journey. In 'Acerca de la situación del intelectual latinoamericano', an open letter to Roberto Fernández Retamar, Cortázar compared the cultural nationalist to an Odysseus that returns to the safety of home:

> Aquí quiero agregar que de ninguna manera me creo un ejemplo de esa 'vuelta a los orígenes' — telúricos, nacionales, lo que quieras — que ilustra precisamente una importante corriente de la literatura latinoamericana [...] hay circunstancias de la vida de los pueblos en que ese sentimiento del retorno, ese arquetipo casi junguiano del hijo pródigo, de Odiseo al final de periplo, puede derivar a una exaltación tal de lo propio que, por contragolpe lógico, la via del desprecio más insensato se abra hacia todo lo demás.[54]

> [I want to add that in no way do I see myself as an example of that 'return to the origins' — telluric, national or otherwise — that precisely illustrates an important trend within Latin American literature [...] there are circumstances in the development of communities in which that sense of return, that almost Jungian archetype of the prodigal son, of Odysseus at the end of his journey, can give rise to such an exaltation of the familiar that logically leads to an unthinking deprecation of what is alien.]

Joyce took a similar stance when he criticized the Irish nativism that developed during the early decades of the twentieth century. In his political and critical writings, he intervenes in the controversial cultural debates of the day, mocking the efforts to implement Gaelic as an official language and the project to renew ancient Celtic literature and culture in modern times. In his essay of 1907, 'Ireland: Island of Saints and Sages', Joyce rejects cultural exclusivism as a decolonizing strategy and argues that self-determination against Britain's colonial control should not rely on the affirmation of linguistic and ethnic purity. He contends that it would be futile to seek an uncontaminated Irish 'essence' in a society that has been heavily transculturated. He presents Ireland as a country with a syncretic culture accumulated during centuries of vigorous contact and exchange with foreign communities. Irish civilization is, in Joyce's words, 'an immense woven fabric in which very different elements are mixed, in which Nordic rapacity is reconciled to Roman law, and new Bourgeois conventions to the remains of a Siriac religion. In such a fabric, it is pointless searching for a thread that has remained pure, virgin and uninfluenced by other threads nearby'.[55]

In addition, Joyce's and Cortázar's involvement with cultural decolonization did not result in the mimetic representation of social conditions that a politically committed conception of literature in a more traditional Marxist sense would expect. Cortázar addressed on several occasions the fraught issue of literature's role within revolutionary struggles, arguing that his creative work strives for a 'revolution in literature' and not to put literature at the service of rigid political programmes.[56] In his essay 'Politics and the Intellectual in Latin America', he expressed this position in unambiguous terms:

> I understand the reproach of hermeticism which I have received through the years; it always comes from those who demand a step backward in creativity in the name of a supposed step forward in the political struggle. It is not in this way that we will contribute to the final liberation of our countries.[57]

Indeed, Cortázar's idea of revolution never aligned itself with unified party orthodoxies or nationalistic programmes. As he showed us through Horacio Oliveira, this sort of unity will just mirror the power structures against which one is rebelling. I suggest, therefore, that what charges *Ulysses* and *Rayuela* with political energy is the counter-mythical capacity to continuously attune readers to latent, unrealized historical forces and ways of thinking, guiding them into what Stephen Dedalus calls 'the room of the infinite possibilities' 'ousted' by the actual events of history (*U* 2.50–51). Thus, I believe that one can tease out the revolutionary energies embedded in these novels by adopting what Morelli would call a 'figural' interpretation of reality and history — that is, by committing ourselves to a revolutionary type of reading that actively considers what could have been but was not as well as what could be but has not been yet.

Fritz Senn has identified in *Ulysses* a process of textual organization analogous to Morelli's *figura*, which he designates 'dynamics of corrective unrest' and describes with the pun 'righting as writing'. 'Righting as writing', he argues, is 'a convenient, compact, synechdochal illustration of a process that characterizes *Ulysses*', adding that the 'book itself tends toward ameliorative diversity. *Ulysses*, as an event in words, seems to try to right itself through more words, as though it wanted to undo the damages of all previous presentations'.[58] In *Ulysses*, the word 'righting' is frequently associated with Leopold Bloom, a modern avatar of Ulysses like Cortázar's Oliveira. From his first appearance in the novel in Chapter 4, he is characterized by his obsession with 'righting' things. Just a few examples should illustrate this point. As he prepares breakfast for his wife Molly while she is still in bed, '[k]idneys were on his mind as he moved about the kitchen softly, *righting* her breakfast things' (*U* 4.6–7; emphasis added). He continues setting Molly's breakfast tray, making sure everything is in order: 'Another slice of bread and butter: three, four: right. She didn't like her plate full. Right' (*U* 4.11–12). Then, his mind turns to whether his wife's pronunciation of Italian is correct: '*Voglio e non vorrei*. Wonder if she pronounces that right: *voglio*' (*U* 4.327–28). In the next chapter, as he observes a Catholic mass, he again uses the term 'right' to describe the religious ceremony: '[p]ious fraud but quite right [...]. Queer the whole atmosphere of the. Quite right. Perfectly right that is' (*U* 5.393).[59] Given that a central trait of his personality is the urge to keep things right, Bloom is at a certain point in the novel called a 'conscious reactor against the void of incertitude' (*U* 17.2210–11).

But like Oliveira's metaphysical search, Bloom's righting process never comes to a halt. *Ulysses* as a textual artefact prevents Bloom from fulfilling his righting obsessions just as *Rayuela* frustrates Oliveira's metaphysical aspirations. By continuously trying to 'right itself through more words', *Ulysses* resists a definitive 'righting', thus confronting Bloom's organizing inclinations with a text that prevents all attempts to impose final orders. To a large degree, the kind of figural interpretation of *Ulysses* that I propose is prefigured in the text by Bloom's attempts to make sense of the events of 16 June 1904. At a certain point during his ramblings around Dublin, he thinks of two people — John Howard Parnell and George Russell — just before running into them. This strange case of coincidence leads him to conclude that '[c]oming events cast their shadow before' (*U* 8.526), a conclusion that could also describe the organization of narrative materials in *Ulysses*.[60] Just one example among many others might illustrate this organizing principle based on coincidence and chance. In 'Circe', Bloom overhears the story of someone who got caught defecating in a plasterer's bucket of porter and then mutters '[c]oincidence too' (*U* 15.593), implicating that he is the person they are talking about, precisely at a point in the episode where he is about to confess to such a 'crime' to Mrs Breen. This infiltration of coincidences into the narrative alters our normal expectations about plot, since the constant possibility of 'shadows' being cast before us unsettles the 'logical' concatenation of cause and effect. Readers aware of this possibility are compelled to change their reading habits, to abandon the comfort of shared logic and sense given by the representation of an ordinary day in Dublin in 1904, and to engage in a frantic search for underlying connections lurking under the surface of the narrated events.

In 'Nausicaa', Bloom realizes that his watch stopped at four thirty — the time he believes sexual intercourse between Molly and her lover, Blazes Boylan, might have been consummated — and wonders whether there is 'any magnetic influence between the person because that was about the time he' (*U* 13.984–85). The fact that there is no empirical way to prove a connection between Bloom's broken watch and Molly's adultery teases Bloom's 'righting' compulsion. At the same time, this alternative 'logic' of coincidence liberates the text from the uniformity of a single time and space and opens it up to multiple possible readings. So we wonder with Bloom, what if there is some unseen connection between his watch and his wife's sexual activity? What if the organization of the text obeys to this elusive system of connections, coincidences and echoes, and not to the narrative coherence provided by causality and plot? This is precisely what Cortázar calls reading 'from the interstices', a sort of reading that keeps colliding with a residue of meaning that cannot be assimilated to the predictability of plot. To perform this kind of reading one should break free from expectations of sequentiality and become aware of a type of order that Borges associated with superstition, magic and James Joyce's novel itself in 'El arte narrativo y la magia'.

This subversion of the superficial causality of plot may be easily read in postmodern or poststructuralist terms, arguing that Joyce's novel is in fact an infinite web of textual elements which, in the absence of transcendental signifiers, abandons all hierarchical pretensions. This interpretation often embraces 'contingency' and 'arbitrariness' as an inescapable state of affairs, inviting the reader to rejoice 'in the patterns of repetition thrown up by the chaos of history'.[61] However, reading history as a textual fabric ruled by arbitrariness and repetition carries with it the unsettling implication that radical change is simply not possible, that revolution is always going to be caught in an inescapable net of linguistic signs, since, to quote Derrida's famous slogan, 'there is nothing outside of the text'. The indeterminacies of postmodern theory can surely act as a corrective to the imperial and nationalistic essentialism which Joyce opposed so fervently. However, the postmodern reaction against common truths also tends to dovetail the crisis of modernity and empire with the claims for liberation emanating from the postcolonial world. That general certainties and principles no longer exist should not become the premise to create a new single picture of the world ruled by free play, indeterminacy and dispersion. Like all universal pictures, this one also robs the peripheral intellectual of his right to generate partial truths and rearrange cultural blocks into configurations motivated by particular historical experiences. As Seamus Deane has clearly put it, to move from 'the search for a legitimating mode of nationalism and origin' to 'the postmodernist simulacrum of pluralism [...] is surely to pass from one kind of colonizing experience into another'.[62] Thus, instead of arguing that meaning in *Ulysses* 'is never grounded or guaranteed; but, as the product of the complexity of our cultural systems, it is always available, utilizable',[63] I contend that meaning in *Ulysses*, like meaning in *Rayuela*, is always unfinished and incomplete, open to possibilities yet to be realized by letting the 'shadow' of alternative beginnings (or counter-myths) puncture and disorient the superficial stability of linear plot and shared sense. This teeming plasticity is powerfully evoked in *Ulysses* by the apparently endless transformations of Bloom's name. Throughout the novel he is called 'Professor Luitpold Blumenduft' (*U* 12.468), 'Senhor Enrique Flor' (*U* 12.1288), 'Jollypoldy the rixdix doldy' (*U* 15.149), 'puffing Poldy, blowing Bloohoom' (*U* 15.157), 'Old Olebo, M. P'. (*U* 17.409) and 'Don Poldo de la Flora' (*U* 18.1428), among other fanciful denominations.

If we heed Morelli's advice, we should generate the multiple readings that *Ulysses* and *Rayuela* can afford through an active process of invention similar to Joyce's playful transformations of Bloom's name, not by letting the ebb and flow of textuality take us adrift. In both novels, we are left with scattered pieces that can be rearranged into endless patterns of meaning, indeed into endless *figuras*. This creative operation embodies what Cortázar calls a 'constantly inventive revolution', an irreverent attitude that punctures closed forms of sense and meaning with 'an opening or a fracture and also, in a sense, a hope'. By engaging readers in this hermeneutic activity, *Ulysses* and *Rayuela* alter established forms of representation and abandon the 'mainstream of Western literature', thus becoming part of a 'literature of exception', a literature that, according to Cortázar, thrives on interrupting rather than establishing narrative coherence and cohesion. This is also a literature that, unlike 'modernist mythopoeia', dispenses with all pretensions of becoming an institutional mode of expression where political and cultural discontinuities can be aestheticized and resolved and where unified world pictures can solidify. Instead, it is a literature that creates and organizes meaning according to patterns that cannot be controlled and reduced to the dialectic of Enlightenment.

Notes to Chapter 3

1. Theodor W. Adorno and Max Horkheimer, *Dialectic of the Enlightenment*, trans. by John Cumming (New York: Herder and Herder, 1972), p. 44.
2. Carlos J. Alonso has referred to this paradox as 'the burden of modernity', a burden he presents as both the legacy of colonial structures of power and as an emancipating force. He affirms that 'the Spanish American text argues strenuously for modernity, while it signals simultaneously in a number of ways its distance from the demands of modernity's rhetoric as a means of maintaining its discursive power' (*The Burden of Modernity*, p. 26).
3. See Djelal Kadir, *Questing Fictions: Latin America's Family Romance* (Minneapolis: University of Minnesota Press, 1986), where the author argues that the search for cultural identity that permeates Latin American literature takes the shape of a self-thwarting 'quest romance', a romance of 'recurrent homelessness' that frustrates the fulfilment of the colonial narrative of discovery and conquest.
4. See: Edmundo O'Gorman, *La invención de América: el universalismo de la cultura de Occidente* (Mexico: Fondo de Cultura Económica, 1958).
5. Roberto González Echevarría, *The Voice of the Masters: Writing and Authority in Modern Latin American Literature* (Austin: University of Texas Press, 1985), p. 102. For postmodernist interpretations of Cortázar's work see also Jaime Alazraki, 'La postmodernidad de Julio Cortázar', in *Hacia Cortázar: aproximaciones a su obra* (Barcelona: Anthropos, 1994), pp. 353–65; Ursula Heise, *Chronoschisms: Time, Narrative, and Postmodernism* (Cambridge: Cambridge University Press, 1997), pp. 77–112; Santiago Juan-Navarro, 'Postmodernist Collage and Montage in Julio Cortázar's *Libro de Manuel*', in *Critical Essays on Julio Cortázar*, ed. by Jaime Alazraki (New York: G. K. Hall, 1999), pp. 173–92; and Dominic Moran, *Questions of the Liminal in the Fiction of Julio Cortázar* (Oxford: Legenda, 2000). I am persuaded by Lucille Kerr's powerful critique of the conflation of poststructuralist theory and contemporary Spanish American fiction in *Reclaiming the Author: Figures and Fictions from Spanish America* (Durham, NC: Duke University Press, 1992); see especially chapter 1, which is devoted to Cortázar. For a cogent critique of deconstructive approaches to Cortázar, see Doris Sommer, 'Grammar Trouble for Cortázar', in *Proceed with Caution, When Engaged by Minority Writing in the Americas* (Cambridge, MA: Harvard University Press, 1999), pp. 211–33.
6. Martin, *Journeys through the Labyrinth*, p. 204.
7. Neil Larsen, 'Cortázar and Postmodernity: New Interpretive Liabilities', in *Julio Cortázar: New*

Readings, ed. by Carlos J. Alonso (Cambridge: Cambridge University Press, 1998), pp. 57–75 (p. 66).

8. On the literary ties between Joyce and Cortázar, see Lida Aronne-Amestoy, *Cortázar: la novela mandala* (Buenos Aires: F. García Cambeiro, 1972) and Antonio Ballesteros González, 'La disgresión paródica en dos modelos narrativos: *Rayuela* y *Ulysses*', in *Joyce en España I*, ed. by Francisco García Tortosa and Antonio Raúl de Toro Santos (A Coruña: Universidade da Coruña, 1994), pp. 93–100. In *The Novels of Fernando del Paso* (Gainesville: University Press of Florida, 2000), Robin Fiddian also addresses the connection between *Ulysses* and *Rayuela*, arguing that Cortázar's novel stands as a bridge between the early 'Joycism' of Leopoldo Marechal's *Adán Buenosayres* and del Paso's *Palinuro de México*.

9. Julio Cortázar and Evelyn Picón-Garfield, *Cortázar por Cortázar* (Jalapa, Mexico: Universidad Veracruzana, 1978), p. 41.

10. Julio Cortázar, *Cartas*, I, 628.

11. Luis Harss and Barbara Dohman, 'Julio Cortázar, or the Slap in the Face", in Alazraki, ed., *Critical Essays on Julio Cortázar*, pp. 33–59 (p. 57).

12. Julio Cortázar, *Rayuela*, ed. by Andrés Amorós (Madrid: Cátedra, 2001), p. 559.

13. Michael Bell, *Literature, Modernism and Myth: Belief and Responsibility in the Twentieth Century* (Cambridge: Cambridge University Press, 1997), p. 9.

14. Ibid., pp. 1–2.

15. Edward Said, *Culture and Imperialism* (New York: Random House, 1993), p. 188.

16. Ibid., p. 189.

17. Julio Cortázar, 'El compromiso del escritor', in *Julio Cortázar: al término del polvo y el sudor* , ed. by Hugo Achugar (Montevideo: Biblioteca de Marcha, 1987), pp. 71–75 (pp. 73–74).

18. Santiago Colás, 'Inventing Autonomies: Meditations on Julio Cortázar and the Politics of Our Time', *CR: The New Centennial Review*, 5, 2 (2005), 1–34 (p. 13).

19. Cortázar, *Rayuela*, p. 234.

20. Ibid., p. 121.

21. Ibid., p. 135.

22. Ibid., p. 212.

23. Ibid., p. 373.

24. Ibid., p. 503.

25. Ibid., p. 410.

26. Ibid., p. 491.

27. Julio Cortázar, *Cuaderno de bitácora*, ed. by Ana María Barrenechea (Buenos Aires: Editorial Sudamericana, 1983), pp. 172–73.

28. Cortázar, *Rayuela*, p. 373.

29. Ibid., p. 410.

30. Georg W. F. Hegel, *Hegel's Phenomenology of Spirit*, ed. by Howard P. Kainz (University Park, PA: Penn State University Press, 1994), pp. 50–51.

31. W. E. B. Du Bois, *The Souls of Black Folk*, ed. by Candace Ward (New York: Dover, 1994), p. 2. On the Hegelian roots of Du Bois's philosophical thought, see Sandra Adell, *Double-Consciousness/Double Bind: Theoretical Issues in Twentieth-Century Black Literature* (Urbana: University of Illinois Press, 1994).

32. Julio Cortázar, *La vuelta al día en ochenta mundos* (Mexico: Siglo Veintiuno, 1967), p. 21.

33. Enrique Dussel, *Philosophy of Liberation* (Maryknoll, NY: Orbis Books, 1985), p. 4.

34. Ibid., p. 14.

35. Cortázar, *Rayuela*, pp. 540–41.

36. Ibid., p. 659.

37. Cortázar, *La vuelta al día en ochenta mundos*, p. 7.

38. Eric Auerbach, 'Figura', in *Scenes from the Drama of European Literature* (Manchester: Manchester University Press, 1984), pp. 11–76 (p. 58).

39. Cortázar, *La vuelta al día en ochenta mundos*, p. 21.

40. Cortázar has frequently commented on the importance of *figura* in Cortázar's fiction. See, for instance Cortázar and Picón-Garfield, *Cortázar por Cortázar*, p. 36.

41. Roland Barthes, *Mythologies*, trans. by Annette Lavers (New York: Hill and Wang, 1972), p. 132.

42. Ibid., p. 128.
43. Ibid., p. 129.
44. Ibid., pp. 135–36.
45. Ibid., p. 136.
46. Borges, *Obras completas*, I, 275.
47. Ibid., p. 277.
48. Ibid., p. 244; emphasis added.
49. Cortázar, *Rayuela*, p. 532.
50. Ibid., p. 531.
51. Fernández Retamar, *Cinco miradas sobre Cortázar*, p. 33.
52. Nehru as quoted in Ganesh Devi, 'India and Ireland: Literary Relations', in *The Internationalism of Irish Literature and Drama*, ed. by Joseph McMinn (Gerrards Cross: Colin Smythe, 1992), pp. 294–308 (p. 300).
53. Diana Sorensen, *A Turbulent Decade Remembered: Scenes from the Latin American Sixties* (Stanford, CA: Stanford University Press, 2007), p. 7.
54. Cortázar, 'Acerca de la situación del intelectual latinoamericano', pp. 270–71.
55. James Joyce, 'Ireland: Island of Saints and Sages', in *Occasional, Critical, and Political Writing*, ed. by Kevin Barry (Oxford: Oxford University Press, 2000), pp. 108–26 (p. 118).
56. See Julio Cortázar's response to the critic Óscar Collazos in 'Literatura en la revolución y revolución en la literatura: algunos malentendidos a liquidar', in *Literatura en la revolución y revolución en la literatura*, ed. by Óscar Collazos (Mexico: Siglo Veintiuno, 1977), pp. 38–77.
57. Julio Cortázar, 'Politics and the Intellectual in Latin America', in *The Final Island: The Fiction of Julio Cortázar*, ed. by Jaime Alazraki and Ivar Ivask (Norman: University of Oklahoma Press, 1976), pp. 37–44 (p. 44).
58. Fritz Senn, *Joyce's Dislocations: Essays on Reading as Translation*, ed. by John Paul Riquelme (Baltimore, MD: Johns Hopkins University Press, 1984), p. 65.
59. Additional examples include: 'Your hat is a little crushed, Mr Bloom said, pointing [...] It's all right now, Martin Cunningham said' (*U* 6.1018–24); 'Must get those old glasses of mine set right' (*U* 8.554).
60. For a discussion of the role of coincidence and chance in *Ulysses* from a postmodernist perspective see Derek Attridge, 'The Postmodernity of Joyce: Chance, Coincidence, and the Reader', in *Joyce Effects: On Language, Theory, and History* (Cambridge: Cambridge University Press, 2000), pp. 117–25. Thomas Rice has connected coincidence to the new physics in *Joyce, Chaos, and Complexity* (Urbana: University of Illinois Press, 1997).
61. Attridge, *Joyce's Effects*, p. 124.
62. Seamus Deane, 'Introduction', in *Nationalism, Colonialism, and Literature*, ed. by Seamus Deane (Minneapolis: University of Minnesota Press, 1986), pp. 3–19 (p. 18–19).
63. Attridge, *Joyce's Effects*, p. 124.

❖

CHAPTER 4

Local Interests: The Aesthetics of the Joycean Novel in Spanish America

Leo *The Waves*, esa puntilla cineraria, fábula de espumas. A treinta centí-metros por debajo de mis ojos una sopa se mueve lentamente en mi bolsa estomacal, un pelo crece en mi muslo, un quiste sebáceo surge imperceptible en mi espalda.

[I am reading *The Waves*, that cinerary piece of lace, a fable of foam. A foot below my eyes some soup is moving slowly in my stomach, a hair is growing on my thigh, an imperceptible sebaceous cyst is growing on my back.]

Julio Cortázar, *Rayuela*

Borges's short story 'El Aleph' draws our attention to the differences between two contrasting strategies to describe the Aleph, a tiny luminous point that contains all space and time. On the one hand, Carlos Argentino Danieri, the poet who finds the minuscule sphere in the basement of his house, believes he can contain it within the *alejandrinos* of a poem he entitles, perhaps with ludicrous grandeur, *La Tierra* (*The Earth*). On the other hand, 'Borges', the narrator, thinks it is futile to use conventional language to capture the seething flux of images radiating from the Aleph and decides to provide a chaotic and fast-paced catalogue of what he sees. Danieri's ambitious literary endeavour is 'static': it sets out to reduce the tumultuous sphere to the recursive patterns and rhythms of poetry; Borges's jumbled list is 'kinetic': it evokes through a rapid succession of phrases an unthinkable conflation of simultaneous acts. *La Tierra* is, of course, the target of a multi-tiered critique. By exposing the limitations of Danieri's project, Borges devastatingly criticizes the attempt to contain a region or a country that characterizes the social realist tradition in Latin American writing, particularly the *novela de la tierra*, a type of novel that engages with the autochthonous aspects of Latin America, with its *tierra*, through close attention to its geography and folklore. However, Danieri's totalizing aspirations and his penchant for formal and linguistic rigor are also redolent of the themes and style of literary modernism. His painstaking search for the *mot juste* and his conscious borrowings from canonical masterpieces relate his creative efforts to James Joyce's linguistic virtuosity and T. S. Eliot's 'mythical method'. Similarly, the detailed descriptions of the planet found in *La Tierra* might be taken as a *reductio ad absurdum* of Joyce's rendering of the events of a single day in *Ulysses*.[1]

Despite what the similarities between *La Tierra* and *Ulysses* might suggest, there is reason to believe that for Borges, Joyce's book resembled his kinetic enumeration more than Danieri's totalizing text. In another of his well-known short stories, 'Funes el memorioso', the Argentine fabulist returns to the incapacity of language to capture and organize reality. Funes, the protagonist, possesses an inordinate memory which keeps him from forgetting, and hence from mapping reality in a meaningful manner. In 'Fragmento sobre Joyce', a short article published in *Sur* in 1941, Borges drafted the basic plot and characters of 'Funes el memorioso', which first appeared a year later.[2] Here he affirms that to read *Ulysses* from beginning to end requires no less than the boundless memory of Funes, a memory that resonates with the immensity of the multifarious Aleph. Just as the multiple styles of *Ulysses* (a feature Borges celebrates) and its indiscriminate attention to details prevent us from perceiving an overarching structure or design in the book — after all, we are told, the gods denied Joyce the gift of plot craftsmanship ('la capacidad de construir') — so Funes's memory frustrates his attempts to arrest and contain a bewildering mass of sensations. Borges goes on to stress the novel's 'chaotic' aspects while dismissing as insignificant 'tics' the Homeric parallels that used to attract so much scholarly attention. In a typically understated and ironic manner, he concludes that mere awareness of those far-fetched correspondences, consecrated by critics like Stuart Gilbert, is enough to make readers perceive and celebrate the 'classical discipline' and 'rigorous construction' of a novel that is essentially formless.

The 'shapelessness' that connects Funes's mind with Joyce's *Ulysses* also characterizes the fragmentary catalogue of the Aleph, which Borges embraces as the origin of a new poetics. Unlike Danieri, who like T. S. Eliot feels compelled to resort to traditional forms and classical texts to render the Aleph amenable to human understanding, Borges reiterates that what he writes is simply what he 'sees': 'Vi el populoso mar, vi el alba y la tarde, vi las muchedumbres de América [...]' [I saw the populous sea, I saw the dawn and the sunset, I saw the multitudes of America].[3] The Argentine writer refuses to accept that the authority to represent can only come from literary predecessors sanctioned by tradition. By claiming the right to 'see' things anew, without the aid of tradition, Borges suggests that bodily sensations and individual experiences should be neither excluded from literary representation nor subjected to the 'impersonal' authority of 'the whole of the literature of Europe from Homer'.[4] As Julio Ortega points out, to 'remake literature, to make a new literature, language must be used in another way', to which he adds that 'the postulation of another language emblematically represents Borges's work, which is a rereading of tradition through criticism'.[5] To Ortega's apposite remark I would add the following observation: to a large degree, such alternative language gains its innovative power and its critical edge by refusing to detach artistic expression from the murmurs of the sentient body and the fluctuating contours of experience.

Borges perceived this attitude in Joyce's *Ulysses*, which he instructs us to read as an attempt to unite rather than separate mind and matter, thought and feeling, abstraction and sensation. As early as 1925, in his review of *Ulysses*, he argued that Joyce's book manifests a 'total reality' where inner and outer experience coexist and interact to evoke the richness and immediacy of life, of 'being in this precise world':

> En las páginas del Ulises bulle con alborotos de picadero la realidad total. No la mediocre realidad de quienes sólo advierten en el mundo las abstraídas operaciones del alma [...] ni esa otra realidad que entra por los sentidos y en que conviven nuestra carne y la acera, la luna y el aljibe. La dualidad de la existencia está en él: esa inquietación ontológica que no se asombra meramente de ser, sino de ser en este mundo preciso, donde hay zaguanes y palabras y naipes y escrituras eléctricas en la limpidez de las noches.[6]

> [A total reality boils incessantly in the pages of *Ulysses*. Not the mediocre reality of those who notice in the world only the abstract operations of the soul [...] nor that other reality that reaches us through the senses and where our flesh coexists with the sidewalk, the moon and the well. The duality of existence is embedded in this book: that ontological unrest that is amazed not only at being, but at being in this precise world where one can find doorways and words and playing cards and electrical writing in the crisp clarity of the nights.]

According to Borges, Joyce does not embrace art as a retreat from the external world nor as a way of controlling, containing and giving shape to experience. The Argentine writer suggests that in the novel the two 'halves' of reality relate to each other horizontally: *Ulysses* does not elevate us from real life into the realm of pure speculation and abstraction; instead, the book shows that the very stuff of life, its overwhelming complexity, can suggest new means for its manifestation. The chaotic enumeration closing Borges's remark ('doorways and words and playing cards and electrical writing in the crisp clarity of the nights') may be one of those forms: a verbal construction that, like the multiple styles of *Ulysses*, evokes rather than restrains the changing shape of reality. As Sylvia Molloy points out, the recurrent enumerations in Borges's writing — which she illustrates through Funes's memory and the catalogue of the Aleph — are series of disparate elements that fail to crystallize into stable images. By disrupting all attempts to achieve closure, to organize materials according to a rigid syntactic causality, the openness of these lists expose the limitations of forms of artistic expression biased toward stasis and order.[7]

Taking my cue from Borges's reflections on *Ulysses*, I would like to propose the 'kinetic' openness of his enumerations, rather than the self-reflexive formalism of literary modernism, as the common aesthetic territory where James Joyce meets those Spanish American novelists frequently labelled 'Joycean'. The modernist artwork has been traditionally appreciated for its formal features and its autonomy from the vicissitudes of the external world. As Virginia Woolf famously claimed in her essay, 'Modern Fiction', literary representation should repudiate the conventions of realism and engage with life by concentrating on the 'spirit' and not the 'body' — by describing experience as a 'luminous halo, a semi-transparent envelope surrounding us from the beginning of consciousness to the end [...] with as little mixture of the alien and external as possible'.[8] This perception of art goes back to Kant's doctrine of 'aesthetic disinterestedness', which maintains that the work of art should remain untouched by 'lower' passions and desires, frequently provoked by what Woolf calls 'the alien and the external'. As Kant explained in the *Critique of*

Judgment (1790), aesthetic taste must be divorced from the empirical world, for art should not appeal to the senses, but provide intellectual gratification 'by means of its form'.[9] I will expand my argument from the previous two chapters to propose that the Spanish American 'Joycism' prefigured by Borges and epitomized by Cortázar engages critically with the Kantian doctrine of 'aesthetic disinterestedness', subverting the separation between the realm of abstract representation and the immediacy of bodily experience. Focusing on the narrative prose of Leopoldo Marechal, José Lezama Lima, Guillermo Cabrera Infante and Fernando del Paso, I set out to demonstrate that these authors redeploy the linguistic and structural innovations commonly associated with Joyce's modernism not to move beyond the world of feeling and phenomena, but rather to express their sense of 'being in this precise world', to use Borges's phrase. Although Spanish American 'Joycism' certainly displays stylistic experiments that overlap with those of Anglo-American modernism, its main representatives 'gave modernist aesthetics a significant inflection of their own'.[10] I argue that this local 'inflection' does not simply involve the representation of native reality with the aid of methods and techniques imported from the metropolis. Most crucially, Spanish American Joycism articulates cultural particularity and locality by consistently frustrating the dematerialized abstractions of modernist formalism, thus staging the breakdown of 'universal' artistic doctrines and demarcating dimensions of lived reality that escape the purview of norms and ideas manufactured in Europe for global consumption. How a Joycean tradition emerged and developed in Spanish America as a reaction against modernist poetics — as an affirmation of local interests against aesthetic disinterestedness — will be the subject of this chapter.

Joycean Genealogies

If we agree with Borges that every writer creates his own precursors, then we should search for the origins of Cortázar's *Rayuela*, the epitome of Joycism in Spanish America, among the several hundred pages of Leopoldo Marechal's *Adán Buenosayres* (1948), a book Cortázar helped rescue from critical oblivion and that prefigures in precise ways the themes and style of *Rayuela*. Both novels revolve around the process of intellectual maturation of their protagonists and address a wide variety of philosophical and cultural issues, ranging from erotic love to questions of nationalism and cultural identity. *Adán Buenosayres* charts in ambitious detail the rambles of the eponymous hero through the streets of Buenos Aires over a forty-eight-hour period and displays a range of cultural reference and a daring mixing of genres unprecedented in Spanish American literature.[11] However, due to Marechal's Peronist affiliation, his work gained critical attention only retrospectively, since it was the victim of a notorious critical silencing that lasted decades. This silence was suddenly broken after *Rayuela* caused a seismic stir in Spanish American letters and critics began to search for the novel's antecedents. It was then that a forgotten review of *Adán Buenosayres* written by Julio Cortázar in 1949, one of the few laudatory appraisals against a backdrop of critical condemnation, was exhumed as evidence of the literary origins of *Rayuela*.[12]

Shortly after Marechal's novel appeared, one of the editors of *Sur*, Eduardo González Lanuza, published a review in that magazine that recalls in its main points H. G. Wells's 1916 review of Joyce's *A Portrait*.[13] González Lanuza, a former literary fellow of Marechal's, scathingly attacks *Adán Buenosayres* for its crude language and its attention to repugnant subjects better left unmentioned. He believes that the combination of the novel's obscenity and the markedly Catholic beliefs that frame the protagonist's spiritual search turn the text into what could be described as a grotesque *Ulysses* written by a priest and then 'splattered with manure'. By including episodes such as high-class women conversing about defecation and constipation (see Section II of Book II) or the scatological details that permeate the account of Adán's descent into the underground 'City of Cacodelphia' (see Book VII), Marechal's novel, like Joyce's *Ulysses*, breaks the rules of literary decorum, letting sordid details improperly intrude in the realm of artistic representation. González Lanuza's condemnation of these aspects tacitly favours a 'disinterested' appreciation of literature based on the separation of aesthetic contemplation from bodily activity and its consequences.

In 1949, Emir Rodríguez Monegal expanded and complemented González Lanuza's views in a piece entitled '*Adán Buenosayres*: Una novela infernal', published in *Marcha*. Here he criticizes the palpable discrepancy between the explicitly religious frame of the work — what he ironically calls its 'angelic tone' — and the scatological details of some of its passages. But his main criticism is perhaps that the novel lacks 'unity'. The multiple details filling the book fail to harden into a static and ordered image of Buenos Aires. Rather than capturing the 'true and definitive face of the city', the novel confronts the reader with a myriad of 'unconnected snapshots, of counterfeit and transitory effigies' ('inconexas instantáneas, efigies aparenciales y transitorias').[14] *Ulysses* is here summoned as a point of reference too, but instead of considering Joyce's book as a source of obscenity and depravation, Rodríguez Monegal presents it as the model of ordered totality that *Adán Buenosayres* tries to imitate without success. Marechal only copies the external details of Joyce's masterpiece without achieving its integral vision, a vision that derives from the attempt to 'cercar la realidad desde todos sus ángulos para agotar su significado y su escandalosa riqueza' [contain reality from all possible angles in order to exhaust its meaning and its scandalous richness].[15] These terms echo the critic's discussion of the modernist novel of Woolf and Kafka in 'Aspectos de la novela del siglo XX' (1948), where it is argued that contemporary novelists should not only invent significant actions or absorbing conflicts, but also create 'estructuras, multiplicar los ángulos, encerrar en la malla ubicua de la narración todo un universo' [structures, multiply angles, capture in the ubiquitous net of the narrative a whole universe].[16] These critical views — which, incidentally, bear an uncanny resemblance to Carlos Argentino Danieri's plan to 'versify the roundness of the world' — associate artistic merit and permanence with abstract form and pattern, that is, with literature's capacity to enclose the elusive circumstances of reality into stable and static forms.

In a postscript added to his review in 1969, six years after the publication of *Rayuela*, Rodríguez Monegal qualifies some of his previous opinions, arguing that in 1949 he did not asses *Adán Buenosayres* for what it really was, namely an

'Argentine' novel. He adds that it was Julio Cortázar who in a 1948 article truly perceived its most 'enduring values'. Cortázar's text stages an almost complete reversal of Rodríguez Monegal's and González Lanuza's opinions. Whereas these two critics censured Marechal's novel for its unfiltered realism and its lack of structural unity, Cortázar perceives in those aspects the beginning of a truly Argentine narrative tradition, of which *Rayuela* might be its triumphal culmination. Carlos Fuentes once quipped that if the Mexicans descended from the Aztecs, the Argentines descended from ships. It is precisely this lack of a distinct Argentine cultural identity that, for Cortázar, *Adán Buenosayres* began to remedy.

In the opening chapter of the novel, Marechal's alter ego, L. M., lays out the plan for the book, carefully emphasizing its unity of purpose. His narrative, which includes his own transcription of some personal documents that Adán bequeathed to him, revolves around the protagonist's search for spiritual salvation:

> Mi plan se concretó al fin en cinco libros, donde presentaría yo a mi Adán Buenosayres desde su despertar metafísico en el número 303 de la calle Monte Egmont, hasta la medianoche del siguiente día, en que ángeles y demonios pelearon por su alma en Villa Crespo, frente a la iglesia de San Bernardo, ante la figura inmóvil del Cristo de la Mano Rota. Luego transcribiría yo el *Cuaderno de Tapas Azules* y *Viaje a la Oscura Ciudad de Cacodelphia*, como sexto y séptimo libros de mi relato.[17]

> [I eventually decided to divide my narrative into five books, where I would present my Adán Buenosayres from his metaphysical awakening in 303 Mount Egmont Street until midnight of the following day, when angels and demons fought for his soul in Villa Crespo, across from San Bernardo Church, under the persistent gaze of the Christ of the Broken Hand. I would then transcribe the *Notebook of the Blue Covers* and the *Journey to the Obscure City of Cacodelphia* as books six and seven of my narrative.]

As Marechal explained in 'Las claves de *Adán Buenosayres*', this metaphysical dimension distances his book from Joyce's *Ulysses*, for Leopold Bloom lacks the spiritual integrity that Adán seeks: Bloom 'no va realizando ningún intento metafísico: viaja según el "error" y según el "errar" (dos palabras de significado casi equivalente), y se "dispersa" en la multiplicidad de sus gestos y andanzas [...]. Adán Buenosayres, en cambio, es un viajero que se desplaza con un objetivo determinado: el fin o finalidad de su viaje' [does not fulfil a metaphysical design: he travels according to 'error' and 'errancy' (two words with almost the same meaning), and he 'dissolves' in his multiple gestures and adventures [...]. By contrast, Adán Buenosayres is a traveller who advances toward a specific goal: the end or destination of his journey].[18] This spiritual dimension also keeps *Adán Buenosayres* from turning into a mere 'catalog of expressive forms' like *Ulysses*. Despite including references to specific episodes from Joyce's novel and drawing on some of its most distinctive narrative techniques, Marechal claims that *Adán Buenosayres* resembles *Ulysses* only because they are both rewritings of Homer's *Odyssey*.

In contrast, Cortázar focuses on the 'erratic' features of *Adán Buenosayres*, underlining the artistic value of the 'deep contradiction' between the protagonist's Neoplatonic inclinations and the novel's chaotic organization and naturalistic details, an aspect that both Rodríguez Monegal and González Lanuza strongly criticized and Marechal underplayed. Instead of considering such contradiction a technical flaw, an unwelcome rift between form and contents, Cortázar finds in the tumultuous, fragmented and at times scatological narrative of Adán's spiritual search an inspiring precursor of the trials of his own character, Horacio Oliveira. As Javier de Navascués aptly notes, both *Adán Buenosayres* and *Rayuela* frame an incessant quest for harmony within a distorted narrative 'que refleja el desorden interior del protagonista' [that projects the internal disorder of the protagonist].[19] Marechal's hero, like the protagonist of *Rayuela*, is uprooted from 'perfection', 'unity' and 'eso que llaman cielo' [that which they call heaven].[20] Cortázar's allusion to 'Heaven' can be read here as an oblique reference to the top square in the chalk pattern of the game of hopscotch, which in *Rayuela* (yet to be published by the time he wrote this review) symbolizes the philosophical horizon of Oliveira's search, the lost paradise that he obsessively seeks to achieve spiritual balance. The elusive nature of this 'heaven', of a sense of metaphysical wholeness, responds to the persistent 'displacement' (*desajuste*) that plagues the Argentine 'en todos los planos mentales, morales y del sentimiento' [at all mental, moral, sentimental levels].[21] It is Cortázar's contention that rather than the folkloric details and local colour that characterize several parts of *Adán Buenosayres*, it is this existential *desajuste* that can best perform the task of articulating a distinctive Argentine voice.

The Argentine novelist describes this sense of dislocation — this inability to organize reality according to abstract notions of 'order' and 'unity' — as an aesthetic force that underlies the works of canonical Argentine writers such as Borges, Güiraldes and Mallea. Cortázar's celebration of the artistic possibilities of not feeling well-adjusted runs counter to González Lanuza's and Rodríguez Monegal's 'disinterested' formalism, while it intersects with the openness of Borges's enumerations. This *desajuste*, like Borges's catalogue of the Aleph, evokes the ungraspable nature of experience, the persistent failure of the categories of the mind to arrest and contain reality — in sum, the triumph of kinesis over stasis. Cortázar's observations about *Adán Buenosayres* imply that to punctuate the 'pure' and 'universal' world of pattern and form with life's ordinary events and amorphous sensations can be an especially powerful means of articulating cultural eccentricity. It should be noted, however, that Adán's *desajuste* as defined by Cortázar refers not only to the displaced status of the Argentine, but also to what he calls the 'angustia occidental contemporánea' [contemporary Western angst]. As is well known, this 'angst' permeated European literature and philosophy during the opening decades of the twentieth century. It created a widespread atmosphere of existentialist pessimism, a deeply felt realization that, following the Nietzschean death of God, the erstwhile universal values of Western culture were on the verge of dissolution. But what in Europe was a source of anguish and desolation, in Argentina became the promise of a new beginning: an 'enérgico empujón hacia lo de veras nuestro' [energetic push toward what is truly ours].[22]

In 'Situación de la novela', an article published in *Cuadernos Americanos* in 1950, Cortázar further discusses how this European sense of cultural crisis affects contemporary narrative. He contends that the modern novel is mainly characterized

by a deep questioning of the 'linguistic conquest' of realism, of its totalizing representational capacities. The realistic novel that predominated in Europe in the
eighteenth and nineteenth centuries deployed 'técnicas racionales para expresar
y traducir los sentimientos' [rational techniques to express and translate feelings],
while the modern novel questions the validity of those conventional forms by either
devising new ones that could reconnect language and the fullness of experience
during a time of crisis (e.g., Virginia Woolf) or by sounding the death knell for
life's inner meanings (e.g., Sartre).[23] A third option is found in Joyce's *Ulysses*, which
for the Argentine writer stands as the prototypical example of an altogether 'new
metaphysics'. According to Cortázar's historical outline, *Adán* is a modern novel
whose characteristic self-questioning features derive directly from 'la empresa
sinfónica que es *Ulysses*' [the symphonic enterprise of *Ulysses*].[24]

But does Cortázar consider this 'new metaphysics' radiating from Joyce's novel
an internal mutation of what he calls 'el espíritu de Manuel Kant' [the spirit of
Immanuel Kant]?[25] In other words, does *Ulysses* offer renovated strategies for
rendering reality tractable once again, thus providing a palliative solution for the
crisis of representation that afflicted Europe? Or does *Ulysses* mark, like *Adán*, a
fresh start, the birth of a radically new form of writing that does not hope to restore
a transcendental view of experience, but instead shows how cultural eccentricity
can provide fertile ground to develop unimagined ways of interpreting the world?
In Chapter 3 we argued that Cortázar favoured this 'eccentric' approach to Joyce's
works. But a cursory perusal of his personal correspondence can cast some new
light on the links between the inception of a truly Argentine narrative tradition
(originating in *Adán Buenosayres* and culminating with *Rayuela*) and Joycean
aesthetics. In 1959, nine years after he wrote 'Situación de la novela', and four years
before the publication of *Rayuela*, Cortázar wrote a letter to Jean Barnabé in which
he illustrated his ideas on fiction by referring to *Ulysses*: 'Piense en algunos capítulos
de *Ulysses*. ¿Cómo escribir una novela cuando primero habría que des-escribirse,
des-aprenderse, partir "a neuf", desde cero, en una condición pre-adamita, por
decirlo así?' [Think of some chapters in *Ulysses*. How can one write a novel when
everything should be first un-written and un-learned; when one needs to start from
scratch, from a pre-Adamic condition, as it were?][26] Rather than interpreting Joyce's
work as a means of 'controlling, of ordering, of giving a shape and a significance
to the immense panorama of futility and anarchy which is contemporary history'
(to use T. S. Eliot's words), Cortázar perceives in it a radically new form of
expression akin to the *desajuste* that infuses Marechal's *Adán Buenosayres*. Therefore,
if *Ulysses* should be considered a model for the modern Argentine novel, Cortázar
suggests, it is not because Joyce's book stands as an example of literary modernity,
or even because it provides a set of methods and techniques that can render Latin
American society and culture in unconventional ways, but because it dispenses with
the authority of established literary and philosophical traditions and starts 'from
scratch', casting aside all the systems, models and referents that seek to organize and
categorize the richness of experience.

The terms that Cortázar uses to refer to *Ulysses* and his projected *Rayuela* recur in
his discussion of another Joycean novel, José Lezama Lima's *Paradiso* (1966). In 'Para

llegar a Lezama Lima' (1967), the Argentine novelist underlines the Cuban writer's distance from the canons and norms of European culture. Unlike European writers, who owe strong allegiance to their cultural backgrounds, Lezama sidesteps fixed literary codes and 'amanece con su alegría de preadamita [...] y no se siente culpable de ninguna tradición directa' [wakes up with pre-Adamic joy [...] and doesn't feel responsible for any direct tradition]. According to Cortázar, this freedom from the constraints of tradition is apparent in *Paradiso*, whose style and message make us wonder how it is possible to dismiss so thoroughly 'los tabúes del saber' [the taboos of knowledge].[27] Although *Paradiso* can be compared with other 'Ulyssean' modernist novels such as Robert Musil's *The Man Without Qualities* and Hermann Broch's *The Death of Virgil*, Lezama's work does not constitute, to use Cortázar's felicitous phrase, 'un eslabón de la cadena' [a link in the chain] of the Western literary tradition. In his essay 'Cortázar y el comienzo de la otra novela', Lezama Lima also perceives this radical novelty in *Rayuela*, a book he describes as the birth of a new genre that releases hidden and ancestral meanings from petrified verbal conventions while at the same time suggesting unsuspected ways of experiencing and representing reality. Evoking Morelli's discussion of *figura*, Lezama argues that *Rayuela* combines an almost magical language that attunes us to 'secuestrados latidos, contracciones, crujimientos, que respiran secretamente detrás de una extendida y visible masa verbal' [kidnapped palpitations, contractions and groans that breathe secretly behind a visible and extended verbal mass] with another kind of verbal code: a boundless and exuberant speech that Lezama compares with *Finnegans Wake*, 'aquella ensalada filológica del último Joyce' [that philological crucible of Joyce's last work]. This dual language, he argues, resonates with the murmurs of a voice and an intellect liberated from 'la *ratio*, como si lo inconexo o la nexitud al azar proyectase más luz que las cadenas causales' [rationality, as if disconnection or the arrangements of chance could be more enlightening than the rules of causality].[28]

It is precisely this combination of bewildering dislocation and exhilarating novelty that distances *Paradiso* (as well as *Adán Buenosayres* and *Rayuela*) from the language and authority of metropolitan literary models. The main thematic thread of the novel is provided by the genealogical tree of José Cemí's family on the maternal and paternal sides. The narrative chronicles the development of this Cuban family, providing a profusion of descriptive details about turn-of-the-twentieth-century Cuba. Cortázar notes that it is not this 'tropical folklore', but the lack of structural unity, and, most importantly, the complex redefinition of the relationship between language and reality, that signal the cultural eccentricity and radical originality of *Paradiso*. According to the Argentine writer, Lezama's book deviates from conventional expectations about genre because despite framing the action within a specific time and place — including precise information on 'geografía, mobiliario, gastronomía e indumentaria' [geography, furniture, gastronomy and clothing] — the characters communicate in an 'oracular' language that transcends the pragmatic value of prosaic information. Cortázar concludes: '¿Por qué no ha de aceptar que los personajes de *Paradiso* hablen siempre *desde la imagen*, puesto que Lezama los proyecta a partir de un sistema poético que ha explicado en múltiples textos y que tiene su clave en la potencia de la imagen como secreción suprema del espíritu humano en busca de la realidad del mundo invisible?' [Why shouldn't we accept that the characters in *Paradiso* always speak *from the image*, since Lezama projects them from a poetic system that he has explained in several texts and that revolves around the power of the image as the highest expression of the human spirit in its search for the reality of the invisible world?][29] The 'image' is indeed one of the most central notions both in the novel and Lezama's poetic system as whole. It is an elusive term that broadly refers to the capacity of poetic inspiration to escape from impersonal historical forces and temporalities. The image, like the esoteric languages that Lezama perceives in *Rayuela* and like Morelli's *figuras*, reunites disparate sensations, trivial incidents and casual memories to configure personal histories that evade the surveillance of standard cultural and cognitive categories. The spiritual manifestation associated with the image breaks free from the dead weight of tradition and clears new ground for alternative literary paths.

During the course of his intellectual conversations with his friends Foción and Fronesis, the protagonist of *Paradiso*, José Cemí realizes that he is destined to walk those untrodden paths by transcending the stifling influence of tradition through his liberated poetic imagination. In a passage that could summarize the contents of these conversations, the narrator tells us that the three friends

> sabían que el conformismo en la expresión y en las ideas tomaba en el mundo contemporáneo innumerables variantes y disfraces, pues exigía del intelectual la servidumbre, el mecanismo de un absoluto causal, para que abandonase su posición verdaderamente heroica de ser, como en las grandes épocas, creador de valores, de formas, el saludador de lo viviente creador y acusador de lo amortajado en bloques de hielo, que todavía osa fluir en el río de lo temporal.[30]

> [knew that conformity in expression and ideas took on in the contemporary world countless disguises, since it demanded of the intellectual servitude to the mechanism of an absolute causality, making him abandon his truly heroic position of being, as in the great eras, creator of values, of forms, greeter of the creative vitality and accuser of what is enshrouded in blocks of ice, which still dares to float in the river of temporality.]

As these lines suggest, Lezama demands from the writer a poetic commitment to establish new and stimulating relations between language and the world. These relations should be fluid, engaged in an incessant 'avanzar retrocediendo y retroceder avanzando' [retreating by advancing and advancing by retreating] as they push in new directions the expressive possibilities handed down by tradition.[31]

One of the fragments that Cortázar selected to offer a panoramic view of *Paradiso* may illustrate this poetic creativity. The fragment revolves around Cemí's impressions as he observes the articles of handicraft in the window of an antiquarian's shop. When he focuses on one of these objects, it moves forward like 'a chess piece' and becomes a point of reference around which the rest of his perceptions gravitate: 'esa pieza que se adelantaba era un punto que lograba una infinita corriente de analogía' [the piece that came forward was a point that gained an infinite current of analogy]. However, the figures in the window fail to organize themselves into a 'ciudad, retablo, o potestades jerarquizadas' [city, an altar screen, or a hierarchy

César A. Salgado has rightly claimed that 'the prominence of the notion of stasis in the aesthetic theory of *A Portrait* is an important influence and component in the evolution of the central topos of *fijeza* in Lezama's system'.[43] However, it is important to stress that the poetic systems of Joyce and Lezama do not rely on 'stasis' or *fijeza* to sustain the sort of pure abstraction that can elevate us from 'real life' and transcend cultural differences. One would be missing Joyce's point about aesthetics if Stephen were taken as a straight mouthpiece of the author's ideas.[44] Certainly, the contrast between Stephen's views and Joyce's creation is the source of much tension and irony in *A Portrait*.[45] Stephen's abstract thoughts are constantly undercut by sexual desire, hunger and other sensory perceptions. Material reality is ever-intrusive in the narrative, acting as a constant ironic reminder that the artist's idealism can never soar above the coarse and repugnant aspects of life. An illustrative example of this sort of irony is found in Chapter 5 of *A Portrait*, when Stephen has already embraced his artistic vocation and sets out to formulate his aesthetic theory. When he comes to a crucial point in the exposition of his theory, his rarefied musings get interrupted by the 'harsh roar of jangled and rattling metal' of a truck carrying iron and by Lynch's curses about the incident.[46] This contrast between the accidents of external reality and Stephen's hyperintellectual consciousness is also a central aspect of *Ulysses*. In Chapter 3, 'Proteus', the artist walks along Sandymount Beach as he speculates about the essential form and meaning of the natural world. In order to organize his perceptions in a systematic and logical manner, he claims that the sand under his feet is 'language' that the tide has silted on the shore. Similarly, when he hears the rustling of the waves, he is compelled to interpret it as 'wavespeech' (*U* 3.457). His medievalistic slant of mind also converts his surroundings into a message to be deciphered, into a system of emblems and symbols with allegorical meaning. For instance, when he sees a rambling dog on the beach, he turns it into the centrepiece of an imaginary coat of arms: 'On a field tenney a buck, trippant, proper, unattired' (*U* 3.336–37). Ironically, however, this dog keeps changing shapes, as he envisions it as a hare, a bear, a buck and a wolf. Despite Stephen's commitment to reading and categorizing the 'signatures of all things' (*U* 3.2), nature proves to be conspicuously recalcitrant to intellectual orders, behaving as a protean mass that exceeds abstract cultural and linguistic grids.

Among other narrative aspects, this subversion of abstract formalism has led Weldon Thornton to claim that far from being modernist texts, *A Portrait* and *Ulysses* are testimony to Joyce's 'antimodernism'.[47] Thornton reads Joyce's subversion of Stephen's ideas as an extended ironic attack against the modernist notion of aesthetic 'stasis' and the related dichotomy between a self-sufficient mind and the vacuous reality of the external world. According to this critic, 'Stephen Dedalus, good modernist that he is, is sufficiently enamored of this empiricist/ Enlightenment view of the self that he does (at least in *Portrait*) aspire to conscious control of all of the various forces at work within him'.[48] While Stephen's Kantian artistic doctrine privileges mind over body, spirit over matter, and form over content, Joyce wishes to expose 'the paltriness of the modernist view of the self', demonstrating the futility of the protagonist's efforts to separate consciousness from experience and to find in art a refuge isolated from the sordid reality of life.[49]

Thornton goes on to suggest that Joyce's 'Irishness' might be an important influence on his antimodernist views. What he calls Stephen's 'Irish shadow' — 'a complex of interrelated images, of attitudes, of fears' that he 'senses to be important but *cannot* render fully conscious' — functions in *A Portrait* like the profuse accidental details that interrupt Stephen's intellectual abstractions.[50] Motifs related to the Irish 'race', the peasants and the countryside recur in the novel as deeply rooted dimensions of Stephen's psyche that escape his self-conscious meditations and prevent him from achieving the ideal of artistic stasis that he pursues. For instance, in Chapter 5 Stephen reflects on the humble subservience of the Irish peasants when they greet the 'patricians of Ireland' — the landowning members of the Protestant Ascendancy that perpetuated Britain's colonial control over Ireland. As he follows this line of thought, he is confronted by the harrowing 'desires of the race to which he belonged flitting like bats, across dark country lanes, under trees by the edges of streams and near the poolmottled bogs'.[51] Just as external reality consistently jars the static harmony of Stephen's aesthetic ideal, the artist's 'Irish shadow' forces him to descend from the airy chambers of intellectual individualism, confronting him with history and the immediacy of a 'sense of place' that disturbs the 'universal' formulations of his thought.

One can draw similar conclusions about the place of *fijeza* within Lezama's wider poetic and cultural system. Lezama, like Joyce, does not embrace 'stasis' to sustain the sort of formalist abstractions promulgated by Stephen, Kant and Eliot. For the Cuban poet, aesthetic 'stasis' or *fijeza* precedes the configuration of the 'image', the poetic phenomenon that rearranges words and perceptions into unconventional designs. The static intensity of 'la mirada que se fija' halts the flow of experience but only to recombine its elements through the incessant dynamism of the 'image'. Perhaps the contrast between artistic disinterestedness and Lezama's notions of *fijeza* and 'image' can be thrown into sharper relief if we briefly consider his theories of history. The 'image' functions not only as the pulse that animates poetic creation and artistic apprehension, but also as the focal point of Lezama's meditations on historiography. For Lezama, history and poetry are indistinguishable: he reads history as a creative text governed by the 'image' and not as an inert sequence of events propelled forward by the abstract notion of progress — by the 'pseudo concepto temporal de que todo se dirige a lo contemporáneo' [by the temporal pseudo-concept that everything advances toward contemporaneity].[52] Historical hermeneutics, like poetic creativity, does not consist of the investigation of universal laws or even the articulation of a cross-cultural morphology that compares homologous historical events; rather, Lezama's understanding of history involves the active participation of a 'metaphorical subject' [*sujeto metafórico*] who combines disparate cultural, historical and natural phenomena into new forms and myths to interpret the universe from a specific perspective.

In the collection of essays *La expresión americana* (1957), Lezama opposes the creative capacity of the 'metaphorical subject' to the 'crepuscular criticism' represented by T. S. Eliot. Lezama's artist–historian, like the English metaphysical poets studied by Eliot in his famous essay, is 'constantly amalgamating disparate experience' and 'always forming new wholes'.[53] However, the Cuban writer draws a sharp distinction between Eliot's theories and his own critical method. While Eliot is interested in recycling old myths and rewriting the masterworks of literary tradition, Lezama embraces the possibility of inventing new myths, new forms of expression, and new and unsuspected cultural and historical configurations: 'Todo tendrá que ser reconstruido, invencionado de nuevo, y los viejos mitos, al reaparecer de nuevo, nos ofreceran sus conjuros y sus enigmas con un rostro desconocido' [Everything will have to be rebuilt and reinvented, and whenever the old myths reappear, they will offer us their spells and enigmas with an unknown face].[54] Eliot's 'new wholes' are permutations of the literary blocks provided by the classics — a nostalgic effort to reactivate the authority of the ancient masters in modern times. As Lezama puts it, his 'mythical method' responds to a 'neoclasicismo *à outrance*, que situaba en cada obra contemporánea la tarea de los glosadores por precisar su respaldo en épocas míticas, pues él es un crítico pesimista de la era crepuscular. Pesimista en cuanto él cree que la creación fue realizada por los antiguos y que a los contemporáneos sólo nos resta el juego de las combinatorias' [Neoclassicism *à outrance*, which demanded from each contemporary work the task of interpreters seeking support in mythical eras, for he was a pessimistic critic of the crepuscular era. He is pessimistic in the sense that he believes that everything was created by the ancients and that the we contemporaries can only engage in a game of combinations].[55] In contrast, Lezama's historical method involves an implacable and mutinous curiosity, an incessant mutation of the elements of tradition, and a transformative ability to combine those elements in an imaginative manner.

Another crucial difference between Eliot's 'mythical method' and Lezama's ideas relates to the cultural specificity that he accords the creative operations of the metaphorical subject. According to the author of *Paradiso*, the process of 'creative assimilation' is deeply rooted in the historical and geographical circumstances of the metaphorical subject. While Eliot's goal is to propose a theory with universal validity, untouched by the particularities of individual emotions or regional attachments, Lezama's reflections ultimately seek to illuminate the defining traits of a truly American mode of expression. The Lezamian historical subject is not a disembodied entity, a Cartesian pure being set apart from the experiences of the world; instead, it arises from the sense of rebelliousness and marginality that characterizes Latin American culture and from the joyful dialogue that the intellect establishes with the exuberance of the American *paisaje* [landscape]. The first avatar of this American subject is 'nuestro señor barroco' ['our Baroque lord'], who acquires a specific ethnic dimension by embodying the *plutonismo* or assimilating force that recycles, reshapes and transforms European forms, frequently combining them with indigenous, Asian and African cultural components to give shape to radically original artistic manifestations. The mixture of classical motifs and elements from Inca cosmology in the portal of San Lorenzo church in Potosí, the Afro-Hispanic style of the Brazilian architect and sculptor Aleijadinho, and the voluptuous lines of Sor Juana Inés de la Cruz's poem *Primero Sueño* are some examples of the American creative imagination. Lezama presents the Spanish American Baroque as the medium of a genuine American expression. In this sense, the New World Baroque does not generate a transcultural formalism or a universal poetics, but rather weaves together disparate fragments into a specific cultural determination that Lezama characterizes as a movement of 'counter-conquest'. In Lezama's words: 'podemos decir que entre nosotros el barroco fue una arte de la contraconquista' [we can say that, among us, the Baroque was an art of the counter-conquest].[56]

Lezama's Baroque 'counter-conquest' and Joyce's 'antimodernism' may be seen as crisscrossing decolonizing strategies, local points of resistance to the authority of universal cultural formations. On closer scrutiny, José Cemí's aesthetic theories in *Paradiso* intersect with a broader interest in cultural self-determination and decolonization and not with Stephen's and Eliot's abstract formalism. The Lezamian operations of *fijeza* and the image infuse the creative process with a specific ethnic dimension that reverses the idealistic stasis of 'disinterested' art by fully historicizing the acts of aesthetic production and consumption. For Lezama, assimilating and recreating myths, works of art, historical events and natural phenomena in an imaginative and irreverent manner is quite literally making history, a particular kind of history that impregnates the abstractions of European culture with a distinctively American nuance. The Cuban poet expressed this American transformation of Western literary and cultural tradition in powerful metaphorical terms through a revised version of the myth of Zeus's abduction of Europa under the guise of a bull. As Emilio Bejel points out, 'Lezama developed the metaphor of the Bull (Taurus) as the image of the force that, by raping Europa, brought about her fecundity. Now, however, he has abandoned the pale European world of abstraction and crossed the sea in order to seek "a new love" in the New World'.[57]

> Taurus [...] siempre ha sido débil con la blancura, con la abstracción de Europa [...]. Pero el toro [...] comenzó a caminar hacia el mar, luego hacia el mar con noche. Europa arrastraba su cuerpo hacia el lomo sin agua, aunque pudiera caerse. Y Europa comenzó a gritar. El toro, antiguo amante de su blancura, de su abstracción, siguió hacia el mar con noche, y Europa fue lanzada sobre los arenales, hinchada con un tatuaje en su lomo sin tacha: tened cuidado, he hecho la cultura.[58]

> [Taurus [...] always had a weakness for the pallor and abstraction of Europa [...]. But the bull [...] began to walk toward the sea, then into the sea at night. Europa dragged herself to the naked back above water, despite the danger of falling. And Europa began to scream. The bull, the old lover of her pallor and abstraction, continued walking into the sea at night, and Europa was thrown on the beach, swollen with a tattoo on her unspoiled back: be careful, I have made culture.]

Given his emphasis on the relevance of a 'sense of place' for the formation of culture and the creation of art, it is no coincidence that Lezama's Joyce is far from being the 'universal', neoclassical architect of Eliot's 'Ulysses, Order and Myth' and Gilbert's *James Joyce's 'Ulysses'*. In 'Sumas críticas del americano', the closing essay in *La expresión americana*, Lezama interprets the originality of Joyce's prose in terms that recall the ability of the poetic image to create and recreate reality continually. When it was first published, *Ulysses* confronted perplexed critics with an unprecedented 'realismo que creaba su propia realidad' [a realism that created its own reality].[59] While these critics interpreted Joyce's unconventional narrative as an abrupt rupture with tradition — reading it as a key manifestation of the *sprit nouveau* of the 1920s — and later as a mythical synthesis of Western culture, Lezama contends that the novelty of *Ulysses* arises from 'una nueva manifestación del hombre en su lucha con la forma' [a new manifestation of man in his fight with form], an artistic manifestation that he describes in ways that echo his analysis of Cortázar's *Rayuela*.[60] Like the American *sujeto metafórico*, Joyce assimilates European literature, philosophy and history, weaving together new forms of expression. As the Cuban author wrote in his obituary of Joyce, 'Muerte de Joyce', the most daring qualities of *Ulysses* do not relate to its linguistic and technical experiments, but to its capacity to open up uncharted cultural territories — to attune us to hidden languages and lead us though secluded cultural passageways long forgotten or never explored before. For instance, Jesuit theology unexpectedly becomes in Joyce's book a frame to explore 'el tema de la carne' [the theme of the flesh], thus closely linking 'apetito a la forma' [appetites to form] and reconciling bodily sensations with spiritual activity to offer a fuller understanding of life.[61]

That Lezama perceives in Joyce's narrative the same poetic dimension that he attributed to the 'image' and the Spanish American Baroque suggests that it is possible to read the literary dialogue between these writers as the result of a shared decolonizing attitude; an attitude that, like Borges's haphazard list in 'El Aleph', incites us to look at reality afresh and to dispense with the abstractions of 'disinterested' aesthetics and the weight of tradition. Despite Borges's well-documented aversion to the aesthetics of the Baroque, his enumeration in 'El Aleph' may be considered Baroque, not in style, but in inflection. According to Lois Parkinson Zamora, 'our reading of Borges will be enriched by an understanding of Baroque modes of expression, and vice versa', and she continues to describe his rendering of the Aleph as a 'trompe l'oeil trick', which is 'more than to simply undermine realistic representation; it is also to amplify the [...] reader's experience of the real by pointing to orders of being that are impossible to represent realistically'.[62] Following Parkinson Zamora, we could also argue that Borges's enumeration evokes the kinetic dynamism shared by contemporary Spanish American fiction and Joyce's narrative, for it encapsulates the displacement, tension and *plutonismo* of the *expresión americana*, the *desajuste* that Cortázar perceived in Marechal's *Adán Buenosayres*, and the innovative creativity that Lezama connected with the image and the metaphorical subject, as well as with *Rayuela* and *Ulysses*.

Bodily Aesthetics

Published a year before *Paradiso*, Guillermo Cabrera Infante's *Tres tristes tigres* (1965) has been frequently compared to both Lezama's novel and to Joyce's *Ulysses*. In 'Joyce and the Contemporary Cuban Novel: Lezama Lima and Cabrera Infante', Leonard Orr contends that *Paradiso* and *Tres tristes tigres* are both Joycean, but in different ways. In Orr's view, Joyce straddles modernism and postmodernism: the 'formalism', 'organicism' and 'stasis' of modernism characterizes *A Portrait* and the first three chapters of *Ulysses*; the 'fragmentation' and 'indeterminacy' of postmodernism informs the language of the second half of *Ulysses* and all of *Finnegans Wake*. According to Orr, while Lezama shares the modernist concern 'for structuring verbal patterns, the use of myth and order and coherence' of *A Portrait* and the opening chapters of *Ulysses*, Cabrera Infante's *Tres tristes tigres* displays the linguistic playfulness of the postmodernist Joyce. This critic underscores the fact that this transition in narrative styles is intimately related to the development of European history. The shock of World War I resulted in the collapse of traditional narrative conventions and in the modernist attempt 'to recreate in art the order that was now lacking in the outside world', an attempt that was later parodied by the fragmentation of postmodernism and the Neobaroque.[63] From this perspective, the Lezamian notion of Baroque 'counter-conquest' and the 'imaginary' historical alternatives associated with it are reinserted within the development of contemporary European culture.

Despite the persuasiveness of Orr's argument, I find it difficult to reconcile his Eurocentric perspective with the explicit caveat which greets the readers of *Tres tristes tigres*: 'El libro está en cubano' [The book is written in Cuban]. It would also be complicated to relate the static formalism of modernist aesthetics — or even the purely linguistic subversion of that formalism — to the author that narrated 'el día en que Moll y Bloom sentadas en la taza defecaron al largo stream-of-consciousness que sería un mojón de la literatura' [the day Moll and Bloom, sitting in the pot, defecated the long stream-of-consciousness that would become a milestone/turd of literature].[64] Cabrera's playful pun on 'mojón' (Spanish for both 'milestone' and 'solid faeces') acknowledges the centrality of *Ulysses* in the history of literature (Joyce's novel is certainly a literary 'milestone') while at the same time associating it with the excremental aspects that most of its early detractors criticized. Some early reviewers of Joyce's fiction, we should recall at this point, interpreted those aspects as symptomatic of Joyce's Irishness, of his provincial backwardness; a backwardness that was at odds with the modern and cosmopolitan characterization of Joyce that Eliot and Pound defended. As Ariela Freedman has observed, '*Ulysses* is a book that celebrates waste; water closets whisk away the offending excreta, allow us to deny the reality of our own shit. Clearly this would have been tempting as a metaphor for colonial denial of the waste products of imperial history'.[65] It seems, then, that the 'Cubanity' that infuses the language of *Tres tristes tigres* and the 'backwardness' manifested in the 'excremental' details of *Ulysses* open up a marginal dimension that contradicts the central place accorded to Joyce and Cabrera Infante within the Eurocentric narrative of modernism/postmodernism.[66]

These details encourage a reading of *Tres tristes tigres* that focuses on Cabrera Infante's efforts to accentuate 'European' forms with a local inflection, to subject experimental techniques to the demands of a truly Cuban expressive mode. This interpretation considers *Tres tristes tigres* a Joycean book not because it is (post-)modernist, but because it is Cuban. In fact, Cabrera Infante's novel might belong to a later stage of the search for a 'Cuban identity' that began with the island's independence from Spain at the turn of the twentieth century. The *americanista* concerns of works such as Nicolás Guillén's *Motivos de Son* (1930), Alejo Carpentier's *Ecue-Yamba-Ó* (1933) and Fernando Ortiz's *Contrapunteo cubano del tabaco y el azúcar*

(1940) provide an idea of the scope and relevance of the question of identity in modern Cuban culture. It is true that *Tres tristes tigres* avoids the local colour that permeates Guillen's poems and Carpentier's novel; but the inflection that Cabrera Infante gives to the polymorphous materials that he includes in his novel successfully marks the distance between the European canon and the Cuban self.

Tres tristes tigres is a gallery of Cuban voices that record the vibrant nights of pre-Revolutionary Havana. The musings and ramblings of Códac, a photographer, Eribó, a bongo player, Arsenio Cué, an actor, and Silvestre, a writer and journalist, intertwine with other minor voices in a kaleidoscopic narrative that reads like an extended conversation about the essence of Havana nightlife. But there are two figures that tower over the rest to shape the texture and style of the novel: La Estrella, a mastodontic black singer of cosmic proportions, and Bustrófedon, an audacious punster and linguistic experimentalist. La Estrella's untrained musical genius (she always sings without musical accompaniment) and Bustrófedon's verbal playfulness are the sources of the language of the novel, and, by extension, of its 'Cubanity'. An obvious approach to compare Joyce and Cabrera would be to concentrate on the shared linguistic experimentalism of *Tres tristes tigres*, *Finnegans Wake* and some sections of *Ulysses*. In fact, Bustrófedon's verbal audacity in *Tres tristes tigres* has usually provided the grounds for considering Cabrera Infante's text Joycean and postmodernist.[67] However, I will direct my attention to the character of La Estrella instead, recognizing in her body a stubbornly material excess that resists the homogenizing gaze of disinterested modes of aesthetic representation. Focusing on this act of resistance will allow me to challenge the use of the metropolitan categories of modernism and postmodernism to address Cabrera Infante's relationship with Joyce.

The relevance of La Estrella is so central that a running section of the novel, 'Ella cantaba boleros' [I heard her sing], is entirely devoted to her. The narrator of this section is Códac, a photographer who spends his nights hopping from club to club, capturing in his snapshots the glittery surface of Havana nightlife. However, La Estrella proves to be persistently recalcitrant to his photographic gaze. During his first encounter with the massive singer, Códac laments not carrying his camera to take a picture of her. Códac describes her perplexing appeal as 'different', 'horrible' and 'new', for it glaringly breaks with traditional canons of feminine beauty. Rather than representing the ideal of refinement and whiteness of the Petrarchan lady, La Estrella embodies 'la salvaje belleza' [savage beauty] which, in any event, would have eluded the lens of Códac's camera had he carried it with him. That this would have been the case is suggested by Códac himself after La Estrella dies. The photographer is only left with her recorded voice and her picture on the jacket cover of her only record. That picture fails to capture the strange and 'savage' beauty that the artist exuded in real life, representing instead 'la mujer más fea del mundo' [the ugliest woman in the world]. Códac argues that those who knew her could clearly see that the woman in the picture is not really La Estrella: 'los que la conocimos sabemos que no es ella, que definitivamente ésa no es La Estrella'.[68] It appears, then, that some fundamental element of the singer's beauty is lost with the arrestedness of the photographic gaze.

In the final part of the book, Silvestre and Cué discuss a variety of topics, including photography. Cué observes that 'una foto transforma la realidad cuando más exactamente la fija' [the more a picture fixes reality, the more it transforms it].[69] According to Silvestre, the image captured by the photograph creates a 'meta-reality' severed from the relentless flow of impressions surrounding the referent. Given that photography holds in abeyance the dynamism of the object and its empirical palpability, one might argue that the arresting effect of the photographic snapshot resembles, to some degree, the isolation of the object by the Kantian operation of aesthetic apprehension. This operation demands the repression of the senses other than sight, the 'noblest' sense, which 'comes nearer to being a *pure intuition* (the immediate representation of the given object, without admixture of noticeable sensation)'.[70] For Kant, the contemplation of an object involves a process of abstraction that distances the observer from his 'interests'. The purgation of the observer's desires and physical urges ensures that the object, 'apart from all matter', will be perceived in rational terms. Since no material or empirical conditions interfere with this pure act of perception, the aesthetic judgment derived from it can claim the universality that Kant bestows on reason. In both the photograph and Kantian apprehension, the teeming details of experience turn into a stable, fixed form that, as Cué puts it, is 'otra realidad. Una irrealidad' [another reality. An irreality].[71] The association of 'disinterested' representation and photography might have been endorsed by Borges himself. Significantly, when Borges the narrator arrives at Danieri's house to witness the Aleph, the housemaid tells him that the writer — who is presumably in his basement observing the luminous sphere to add some new lines to his monstrous poem, *The Earth* — is developing pictures: 'El niño estaba, como siempre, en el sótano, revelando fotografías' [the master was, as usual, in the basement, developing pictures].[72] This elusive yet revealing comment entwines the fixity of photographic images and Danieri's efforts to contain the limitless Aleph within the harmonic rhythms and structures of poetic language and literary form — a strategy that sustains Kant's concept of aesthetic perception, notably its emphasis on stasis, self-sufficient form and universality.

Adding new layers of meaning to Borges's suggestive detail, Cué goes on to tell Silvestre that 'lo que a ti te perturba de las fotos es la fijeza. No se mueven' [what perturbs you about photos is their fixity. They don't move].[73] These words could also describe Códac's reaction to La Estrella's picture. His perception of the singer when she was alive felt very much like 'another reality', the difference being so great that the photographer does not even recognize her in the picture. When he observes La Estrella in real life, Códac is caught between the involvement of the music enthusiast and the detachment of the professional photographer. When he listened to her singing for the first time, we are told that he experienced 'verdadero sentimiento' [true feeling] as the singer's almost palpable voice flowed from her body and reached him, making him shudder and laugh frantically: 'Hacía tiempo que algo no me conmovía así y comencé a sonreirme en alta voz' [it had been a while since something moved me like this, and I started laughing out loud].[74] Far from partaking in a dehumanized or disinterested appreciation of her music,

Códac is compelled to abandon his position as a spectator and become part of La Estrella's spectacle.

In *The Cuban Condition*, Gustavo Pérez Firmat identifies this liminal position between involvement and detachment as a defining aspect of the Cuban and Spanish American intellectual, of his peculiar condition as someone whose voice rings with a foreign, acquired accent 'even when he speaks most personally or provincially'. The distance between the culture of the Old World and the 'derivativeness of New World culture' turns this intellectual into an 'impassioned spectator'. In Pérez Firmat's words, an 'impassioned spectator', a term he borrows from Juan Marinello, 'is someone who is both involved in and removed from the objects of his attention. Even if he is physically distant, his passion constitutes an effective link to the reality he contemplates. To some degree, such a spectator is himself part of the spectacle'.[75] Códac's attraction to La Estrella illustrates with great precision this process of involvement and detachment: the *verdadero sentimiento* the photographer experiences when he hears her sing consists of a kind of aesthetic pleasure that involves all the senses, an almost orgasmic sensation caused by the intensity of the singer's voice and the 'savage' allure of her body rather than by the organized patterns of the melody — by the form of music.

This type of interested contemplation evidently deviates from the arrestedness that characterizes the photographic image, but also from the formalism of Kantian aesthetic judgment. In this sense, La Estrella's beauty may be compared to the Neobaroque excess that, in Lezama's poetic system, ultimately transcends *fijeza*, the gaze that contains reality, holding it still. Lezama's *fijeza* is an aesthetic stage leading not to the postulation of a universal artistic creed, but to the constant tension of the plutonic 'image', a tension that resonates with the echoes of La Estrella's untrained voice. Both the Lezamian 'image' and La Estrella's unconventional 'beauty' tap into esoteric sources of knowledge and open up dimensions of experience neglected or denigrated by the formative discourses of Western modernity, notably Hegelian history and Kantian aesthetics. As noted above, the 'image' was the origin of a truly American culture, a 'gnostic space' where the metaphorical subject could devise an artistic 'counter-conquest' after assimilating, recycling and reshaping metropolitan forms and combining them with African and Asian elements. This creative operation ultimately involves the redemptive power of the artistic imagination to transform the cultural sediments accumulated after centuries of colonial domination into a form of expression liberated from the authority of metropolitan paradigms. Significantly, Códac explicitly relates La Estrella to the effects of colonialism and racial diversity in the historical configuration of modern Cuban society. She is a descendant of the African slaves brought to Cuba following Bartolomé de las Casas's advice to spare the indigenous population of the island from hard labour. Instead of lamenting this historical event, Códac celebrates it, because if black slaves had never made it to the shores of Cuba, he would have never been able to enjoy La Estrella's music: 'qué país más aburrido sería éste si no hubiera existido el padre Las Casas y le dije, Te bendigo, cura, por haber traído negros del África como esclavos para aliviar la esclavitud de los indios' [what a boring country this would be if Father Las Casas had not existed, and I told him, I bless you, father, for bringing blacks from Africa as slaves to ease the slavery of the Indians].[76] Or, to put it differently, if colonialism had not transformed the pre-Columbian social texture of the island, the raw power of La Estrella's voice and body would have never come into being. The racial layering that in the sixteenth century upheld colonial domination now provides the grounds for the transgressive force that La Estrella embodies.

By evading the arresting gaze of the photographic lens and demanding a different kind of aesthetic perception, La Estrella eludes what might be called 'rationalistic' or 'static' ways of looking; that is, modes of apprehension that repress the senses other than sight and favour the capacities of the Kantian mind to abstract form from matter, thought from feeling, and contemplation from passion. Contemporary postcolonial theory has underlined the repressive dimension of this mode of observation, of colonial *aesthesis*, by invoking the metaphor of the 'gaze' and 'the look of surveillance' to refer to the disciplinary process of stereotyping the 'other' carried out by the colonial 'self'. A familiar case is Homi Bhabha's notion of the 'structured gaze of power whose objectivity is authority'.[77] For Bhabha, the colonized can subvert those structures of power only by imitating the cultural and linguistic gestures of the occupier, by performing a type of 'mimicry' which returns the colonizing gaze and transforms the observer into the observed. But whereas this operation still takes place 'under the eye of power, through the production of "partial" knowledges and positionalities', the resistance of La Estrella's 'strange beauty' to the camera lens suggests an 'other' dimension of experience that fully evades the 'eye of power'.[78] La Estrella demands looking otherwise, not looking back.

Let me return now to my central argument to relocate the intersection between Joyce and Cabrera Infante beyond the scope of Anglo-American modernism. To do so, it would be instructive to compare Códac's 'impassioned' engagement with the Afro-Cuban singer and Leopold Bloom's voyeuristic escapade in Chapter 13 of *Ulysses*, focusing on the counterpoint the episode poses to Stephen Dedalus's well-known vision of the angel-girl at the end of *A Portrait*. In particular, I want to read Códac's 'interested' contemplation and Bloom's ironic subversion of Stephen's modernist bias toward 'stasis' as intersecting acts of cultural 'counter-conquest' and decolonization. As discussed above, critic Weldon Thornton reads Joyce's subversion of Stephen's theories in *A Portrait* as a sustained critique of modernist aesthetics. The Irishman's ironic approach to Stephen's modernism is carried over into the contrasts he establishes between the young artist and Bloom in *Ulysses* — although it should be noted that Stephen's adherence to intellectual abstractions is attenuated during the course of this novel, particularly in 'Scylla and Charybdis', where he confronts the contention of the poet A. E. (George Russell) that 'Art has to reveal to us ideas, formless spiritual essences' (*U* 9.48–49) with the pithy remark that 'The life esoteric is not for ordinary person' (*U* 9.69–70) and with the refusal to evade this 'vegetable world', holding instead to the 'the now, the here, through which all future plunges to the past' (*U* 9.89). In many ways, however, Bloom is what Stephen is not. Bloom is a pragmatic empiricist where Stephen is an idealist rationalist. Bloom does not compare his life to a 'theorem of divine power' as Stephen does in *A Portrait*, but to the movement of his bowels while defecating: 'Midway, his last resistance yielding, he allowed his bowels to ease themselves quietly as he read [...] Hope it's not too big bring on piles again. No, just right. So. Ah! Costive. One tabloid of cascara sagrada. Life might be so' (*U* 4.506–11). If Stephen sees the world through literature, Bloom uses a literary magazine he reads in the bathroom to wipe himself. While Stephen goes to Dublin's National Library to discuss literary and philosophical matters with a group of artists and intellectuals, Bloom visits the museum to admire the naked anatomy of the classical statues with carnal interest, wondering about the intestinal physiology of the stone 'goddesses': 'Lovely forms of women sculped Junonian. Immortal lovely. And we stuffing food in one hole and out behind: food, chyle, blood, dung, earth, food: have to feed it like a stoking engine. They have no. Never looked. I'll look today. Keeper won't see. Bend down let something drop. See if she' (*U* 8.928–32).

The contrast between Stephen's bookishness and Bloom's down-to-earth attitude is first announced by the sharp transition between the metaphysical musings of 'Proteus' and the almost naturalistic invocation of Bloom's culinary preferences at the beginning of 'Calypso' (the first chapter in the novel that has a part of the body attached to it in the Linati Schema that Joyce circulated to explain the fundamental structure of *Ulysses*). Bloom delights, we are told, in the taste of 'the inner organs of beast and fowls', especially in grilled mutton kidneys, which give to his palate 'a fine tang of faintly scented urine' (*U* 4.1–5). Similarly, some episodes of Bloom's day can be read as an ironic recasting of Stephen's epiphanic moments in *A Portrait*. For instance, the climactic scene at the end of Chapter 4 in *A Portrait*, where Stephen embraces his artist vocation after he observes a girl wading in the sea, is ironically echoed in Chapter 13 ('Nausicaa') in *Ulysses*. Here Leopold Bloom also observes a girl by the sea, Gerty MacDowell, and the scene contains certain elements that invite a comparison between Stephen's divine muse and Gerty. For instance, both episodes take place in similar locations and the girls are both described in religious terms. Stephen invokes heaven and God when he first sees his girl-muse; Bloom looks at Gerty as if he was 'worshipping at her shrine' (*U* 13.564). The religious overtones of Bloom's description of Gerty are sustained throughout the episode by the periodic interpolations of prayers to the Virgin Mary wafting from a nearby chapel. She comes to resemble Stephen's muse even more when Bloom says that her neck is so beautiful and flawless that it 'seemed one an artist might have dreamed of' (*U* 13.583–84). However, instead of inspiring an aesthetic theory, as Stephen's girl does, Gerty incites Bloom to masturbation.

After Bloom reaches his climax, his idealized portrayal of Gerty quickly dissolves. She ceases to be a perfect goddess to become a vulgar girl who limps and wears cheap perfume. Just as she becomes a caricature of Stephen's muse, so Bloom's thoughts after he masturbates invite us to cast an ironic glance at the young artist's modernist theory. Rather than positing a transcendental realm where the artist can detach himself from the material world, Bloom proceeds to ruminate on the qualities of different kinds of odours. He concludes that humans, like animals, use odours to orient themselves, but also as a system of communication to convey specific messages. For instance, he meditates on how the female menstrual scent may be intended as a warning against sexual intercourse. Bloom's unscrupulous attention to the functions and desires of the body constantly reminds readers of the limitations of Stephen's modernist conception of art and life. His voyeurism, like Códac's 'impassioned' surrender to La Estrella's living voice and body, turns the 'noble' sense of sight not into the source of 'pure intuitions', but rather into the catalyst of desire and physical gratification. As severe deviations from the regulations of disinterested perception, Bloom's and Códac's fully 'interested' acts of gazing expose the precariousness of Stephen's use of art as a shield against the external world and the brute force of carnal needs. Joyce underscores this vulnerability by playing Stephen's celebration of aesthetic 'stasis' against Bloom's 'kinesis' in a patently ironic way. Later in the novel, Bloom is defined as a 'kinetic poet' (U 17.410) who has a 'kinetic temperament' (U 17.638). So while he describes himself as a 'waterlover' that enjoys the 'hydrokinetic turgidity' of water and its protean changes of state (from vapour to mist to rain to hail), Stephen can only be a 'hydrophobe' due to his scholastic distrust of 'aquacities of thought and language' (U 17.240).

Gerty's physical imperfections and Bloom's sensuality — like La Estrella's 'savage' beauty and Códac's involvement with the singer — can be interpreted not only as deviations from canonical models of beauty and the maxims of artistic disinterestedness, but also as part of a wider critique of colonialism. The section of 'Nausicaa' that revolves around Gerty's goals and aspirations adopts the language and style of feminine magazines such as *The Princess's Novelettes* and *Ladyland*, thus stressing the overwhelming influence that these publications have on the provincial girl's psyche. Karen Lawrence suggests that by casting Gerty's thoughts in the overblown oratory supplied by these journals Joyce exposes the character's delusional views in an ironic way, making us aware of the rift between the paltriness of her life and the romantic ideals that captivate her imagination.[79] However, Gerty may not be the only target of Joyce's irony. As Andrew Gibson has suggested, 'Nausicaa' also subverts the conceptions of womanhood promoted by the magazines she reads, which, this critic argues, were 'part of a colonial culture'.[80] By casting women in the role of angelic wives, the British establishment created normative gender models that paralleled and supported colonial and patriarchal structures of power. These magazines had wide circulation, reaching the furthest corners of the British Empire, and so they became an effective way to impose metropolitan norms in the field of cultural politics. However, despite Gerty efforts to follow the dictates of these publications, she emerges as a recalcitrant deviation from the norms of conduct that they propose. Her physical imperfections, along with Bloom's furtive masturbation, effects an ironic reversal of the ideal of femininity she embraces so fervently. For instance, her aspirations to become a loving spouse and a devoted housewife do not elicit the attentions of a hard-working and protective husband, but only Bloom's leering glances. The masturbatory act brutally dissolves the rhetorical smokescreen of the magazines and lays bare the mismatch between normative discourses manufactured in the metropolis and the material reality of the colonial periphery. Bloom's sexual activity and Gerty's deformity bring about the breakdown of imported beliefs in a way that resonates with Joyce's ironic treatment of Stephen's modernist aesthetics. The weakness that Stephen's artistic creed displays when faced with the empirical world intersects with the shortcomings of imported forms of imperial knowledge in the colonies. In both cases, immediate interests, frequently related to the experience of local reality, dismantle the rhetoric of disinterestedness and universality that permeates the pedagogical and artistic norms and practices sanctioned and supplied by the metropolis. The result is an ironic exposure of the limits of the colonial culture akin to the redefinition of race hierarchies and Kantian disinterestedness enacted by La Estrella's 'strange beauty' and Códac's passionate involvement with her musical performances.

The subversive treatment of aesthetic autonomy that connects *Tres tristes tigres* with *Ulysses* effectively undermines totalizing theories of representation and disembodied notions of subjectivity. By celebrating the senses and embracing the affective elements that Kant, like Stephen in *A Portrait*, held in abeyance, Joyce and Cabrera Infante infuse the literary text with decolonizing potential: with the ability to demarcate dimensions of lived experience that evade enlightened theories of art and the subject. H. G. Wells might have been right when he established a link between the sordid details of *A Portrait* and Joyce's 'Irishness', since, as we have seen in our analysis of 'Nausicaa', such scatological details can be instrumental in marking the distance between imperial models of subjectivity and the colonized mind. Whereas Wells interpreted Joyce's 'cloacal' obsession as a sign of 'backwardness', we have shown that attention to the external world — to those details, experiences and sensations repressed and concealed by the eye of reason — can also be the origin of local forms of cultural expression. Hence, *Tres tristes tigres* intersects with *Ulysses* not because its language and structure reflect historical changes in contemporary Europe, but because it asserts that metropolitan paradigms are as displaced in the Tropics as they are in Ireland.

Sexing *Ulysses* in Mexico

The linguistic experiments and formal innovations shared by *Tres tristes tigres* and *Ulysses* also characterize contemporary Mexican novels as relevant as Salvador Elizondo's *Farabeuf* and Fernando del Paso's *Palinuro de México*. While Elizondo openly acknowledged Joyce's influence and even translated a portion of *Finnegans Wake*, del Paso is perhaps the contemporary Mexican novelist who has shaped his narrative according to Joycean patterns most consciously and conscientiously. *Palinuro de México* (1977), an audacious and polymorphous text recounting the trials of a twenty-year old medical student in Mexico City during the tumultuous late 1960s, parallels *Ulysses* in numerous stylistic and thematic ways — from its encyclopaedic scope and use of a mythical subtext to its disruption of linear storytelling. But the ties between Joyce and del Paso, like those that connect Joyce and Marechal, Lezama Lima and Cabrera Infante, would be inadequately addressed if we limited ourselves to discussing formal aspects or thematic parallels between specific passages. By stressing the interconnection between the textual and the political in Joyce's *Ulysses*, del Paso himself suggested the guidelines that should inform an integral comparison between his fiction and that of the Irish writer:

> I consider that *Ulysses* is a sort of sun installed at the center of the Gutemberg Galaxy, which illuminates not only all the works which followed it but all of

universal literature that preceded it. [...] Joyce's most important aspect for me is what has been called his 'total' or 'totalizing' practice of fiction, because I'm interested in books not only as macrocosms but also as microcosms. This attitude implies two further aspects: the mythical background and linguistic revolution. But it also implies an anti-colonial posture, because it presupposes a very highly personal analysis by the writer of history, that of his country, the West as a whole, and the world — quoting from memory, 'History, that nightmare from which I am trying to awake'. But it also implies sexuality, of course, which only acquires human dignity when it is liberated.[81]

Del Paso suggests that if one is looking for affinities between his work and *Ulysses*, one should not simply document a shared interest in linguistic playfulness and structural complexity. Robin Fiddian has convincingly shown that 'the structural and thematic coherence of *Palinuro de México*, together with its mythical and archetypal scaffolding, narrative exuberance, and message of life sacrificed and then restored' constitute a common rhetorical ground that enable us to compare del Paso's novel and Joyce's *Ulysses*.[82] This critic goes on to argue that the strong similarities between *Palinuro de México* and *Ulysses* places the Mexican novel in 'an undifferentiated community of world literature' which can be conveniently segmented into transcontinental literary categories such as modernism and postmodernism.[83]

Although Fiddian fully addresses the postcolonial dimension of del Paso's writing, relating his novels to the political themes and ideas of Leopoldo Zea's radical philosophy, he insists that such dimension overlaps with the 'decentering processes that are fundamental to postmodernism'.[84] To assert that 'the postmodern and the postcolonial are homologous' certainly stresses the political meaning of literary form, forcing us read with an awareness of the historical implications of unequal relations of power; but imbricating both categories — postmodernism and postcolonialism — also makes it difficult to demarcate the particularity of marginal writers against the backdrop of what Simon Gikandi has termed an essentially '"Western" theoretical project'.[85] One way to approach the 'anti-colonial posture' shared by Joyce and del Paso without reducing it to the indeterminacies of poststructuralist theory might be by focusing on another important aspect that del Paso highlighted in his assessment of Joyce's novel: the liberation of desire and sexuality. The presence of the body is as central in *Palinuro de México* as it is in *Ulysses*, *Adán Buenosayres* and *Tres tristes tigres*. In an episode that echoes Bloom's defecating scene in 'Calypso', Palinuro describes his toilet as a library where pornography and high literature stand side by side: 'tengo en el baño toda la literatura que te puedas imaginar, desde Pentesilea hasta las revistas que se leen con una sola mano como el Playboy' [in the toilet I have all the kinds of literature you can imagine, from *Penthesilea* to magazines you can read using only one hand like *Playboy*].[86] Palinuro then adds that he, like Leopold Bloom, reads while defecating and then uses the pages he has read to wipe himself. The implication here is that for Palinuro, as for Bloom, literature is far from being an aseptic sphere detached from unsavoury experiences. Bloom and Palinuro bring literature, quite literally, face to face with the most repugnant and unpleasant aspects of life. This combination of high culture and physiological needs and urges also informs del Paso's subversions of canonical representations of female beauty and erotic love. For instance, Palinuro's complex description of his cousin and lover in the section entitled 'Unas palabras sobre Estefanía' [A few words about Estefanía] shockingly juxtaposes the lyric commonplaces of Petrarchan love poetry with crude scenes of sexual intercourse. Estefanía is, we are told, 'pure', 'angelic' and 'faultless', like 'the God of St. Anselm, of Leibniz and of Spinoza'; but her perfection 'never had anything to do with what she was in reality, in this world, in Santo Domingo Square', within the confines of their room, where she is 'full of imperfections' (athlete's foot, bad breath, eyes gummed with sleep) and where, among other things, she lets his cousin sodomize her, ejaculate in her nostrils and cover her entire body with his semen.[87] The result here, as in the toilet scene, is an 'antimodernist' violation of the barriers between 'disinterested' conceptions of beauty and the kinetic affects and physiological functions of the body.

The transgressive implications of sex and desire are further developed in del Paso's novel through the incestuous relationship between Palinuro and Estefanía, which occupies well over half of the novel's twenty-five chapters. The descriptions of the often sadistic sexual intercourse between Palinuro and his cousin are frequently related to his recurrent concern about the nature of language. The elaboration of a utopian language of the body is inextricably bound with the protagonist's erotic experiences, which allow him to expose the limits of conventional ways of expression and sexuality. These activities closely relate del Paso's text with the revolutionary counterculture of the 1960s and the reaction against the mechanisms of control and coercion that underpin Western civilization and capitalist modernity. In the section entitled 'La muerte de nuestro espejo' [the death of our mirror], Palinuro and Estefenía discuss the inability of words to contain the material world around them and to express their feelings for each other. Palinuro's uneasiness with language drives him to experiment with surrealist metaphors, to obsessively interrogate the meaning of the most trivial utterances, and, eventually, to embrace silence as a radical reaction against the limitations of verbal communication. At this point Palinuro and Estefanía reach for each other to make love in silence, uttering

> el lenguaje de nuestras lágrimas, nuestros besos y caricias, nuestros eructos y nuestros gestos, sin decirnos ni una sóla cosa ni en español ni en ningún otro idioma. Pero a cambio de esto, y para que mi prima viera que en efecto yo hablaba más de un idioma vivo y más de una lengua muerta, un día la besé en francés. Ella se limitó a bostezar en sueco. Yo la odié un poco en inglés y le hice un ademán obsceno en italiano. Ella fue al baño y dio un portazo ruso. Cuando salió, yo le guiñé un ojo en chino y ella me sacó la lengua en sánscrito. Acabamos haciendo el amor en esperanto.[88]

> [the language of our tears, our kisses and caresses, our burps and our gestures, without saying a single thing either in Spanish or in any other language. But to compensate for this, and to show my cousin that I could actually speak more than one living language and more than one dead tongue, one day I kissed her in French. She merely yawned in Swedish. I hated her a little in English and made an obscene gesture in Italian. She left for the bathroom, slamming the door in Russian. When she came out, I winked at her in Chinese, she stuck out her tongue at me in Sanskrit. We ended up making love in Esperanto.]

After this cathartic scene, the lovers decide to look upon reality without letting language 'bewitch' their intellect, thus refusing to express the material world in 'symbolic terms'. Palinuro realizes that abandoning language involves an act of 'unlearning', a return to 'la infancia misma de la especie humana' [to humanity's infancy] that would allow him to rediscover the exhilaration of renaming the universe without the mediation of reified words.[89] The revolutionary force of unrestrained sexuality reveals to Palinuro areas of experience occluded and repressed by words, which must therefore be discarded as abstract tokens worn out by time and use.[90]

Del Paso's search for alternative modes of expression, as well as his critique of normative discourses about the body and sexuality, affiliates his work with the iconoclastic stance of Surrealist poetics and the Freudian exploration of the subconscious, as well as with Rabelaisian literature and the anti-systemic philosophy of Herbert Marcuse. But what makes del Paso's transgressive use of sexuality in the novel an anti-colonial strategy? What distinguishes the book's linguistic *jouissance* and affirmation of the body from other metropolitan subversions of sexual, moral and literary norms? I believe that to answer to these questions we must return to the central theme of incest. As Robin Fiddian has aptly noted, del Paso's reclamation of the body from repressive discourses is common to a large list of European and Spanish American authors, including George Bataille, Octavio Paz and Julio Cortázar; but where he 'breaks new ground is in the elaboration of a utopian scenario of incest, independent of the regime of Oedipal prohibitions that has exercised so profound an influence on the organization of western societies and the theoretical apparatuses that have served to legitimate them'.[91] As Michel Foucault has taught us, the economic and social structure of Western civilization largely rests on a set of moral codes that regulate the appropriate uses of sexuality. According to these codes, incest is (to use Christian terminology) a 'sin contrary to nature', a 'nature' that, as Foucault reminds us, is 'still a kind of law'[92] — an *interpretation* of nature, not nature itself — that establishes norms of conduct and represses transgressive forms of sexuality. Incest occupies a central position within this system of taboos and prohibitions, since the 'threshold of all culture' — understanding 'culture' in the Western, anthropological sense of the term — might be 'prohibited incest'.[93]

Although there is nothing intrinsically anti-colonial in the literary use of incest, this theme has featured prominently in modern and contemporary Spanish American fiction, which has approached sex within the boundaries of the family not so much as an 'anti-natural' transgression of a 'social universal' (Foucault) as a foundational act for the formation of postcolonial societies. According to Efraín Kristal, the incest motif, 'one of the master plots of Spanish American literature from the 19th century until the present', indicates the 'ambiguous uncertainties about transitions from hierarchical societies to more egalitarian ones'.[94] Indeed, the multiple incestuous relationships among the Buendías in Gabriel García Márquez's *Cien años de soledad* or the mysterious affair between Alejandra and her father Fernando in Ernesto Sábato's *Sobre héroes y tumbas* mark the beginnings or continuations of family romances that symbolically represent the origins and development of Latin American society.[95] Even though the outcome of incest in *Cien años de soledad* and

Sobre héroes y tumbas is ultimately disastrous — a son with a pig's tail followed by apocalyptic destruction in García Márquez's novel; death, suicide and desolation in Sábato's book — the consummation of forbidden longings, especially those that involve one of the primordial interdictions of civilization, poses a sharp critique of Western institutions and models of societal organization, laying bare the artificiality of the 'natural' laws regarding sexual conduct.

Del Paso's *Palinuro de México*, where incest goes unpunished, valorizes the 'sin' as a form of joyful liberation from inherited social, cultural and linguistic constraints. In *The Political Unconscious*, Fredric Jameson alerts us to the deep connections between the social and the aesthetic, arguing that literary production is indeed an ideological act 'with the function of inventing imaginary or formal "solutions" to unresolvable social contradictions'.[96] The theme of incest in contemporary Spanish American fiction symbolizes a social contradiction, but a contradiction of a peculiar kind, since it derives from a colonial structure of power. By relating the origin of postcolonial societies to the repressed taboo of incest, these novels not only engage in a deconstruction of the codes and regulations that gave shape to European society and propelled its imperial expansion under the guise of universal truths; they also suggest that civilization never effaces what it buries and that taboos might take on new meanings after getting charged with the energy to imagine a culture yet to come. Since freedom and creativity are closely intertwined with incest in *Palinuro*, it might be argued that the text's 'formal solution' to the deep contradiction of resorting to metropolitan forms (aesthetic, cultural, social, linguistic) for self-expression and social organization in postcolonial settings might be the transformation of prohibitions and taboos into fertile spaces of cultural and social production.

As Arturo Uslar Pietri contended in 'La tentativa desesperada de James Joyce', this subversive and irreverent treatment of the proscriptions of civilization is also central to Joyce's aesthetics. According to the Venezuelan writer Western culture is laced with 'cosas y regiones tabú' [taboo things and areas] which impoverish our experience of life. Echoing Borges's 1925 review of *Ulysses*, Uslar argues that Joyce's book engages in an iconoclastic subversion of these taboos, mixing obscenity and abstraction, the flesh and the spirit, to offer a 'reconstruction total del hombre'.[97] Joyce's holistic perspective, what del Paso calls 'his "total" or "totalizing" practice of fiction', drives him to explore new poetic forms and cultural meanings, often tapping into neglected and repressed dimensions of existence. David Lloyd, whose analysis of *Ulysses* in *Anomalous States* supports and expands Uslar Pietri's ideas, contends that the novel is governed by a stylistic principle of 'adulteration'. This principle undermines the idea of an autonomous speaking subject through the interpolation of extraneous textual material from a variety of sources. Certainly, the 'citational' style of *Ulysses*, its indiscriminate intermingling of high literature and colloquial speech, of legal writing and journalese, of scientific discourse and liturgical formulas, transforms the text into a site where no stable voice or 'normative mode of representation' can be ascertained. Lloyd goes on to argue that this stylistic adulteration is analogous to the threat that adultery poses to patriarchal structures and the nation state. Against the anxiety of contaminated origins and essences that always haunts cultural nationalism, Joyce refuses to produce, in stylistic terms, 'a singular voice', placing the 'narrative as a whole' in 'aesthetic, cultural, and sexual terrains in a manner that continually runs counter to nationalist ideology' and, we might add, to one of the basic regulations that sustains society's stability and guarantees its permanence.[98] Bloom's constant preoccupation with adultery throughout the novel, obsessed as he is with his wife's sexual involvement with Blazes Boylan, provides a thematic leitmotif linking style and ideological content metaphorically. As we have seen, a similar point could be made about Palinuro's intense sexual involvement with his cousin and its revolutionary ramifications regarding language, style and representation. Indeed, the transgressive force of incest and adultery, both as thematic motifs and stylistic principles, breaks new, untrodden grounds for comparing *Ulysses* and *Palinuro* de México, allowing us to take their fully 'interested' aesthetics as a standard of equivalence that places both works beyond the idealist, disinterested self-sufficiency of High Modernism and the delocalized playfulness and indeterminacy of postmodernist art.

Notes to Chapter 4

1. Suzanne Jill Levine suggests in 'Notes on Borges's Notes on Joyce' that Borges's Aleph 'supersedes and mocks' Joyce's totalizing attempt in *Ulysses* (p. 349).
2. Jorge Luis Borges, 'Fragmento sobre Joyce', *Sur*, 60–62 (1941), 59–61.
3. Borges, *Obras completas*, I, 666.
4. Eliot, 'Tradition and the Individual Talent', p. 100.
5. Julio Ortega, *Poetics of Change: The New Spanish-American Narrative*, trans. by Galen Greaser (Austin: University of Texas Press, 1984), p. 15.
6. Jorge Luis Borges, 'El *Ulises* de James Joyce', *Proa*, 6 (1925), 3–6 (p. 5). See also his translation of the last page of *Ulysses*: 'La última hoja del *Ulises*', *Proa*, 6 (1925), 8–9.
7. Molloy, *Signs of Borges*, pp. 112–29.
8. Virginia Woolf, 'Modern Fiction', in *Selected Essays*, ed. by David Bradshaw (Oxford: Oxford University Press, 2008), pp. 6–12 (p. 9).
9. Immanuel Kant, *The Critique of Judgment*, trans. by J. H. Bernard (Amherst, NY: Prometheus, 2000), p. 75.
10. Maarten van Delden, 'The Spanish-American Novel and European Modernism', in *Modernism*, ed. by Astradur Eysteinsson and Vivian Liska, 2 vols (Amsterdam: Johns Benjamins, 2007), II, 947–65 (p. 947).
11. *Adán Buenosayres* is one of the first 'Joycean' or 'Ulyssean' novels published in Spanish America. On the parallels in themes, style and content between *Ulysses* and *Adán* see Ambrose Gordon, 'Dublin and Buenos Aires, Joyce and Marechal', *Comparative Literature Studies*, 19, 2 (1982), 208–19; Robin Fiddian, 'James Joyce and Spanish-American Fiction', pp. 30–31; and Javier de Navascués, 'Marechal frente a Joyce y Cortázar', *Cuadernos Hispanoamericanos*, 538 (1995), 45–56. For Marechal's opinions about the links between his novel and Joyce's, see 'Las claves de *Adán Buenosayres*', in *Adán Buenosayres*, ed. by Jorge Lafforge and Fernando Colla (Madrid: ALLCA XX, 1997), pp. 863–70.
12. Other studies that also assessed Marechal's novel positively include Adolfo Prieto, 'Los dos mundos de *Adán Buenosayres*', in Lafforge and Colla, eds, *Adán Buenosayres*, pp. 897–907 and Graciela de Sola, 'La novela de Leopoldo Marechal: *Adán Buenosayres*', in ibid., pp. 908–22.
13. Eduardo González Lanuza, 'Leopoldo Marechal: *Adán Buenosayres*', in Lafforge and Colla, eds, *Adán Buenosayres*, pp. 876–79.
14. Emir Rodríguez Monegal, '*Adán Buenosayres*: Una novela infernal', in Lafforge and Colla, eds, *Adán Buenosayres*, pp. 923–29 (p. 924).
15. Ibid., p. 925.

16. Rodríguez Monegal, 'Aspectos de la novela del siglo XX', p. 96.

17. Leopoldo Marechal, *Adán Buenosayres*, p. 6.

18. Leopoldo Marechal, 'Las claves de *Adán Buenosayres*', in Lafforge and Colla, eds, *Adán Buenosayres*, pp. 863–70 (p. 869).

19. Javier de Navascués, 'Sobre la novela argentina: *Rayuela* y *Adán Buenosayres*', in Lafforge and Colla, eds, *Adán Buenosayres*, pp. 957–66 (p. 965).

20. Julio Cortázar, 'Leopoldo Marechal: *Adán Buenosayres*', in Lafforge and Colla, eds, *Adán Buenosayres*, pp. 879–83 (p. 880).

21. Ibid., p. 880.

22. Ibid., p. 883.

23. Julio Cortázar, 'Situación de la novela', *Cuadernos Americanos*, 9, 4 (1950), 223–43 (p. 230).

24. Ibid., p. 233.

25. Ibid., p. 231.

26. Cortázar, *Cartas*, I, 396.

27. Cortázar, 'Para llegar a Lezama Lima', in *La vuelta al día en ochenta mundos*, pp. 134–55 (p. 141).

28. José Lezama Lima, 'Cortázar y el comienzo de la otra novela', in *Obras completas*, II, 1187–1207 (pp. 1192–94).

29. Cortázar, 'Para llegar a Lezama Lima', in *La vuelta*, p. 144.

30. José Lezama Lima, *Paradiso*, ed. by Eloísa Lezama Lima (Madrid: Cátedra, 2001), p. 499.

31. Ibid.

32. Ibid., p. 530.

33. Ibid., p. 532.

34. Ibid., p. 533.

35. Cortázar, 'Para llegar a Lezama Lima', in *La vuelta*, p. 148.

36. Lezama Lima, *Paradiso*, pp. 529–30.

37. James Joyce, *Stephen Hero* (London: Granada, 1977), p. 188.

38. Gustavo Pellón, *José Lezama Lima's Joyful Vision: A Study of 'Paradiso' and Other Prose Works* (Austin: University of Texas Press, 1989), p. 79.

39. Ibid., p. 82.

40. Joyce, *A Portrait of the Artist as a Young Man*, p. 213.

41. Kant, *The Critique of Judgment*, p. 75.

42. Joyce, *A Portrait of the Artist as a Young Man*, pp. 208–09.

43. Salgado, *From Modernism to Neobaroque*, p. 73.

44. The relationship of the author to his character in *A Portrait* has attracted considerable scholarly attention. While authors such as Harry Levin defend an identification between Joyce and Stephen in *James Joyce: A Critical Introduction* (Norfolk, CT: New Directions, 1960), others, such as Maurice Beebe, in 'Joyce and Stephen Dedalus: The Problem of Autobiography', in *A James Joyce Miscellany: Second Series*, ed. by Marvin Magalaner (Carbondale: Southern Illinois University Press, 1959), pp. 67–77, argue against such an identification. For a discussion of this relationship regarding Stephen's aesthetic theory, see A. D. Hope, 'The Esthetic Theory of James Joyce', in *James Joyce's 'Portrait': Criticism and Critiques*, ed. by Thomas E. Connolly (London: Owen, 1964), pp. 183–203, where it is argued that this theory can be attributed to Joyce himself. While this contention might hold true when discussing the aesthetic reflections of the young Joyce, it begins to lose strength when faced with the writer's mature critical views and literary creation. See Jacques Aubert, *The Aesthetics of James Joyce*, for an analysis of the progression of Joyce's aesthetic thought from a Hegelian conception of art to a complex questioning of aesthetic formalism.

45. Joyce's ironic stance regarding Stephen Dedalus was first articulated by Wayne C. Booth in 'The Problem of Distance in *A Portrait of the Artist*', in *The Rhetoric of Fiction* (Chicago: University of Chicago Press, 1961), pp. 322–36. For a recent consideration of Joyce's use of irony, see Tim Conley, *Joyce's Mistakes: Problems of Intention, Irony and Interpretation* (Toronto: University of Toronto Press, 2003).

46. Joyce, *A Portrait of the Artist as a Young Man*, p. 209.

47. See Weldon Thornton, *The Antimodernism of Joyce's 'A Portrait of the Artist as a Young Man'* (Syracuse, NY: Syracuse University Press, 1994) and 'Authorial Omniscience and Cultural Psyche: The Antimodernism of Joyce's *Ulysses*', in *Irishness and (Post)Modernism*, ed. by John S.

Rickard (Lewisburg, PA: Bucknell University Press, 1994), pp. 84–102.

48. Thornton, *The Antimodernism of Joyce's 'A Portrait of the Artist as a Young Man'*, pp. 57–58.
49. Ibid., p. 57.
50. Ibid., p. 146.
51. Joyce, *A Portrait of the Artist as a Young Man*, p. 238.
52. José Lezama Lima, 'La expresión americana', in *Obras completas*, II, 277–390 (p. 290).
53. Eliot, 'The Metaphysical Poets', p. 231.
54. Lezama Lima, 'La expresión americana', in *Obras completas*, II, 286.
55. Ibid., p. 285.
56. Ibid., p. 303.
57. Emilio Bejel, *José Lezama Lima, Poet of the Image* (Gainesville: University Press of Florida, 1990), p. 125.
58. José Lezama Lima, 'Las imagines posibles', in *Obras completas*, II, 152–82 (p. 181).
59. Lezama Lima, 'La expresión americana', in *Obras completas*, II, 285.
60. Ibid., p. 372.
61. Lezama Lima, 'Muerte de Joyce', in *Obras completas*, II, 236–38 (pp. 237–38).
62. Parkinson Zamora, *The Inordinate Eye*, p. 244.
63. Leonard Orr, 'Joyce and the Contemporary Cuban Novel: Lezama Lima and Cabrera Infante', *Neohelicon*, 19, 2 (1992), 17–25 (pp. 20–21).
64. Guillermo Cabrera Infante, *Tres tristes tigres* (Barcelona: Seix Barral, 2005), p. 162.
65. Ariela Freedman, 'Did it Flow? Bridging Aesthetics and History in Joyce's *Ulysses*', *Modernism/modernity*, 13, 1 (2006), 853–68 (p. 864).
66. On Joyce's use of scatological details, see Vincent J. Cheng, '"Goddinpotty": James Joyce and the Language of Excrement', in *The Languages of Joyce*, ed. by Rosa Maria Bolletieri Bosinelli, Carla Marengo and Christine van Boheemen (Amsterdam: John Benjamins, 1992), pp. 85–102.
67. On the linguistic similarities between Joyce's work and *Tres tristes tigres*, see Michael Wood, 'Cabrera Infante: Unruly Pupil', in *Transcultural Joyce*, ed. Karen Lawrence (Cambridge: Cambridge University Press, 1998), pp. 49–62. In 'Stalking the Oxen of the Sun and Felling the Sacred Cows: Joyce's *Ulysses* and Cabrera Infante's *Three Trapped Tigers*', *Latin American Literary Review*, 3, 8 (1976), 15–22, Djelal Kadir argues that Joyce's and Cabrera's novels stage an analogous parodic subversion of tradition and 'Literature', but a subversion that is ultimately reinscribed within 'the evolving book which the pantheistic scribe of Emerson or Coleridge's Spirit of Literature have been elaborating' (p. 18). I should like to take a different route in my analysis to demonstrate how the subversive dimension of these novels exceeds the universalistic coordinates of Emerson's or Coleridge's 'Spirit' and the Western literary tradition.
68. Cabrera Infante, *Tres tristes tigres*, p. 312.
69. Ibid., p. 372.
70. Immanuel Kant, *Anthropology from a Pragmatic Point of View*, ed. by Robert B. Louden (Cambridge: Cambridge University Press, 2006) p. 48.
71. Cabrera Infante, *Tres tristes tigres*, p. 373. For a more extensive discussion of the cultural implications of Cabrera Infante's thematic use of photography in the novel, see José Luis Venegas, 'Exile, Photography, and the Politics of Style in Guillermo Cabrera Infante's *Tres tristes tigres*', *Latin American Literary Review*, 36, 72 (2008), 107–33.
72. Borges, *Obras completas*, I, 665.
73. Cabrera Infante, *Tres tristes tigres*, p. 375.
74. Ibid., p. 73.
75. Gustavo Pérez Firmat, *The Cuban Condition: Translation and Identity in Modern Cuban Literature* (Cambridge: Cambridge University Press, 1989), pp. 10–12.
76. Cabrera Infante, *Tres tristes tigres*, p. 70.
77. The interrelation between colonialism and photography has been explored by Wolfram Hartmann, Jeremy Silvester and Patricia Hayes in *The Colonizing Camera: Photographs in the Making of Namibian History* (Cape Town: University of Cape Town Press, 1998). These authors underline the central role of photographic technology for the production and circulation of colonial images in the late nineteenth century, cogently arguing that photography was an active agent in the construction of colonialist discourse in the British Empire.

78. Bhabha, *The Location of Culture*, p. 169.
79. Karen Lawrence, *The Odyssey of Style in 'Ulysses'* (Princeton, NJ: Princeton University Press, 1981), pp. 122–23.
80. Andrew Gibson, *Joyce's Revenge*, p. 145.
81. Fernando del Paso, as quoted in Gerald Martin, *Journeys through the Labyrinth*, p. 140.
82. Fiddian, *The Novels of Fernando del Paso*, p. 92.
83. Ibid., p. 99.
84. Ibid., p. 104.
85. Simon Gikandi, 'Poststructuralism and Postcolonial Discourse', in *The Cambridge Companion to Postcolonial Literary Studies*, ed. by Neil Lazarus (Cambridge: Cambridge University Press, 2004), pp. 97–119 (p. 117).
86. Fernando del Paso, *Obras I: José Trigo y Palinuro de México* (Mexico: Fondo de Cultura Económica and El Colegio Nacional, 2000), p. 643.
87. It is also worth noting the significance of the setting where their sexual intercourse takes place. The 'room in Santo Domingo Square' becomes a utopian space that literally comes to life with Palinuro and Estefanía's erotic and linguistic playfulness. Significantly, the first object that they bring to the room is a picture of Estefanía taken by her Francophile aunt, Luisa. For the lovers, the static photograph becomes a starting point to reinvent a plastic universe around it.
88. Del Paso, *Obras I*, p. 672.
89. Ibid., p. 673.
90. For a discussion of the intersection of language and sex in the novel from a Bakhtinian perspective, see Claude Fell, 'Sexo y lenguaje en *Palinuro de México*, de Fernando del Paso', in *Escritura y sexualidad en la literatura hispanoamericana*, ed. by Alain Sicard and Fernando Moreno (Madrid: Fundamentos, 1990), pp. 181–94.
91. Fiddian, *The Novels of Fernando del Paso*, p. 81. In an interview with Ignacio Trejo, del Paso stressed the liberating power of those 'incestuous bonds' which could be wonderful had not our society condemned them as something appalling. See Ignacio Trejo Fuentes, 'El que despalinurice a Palinuro será un buen despalinurizador: entrevista con Fernando del Paso', *La Semana de Bellas Artes*, 138 (1980), 6–11.
92. Michel Foucault, *The History of Sexuality: An Introduction* (New York: Vintage, 1990), p. 38.
93. Ibid., p. 109.
94. Efraín Kristal, 'The Incest Motif in Narratives of the United States and Spanish America', in *Internationalität nationaler Literaturen*, ed. by Udo Schöning (Göttingen: Wallstein Verlag, 2000), pp. 390–403 (p. 390).
95. The theme of incest in García Márquez has been amply studied; see Donald Shaw, 'El tema del incesto en Faulkner y García Márquez', *Anthropos*, 187 (1999), 100–05; Suzanne Jill Levine, 'La maldición del incesto en *Cien años de soledad*', *Revista Iberoamericana*, 37 (1971), 711–23; and Benjamín Torres Caballero, *Gabriel García Márquez o la alquimia del incesto* (Madrid: Playor, 1987). In *Sobre héroes y tumbas* Martín's Oedipal involvement with his mother and Alejandra, and Fernando's troubled relationship with his daughter, are related to his Argentinness and to the origins of Argentine history and identity. Otto Rank's classic book, *The Theme of Incest in Literature and Legend: Fundamentals of a Psychology of Literary Creation* (Baltimore, MD: Johns Hopkins University Press, 1991) remains a standard reference for those interested in this topic.
96. Fredric Jameson, *The Political Unconscious: Narrative as a Socially Symbolic Act* (Ithaca, NY: Cornell University Press, 1981), p. 79.
97. Uslar Pietri, 'La tentativa desesperada de James Joyce', p. 262.
98. David Lloyd, *Anomalous States*, p. 110.

CONCLUSION

❖

Literary History Otherwise

The eponymous protagonist of Carlos Fuentes's *Cristóbal Nonato* is an unborn child, a disembodied consciousness, encircled and nurtured by language, like the fluid in the motherly womb. But, as his mother, Dolores, asks his father, Ángel, what *lengua* is Cristóbal really going to speak when he is finally born and grows up? To answer this question, he alludes to the hybrid nature of contemporary Mexican society, where pre-Columbian words mix with English expressions and the Spanish language, forming a Janus-faced linguistic culture that seems to find an appropriate vehicle for self-expression in the Spanish American 'Joycean' novel:

> J'AIME JOYCE o GÓCELA CON JOYCE: lo cierto es que Leopoldo BOOM sustituyó al desgastado astro del auge de la novela latinoamericana, Marcelo Chiriboga, como principal bautizador de las calles de la ciudad que crecía tan rápido y tan vástamente rebasaba la capacidad nominativa de sus propios habitantes [...] .[1]

> [J'AIME JOYCE or REJOICE WITH JOYCE: the truth is that Leopold BOOM replaced the worn-out star of the rise of the Latin American novel, Marcelo Chiriboga, as the main name-giver of the streets in the city, which grew so fast and so vastly that it exceeded the naming capacity of its own inhabitants.]

Besides connecting Mexico's hybrid modernity with narrative playfulness (as if the country's liminal historicity, caught between traditions that have not yet gone and an incipient though never fully realized modernization, could only be rendered by the puns and verbal games of a language that, emptied of its referential capacity, folds upon itself) these lines also describe the evolution of Latin American narrative during the second half of the twentieth century. It was then that the experimental novel represented by the allegorical 'Leopoldo BOOM' — an obvious pun on 'Leopold Bloom' and the literary 'boom' — superseded the 'worn out' autochthonous discourse of the fictional Ecuadorian writer, Marcelo Chiriboga. This scheme of periodization suggests that the influence of Joyce's *Ulysses* set the works of the boom writers apart from the regionalist novel — the so-called *novela de la tierra* — and integrated Spanish American literature within an international literary canon. This qualitative leap from 'regionalism' to 'modernism' was achieved, to a large degree, after assimilating the playful language that permeates the pages of Fuentes's *Cristóbal Nonato*, a Joycean novel that certainly abandons the conventions of mimetic realism to embrace a self-sufficient style.

But Joycean fiction in Spanish America also challenges the belief that local attachments can dissolve in a whirl of puns and stylistic contortions — that the provincial artist's commitment to formal and linguistic innovation necessarily involves a disconnection from the social world and the logic of historical change. As these chapters have shown, Joyce's work, particularly *Ulysses*, intertwines with the narrative of Marechal, Borges, Cortázar, Lezama Lima, Cabrera Infante and del Paso — customarily categorized as 'modernizers' of Spanish American literature — to constitute a literary web of transnational affiliations that remains resilient to the teleological patterns of Eurocentric literary history. From this perspective, the 'newness' of Spanish American Joycism is not simply the result of the belated assimilation of modernist art forms that emerged in Europe between the late 1890s and the first decades of the twentieth century. Rather, the crossing literary pathways of Joyce and the authors considered here are part of a quest for a liberated means of expression, for a voice that could encode the displacement of those caught between an inherited tradition and the desire for cultural emancipation. As Néstor García Canclini has suggested, the paradox of a 'modernism without modernization', a phenomenon that applies as accurately to contemporary Spanish American culture as it does to Joyce's Ireland, should not be understood as a 'question of a transplant, above all in the main artist and writers, but rather of reelaborations eager to contribute to social change'.[2] These 'reelaborations' are not restricted to the use of imported models to render local events and situations; they also extend to the subversion of artistic disinterestedness — of 'universal' abstractions that fail to explain away 'local interests' — and to the active production of innovative forms of representation. However, this emphasis on the relevance of locality for the production, reception and classification of experimental literature does not necessarily support a nationalist or ethnocentric argument that extols indigenous aspects of culture untouched by foreign elements or by the contingencies of modernity. (As Linda Hutcheon has correctly remarked, there is an urgent need to 'rethink the dominance of the national model of literary history, a model that has always been premised on ethnic and often linguistic singularity, not to say purity').[3] Instead, the parallelisms and intersections between Joyce's local interests and those that permeate Spanish American literature encourage new approaches to the interface between the native and the foreign, the national and the global, that elude the authority of totalizing versions of literary history. This alternative mapping of cross-pollinating cultural traditions transcends autarchic national bounds while at the same time eschewing universal aesthetic standards and common measures of periodization.

Borges once remarked that Joyce is a whole literature rather than an individual writer, *menos un literato que una literatura*. Indeed, no one would contest that the publication of *Ulysses* and *Finnegans Wake* marked a watershed in world literature, forever changing established notions of novelistic discourse and inspiring such prominent writers as Samuel Beckett, Vladimir Nabokov, John Barth and Salman Rushdie. But the category 'Joycean' is far from being an unchanging monolith. Revising Borges's observation, we could say that Joyce is many literatures, or that there are many 'Joyces', woven and unwoven into multiple images of the artist as his texts are read, translated and reviewed in cultural contexts divided by oceans and separated by decades. Like the elusive figure of Homer in Borges's short story, 'El Inmortal', Joyce tends to become what his successors make of him, thus turning into a precursor of a peculiar kind, one who inherits as much as creates his own literary legacy. The variegated and unpredictable nature of this legacy would have no doubt pleased Joyce, a writer who was convinced that there is no act of conscious begetting, that paternity might be after all just a 'legal fiction' (*U* 9.844). As is well known, the author of *Ulysses* has been canonized as an icon of modernism, but also as a precursor of poststructuralism and a pioneer of *écriture féminine* and hypertext technology. It was not until recently, however, that critics have explored the national and vernacular dimensions of Joyce's texts, restoring them to the Irish context of their original production and reception. As Karen Lawrence has aptly put it, Joyce occupies a 'borderline position' between the European canon and the experience of British colonialism in Ireland, thus becoming 'both canonical authority and disruptive iconoclast' at once.[4] Just as the 'canonical' Joyce stands as an uncontested model of modernist and postmodernist aesthetics, so the 'iconoclastic' and 'Irish' Joyce has engendered marginal traditions, emerging as an influential example for peripheral artists who set out to recycle the shards of Western culture and history into novel configurations. Within this marginal context, Joyce is not so much an original model to be assimilated and transformed as a model of creative assimilation and transformation.

As Cuban writer Edmundo Desnoes — who translated *A Portrait* into Spanish — pointed out, Joyce's experience 'tiene muchos puntos de contacto con la circunstancia social del escritor hispanoamericano. Irlanda, en la época en que escribió, era una colonia subdesarrollada de Inglaterra' [has many points of contact with the social situation of the Spanish American writer. At the time when he wrote, Ireland was an underdeveloped English colony].[5] Desnoes's comment is reminiscent of Borges's arguments in 'El escritor argentino y la tradición', where he stresses the parallels and similarities between the peripheral and irreverent literary traditions of Ireland and South America. The contact zone that emerges from the encounter of these traditions, a postcolonial Irish-Hispanic Atlantic, resists a single line of progress and periodization, allowing us to frame literary exchange within the often neglected cultural space between peripheries. This perspective prevents us from assimilating marginal authors to a global literary canon, thus converting Borges, Cortázar or Lezama Lima into modernist or postmodernist writers; instead we are forced to recognize alternative forms of cultural interaction: elusive networks uniting the double-voiced texts of those writing from what Walter Mignolo calls 'the colonial difference', from the abrasive space between emancipatory longings and imposed modes of expression and categories of thought.[6] Read in this way, *Ulysses* is indeed a 'symphonic enterprise' of global proportions, as Cortázar declared, or 'a sort of sun installed at the center of the Gutemberg Galaxy', to use del Paso's words; but if the book rises to those heights it is not only to postulate a linguistic totality devoid of historical content, or a universal aesthetic standard that all literary cultures worldwide should strive to imitate and assimilate. *Ulysses* also illuminates the many ways in which literary innovation can lead to cultural self-determination, and in doing so it becomes a decolonizing manifesto, a text with the capacity to inspire marginal artists to encode utopian messages of cultural autonomy in the words and structures of an acquired speech. Therefore, Joyce's book stands as a powerful response to Stephen Dedalus's anxieties about the English language in *A Portrait*, a language 'so familiar and so foreign' that he could not speak its words 'without unrest of spirit'.[7]

In recent years, the prose of the 'Irish' and 'iconoclastic' Joyce has remained a suggestive cultural referent for younger generations of Spanish American writers, a topic that merits a study of its own. For instance, the Mexican writer Gustavo Sainz has used the symbolic implications of *Ulysses* to great effect in *Obsesivos días circulares* (1969). Throughout the novel, the protagonist, Terencio, struggles to finish Joyce's book, but his reading experience remains episodic at best, for he is constantly distracted by the demands of his daily life as a school janitor. The disconnected bits and pieces of *Ulysses* that permeate Terencio's interior monologues evoke a sense of fragmentation that collides with the homogeneous narratives of state power that lost so much credence in Mexico after 1968. But Terencio's jagged rendering of the text also invites the reader to approach *Ulysses* less as a modernist monument, whole in its structure and univocal in its message, and more as a porous text open to multiple meanings, particularly those that can escape the gaze of established forms of power and culture. In a similar vein, the Argentine novelist and critic Ricardo Piglia has often evoked Joyce's marginal side, identifying particularly with his dismissal of totalizing version of history and his celebration of parody as a means to generate a dissident type of discourse that can elude the purview of the canon and the state. In *Respiración artificial* (1980), Piglia brings Borges and Joyce together under the sign of parody, suggesting that vernacular traditions can emerge from the irreverent citation and mistranslation of original sources: if Joyce, 'una parodia de Shakespeare', might agree that there are only parodies, that 'la parodia ha sustituido por completo a la historia' [parody has completely replaced history], Borges's texts are essentially 'cadenas de citas fraguadas, apócrifas, falsas, desviadas" [chains of forged, apocryphal, false, distorted quotations].[8] Likewise, in the afterword to the English translation of *La ciudad ausente* (1992) — a novel that, as Piglia admits, is influenced by *Finnegans Wake* — the Argentine writer reiterates the shared dissidence toward metropolitan culture that unites Ireland and Spanish America. Echoing Borges's 'El escritor argentino y la tradición', Desnoes's observations in 'La mirada de Joyce' and Roberto Fernández Retamar's remarks about *Ulysses* and *Rayuela* in *Cinco miradas sobre Cortázar*, Piglia writes:

> Dublin and Buenos Aires share the fact that they are both literary cities, in the sense that they have had a large density of writers (in the 1930s and 1940s, Macedonio, Borges, Arlt, Cortázar, among others, all lived in Buenos Aires), who have had a tense relationship with the Metropolis. For example, the tension Stephen Dedalus feels with English, which he considers to be an imperial tongue. Similarly, the issue of the inheritance of the Spanish language and the struggle to become independent from Spain was very much present in Argentina. One can see an analogy between Joyce's relationship with Shakespeare, and Macedonio's with Cervantes. The question becomes: whose language is it? And: how do we overcome the political control associated with this language to reach Shakespeare, for example, thinking of Joyce's parodies in *Ulysses*, and the position that Macedonio takes with respect to Spain's Golden Age?[9]

As these questions continue to occupy Spanish American novelists marching into the twenty-first century, Joyce's work remains a provocative source of imaginative wisdom, a bewildering puzzle that teaches us to reconceive literature, history and the world beyond restrictive binaries such as original and copy, colonizer and colonized. Indeed, it would be misleading to say that Joyce's fertile interaction with Spanish American literature ceased after the last glimmers of the boom died out, as contemporary writers as prominent as Gustavo Sainz and Ricardo Piglia continue to take him beyond the cultural contexts of the early twentieth century to explore the ways in which his unprecedented literary techniques can open up new forms of interaction between individuals, culture and community.

Notes to the Conclusion

1. Carlos Fuentes, *Cristóbal Nonato* (Mexico: Fondo de Cultura Económica, 1987), p. 104.
2. Néstor García Canclini, *Hybrid Cultures: Strategies for Entering and Leaving Modernity*, trans. by Christopher L. Chiappari and Silvia L. López (Minneapolis: University of Minnesota Press, 2005), p. 51.
3. Linda Hutcheon, 'Rethinking the National Model', in *Rethinking Literary History: A Dialogue on Theory*, ed. by Linda Hutcheon and Mario J. Valdés (Oxford: Oxford University Press, 2002), pp. 3–49 (p. 3).
4. Karen Lawrence, 'Introduction: Metempsychotic Joyce', in *Transcultural Joyce*, ed. by Karen Lawrence (Cambridge: Cambridge University Press, 1998), pp. 1–10 (p. 4). In his analysis of *Ulysses*, Fredric Jameson has also highlighted Joyce's liminal position between the social reality of the First World and the power structures of the Third World. See Fredric Jameson, 'Modernism and Imperialism', in *Nationalism, Colonialism and Literature*, by Seamus Deane, Terry Eagleton, Fredric Jameson and Edward Said (Minneapolis: University of Minnesota Press, 1990), pp. 43–68.
5. Edmundo Desnoes, 'La mirada de Joyce', *Edita*, 1, 4 (1964), 1–4 (p. 4).
6. Mignolo contends that 'what is missing in literary histories written until today is precisely the focus on double consciousness, which is to say, on the enunciation from the colonial difference' (p. 175). See Walter Mignolo, 'Rethinking the Colonial Model', in Hutcheon and Valdés, eds, *Rethinking Literary History*, pp. 155–93.
7. Joyce, *A Portrait of the Artist as Young Man*, p. 189.
8. Ricardo Piglia, *Respiración artificial* (Barcelona: Anagrama, 2001), pp. 112, 131.
9. Ricardo Piglia, 'Afterword', in *The Absent City*, trans. by Sergio Waisman (Durham, NC: Duke University Press, 2000), pp. 141–47 (pp. 142–43). For a lucid discussion of the points of contact between Piglia and Joyce, see Waisman, 'Epilogue: Reading Argentina, Translating Piglia', in *Borges and Translation*, pp. 207–18.

BIBLIOGRAPHY

❖

Adell, Sandra, *Double-Consciousness/Double Bind: Theoretical Issues in Twentieth-Century Black Literature* (Urbana: University of Illinois Press, 1994)

Adorno, Theodor W., and Max Horkheimer, *Dialectic of Enlightenment*, trans. by John Cumming (New York: Herder and Herder, 1972)

Alazraki, Jaime, 'La postmodernidad de Julio Cortázar' in *Hacia Cortázar: aproximaciones a su obra* (Barcelona: Anthropos, 1994), pp. 353–65

——ed., *Critical Essays on Julio Cortázar* (New York: G. K. Hall, 1999)

Alifano, Roberto, *Conversaciones con Borges* (Madrid: Debate, 1986)

Alonso, Carlos J., *The Burden of Modernity: The Rhetoric of Cultural Discourse in Spanish America* (New York: Oxford University Press, 1998)

——'Borges y la teoría', *Modern Language Notes*, 120, 2 (2005), 437–56

Altschul, Carlos, 'Hacia una interpretación del hombre James Joyce', *Sur*, 260 (1959), 24–36

Anderson, Benedict, *Imagined Communities: Reflections on the Origin and Spread of Nationalism* (London: Verso, 1991)

Arguedas, José María, *El zorro de arriba y el zorro de abajo*, ed. by Eve-Marie Fell (Nanterre, France: ALLCA XX, 1990)

Aronne-Amestoy, Lida, *Cortázar: la novela mandala* (Buenos Aires: F. García Cambeiro, 1972)

Attridge, Derek, *Joyce Effects: On Language, Theory, and History* (Cambridge: Cambridge University Press, 2000)

Aubert, Jacques, *The Aesthetics of James Joyce* (Baltimore, MD: Johns Hopkins University Press, 1992)

Auerbach, Eric, 'Figura', in *Scenes from the Drama of European Literature* (Manchester: Manchester University Press, 1984), pp. 11–76

Balderston, Daniel, 'The Argentine Writer and the "Western" Tradition', in Fishburn, ed., *Borges and Europe Revisited*, pp. 37–48

Ballesteros, González Antonio, 'La digresión paródica en dos modelos narrativos: *Rayuela* y *Ulysses*', in *Joyce en España I*, ed. by F. García Tortosa and A. R. de Toro Santos (A Coruña: Servicio de Publicaciones de la Universidade da Coruña, 1994), pp. 93–100

——'Controversias, exilios, palabras y cegueras: Joyce en Borges', in *James Joyce: límites de lo diáfano*, ed. by C. Medina and others (Jaén: Publicaciones de la Universidad de Jaén, 1998), pp. 61–71

Barthes, Roland, *Mythologies*, trans. by Annette Lavers (New York: Hill and Wang, 1972)

Beebe, Maurice, 'Joyce and Stephen Dedalus: The Problem of Autobiography', in *A James Joyce Miscellany: Second Series*, ed. by Marvin Magalaner (Carbondale: Southern Illinois University Press, 1959), pp. 67–77

——'*Ulysses* and the Age of Modernism', *James Joyce Quarterly*, 10, 1 (1972), 172–88

Begam, Richard, 'Joyce's Trojan Horse: *Ulysses* and the Aesthetics of Decolonization', in *Modernism and Colonialism: British and Irish Literature, 1899–1939*, ed. by Richard Begam and Michael Valdez Moses (Durham, NC: Duke University Press, 2007), pp. 185–208

——*Strange Country: Modernity and Nationhood in Irish Writing since 1790* (Oxford: Oxford University Press, 1997)

DELEUZE, GILLES, and FÉLIX GUATTARI, *Kafka: Toward a Minor Literature*, trans. by Dana Polan (Minneapolis: University of Minnesota Press, 1986)

DEL PASO, FERNANDO, *Obras I: José Trigo y Palinuro de México* (Mexico: Fondo de Cultura Económica and El Colegio Nacional, 2000)

DEMING, ROBERT H., ed., *James Joyce: The Critical Heritage*, 2 vols (New York: Routledge and Kegan Paul, 1970)

DERRIDA, JACQUES, *Spurs: Nietzsche's Style / Eperons: Les Styles de Nietzsche*, trans. by Barbara Harlow (Chicago: University of Chicago Press, 1981)

DESNOES, EDMUNDO, 'La mirada de Joyce', *Edita*, 1, 4 (1964), 1–4

DETTMAR, KEVIN J. H, 'Joyce/"Irishness"/Modernism', in *Irishness and (Post)Modernism*, ed. by John S. Rickard (Lewisburg, PA: Bucknell University Press, 1994), pp. 103–58

DEVI, GANESH, 'India and Ireland: Literary Relations', in *The Internationalism of Irish Literature and Drama*, ed. by Joseph McMinn (Gerrards Cross: Colin Smythe, 1992), pp. 294–308

DONOSO, JOSÉ, *Historia personal del 'boom'* (Madrid: Alfaguara, 1999)

DOYLE, LAURA, and LAURA WINKIEL, 'Introduction: The Global Horizons of Modernism', in *Geomodernisms: Race, Modernism, Modernity*, ed. by Laura Doyle and Laura Winkiel (Bloomington and Indianapolis: Indiana University Press, 2005), pp. 1–14

DU BOIS, W. E. B., *The Souls of Black Folk*, ed. by Candace Ward (New York: Dover, 1994)

DUFF, CHARLES, '*Ulises* y otros trabajos de James Joyce', *Sur*, 5 (1932), 86–127

DUFFY, ENDA, *The Subaltern 'Ulysses'* (Minneapolis: University of Minnesota Press, 1994)

DUSSEL, ENRIQUE, 'Eurocentrism and Modernity (Introduction to the Frankfurt Lectures)', *boundary 2*, 20, 3 (1993), 65–76

——*Philosophy of Liberation* (Maryknoll, NY: Orbis Books, 1985)

——*The Invention of the Americas: Eclipse of 'The Other' and the Myth of Modernity*, trans. by Michael D. Barber (New York: Continuum, 1995)

——*The Underside of Modernity: Apel, Ricoeur, Taylor, and the Philosophy of Liberation*, ed. by Eduardo Mendieta (Atlantic Highlands, NJ: Humanities Press, 1996)

ECO, UMBERTO, *The Aesthetics of Chaosmos: The Middle Ages of James Joyce*, trans. by Ellen Esrock (Tulsa, OK: University of Tulsa Press, 1982)

ELIOT, T. S., *Points of View* (London: Faber and Faber, 1941)

——'The Metaphysical Poets', in *'The Waste Land' and Other Writings* (New York: Random House, 2002), pp. 224–34

——'The Waste Land', in *'The Waste Land' and Other Writings*, pp. 38–56

——'Tradition and the Individual Talent', in *'The Waste Land' and Other Writings*, pp. 99–108

——'*Ulysses*, Order and Myth', in DEMING, ed., *James Joyce: The Critical Heritage*, 1, 268–71

EVANS, MICHAEL, 'Intertextual Labyrinth: "El Inmortal" by Borges', *Forum for Modern Language Studies*, 23, 3 (1984), 275–81

EYSTEINSSON, ASTRADUR, *The Concept of Modernism* (Ithaca, NY: Cornell University Press, 1990)

FABIAN, JOHANNES, *Time and the Other: How Anthropology Makes its Object* (New York: Columbia University Press, 1983)

FANON, FRANTZ, *The Wretched of the Earth*, trans. by Richard Philcox (New York: Grove, 2004)

FARIS, WENDY, '"Desyoización": Joyce/Cixous/Fuentes and the Multi-Vocal Text', *Latin American Literary Review*, 19 (1981), 31–39

FELL, CLAUDE, 'Sexo y lenguaje en *Palinuro de México*, de Fernando del Paso', in *Escritura y sexualidad en la literatura hispanoamericana*, ed. by Alain Sicard and Fernando Moreno (Madrid: Fundamentos, 1990), pp. 181–94

FERNÁNDEZ RETAMAR, ROBERTO, *Calibán y otros ensayos* (Havana: Editorial Arte y Literatura, 1979)

—— 'Fanon y América Latina', in *Algunos usos de civilización y barbarie* (Havana: Letras Cubanas, 2003), pp. 225–35

—— *Para una teoría de la literatura hispanoamericana* (Santafé de Bogotá: Instituto Caro y Cuervo, 1995)

FERRO, ROBERTO, ed., *La parodia en la literatura latinoamericana* (Buenos Aires: Universidad de Buenos Aires, 1993)

FIDDIAN, ROBIN, 'Latin America and Beyond: Transcontinental Dialogue in the Work of Leopoldo Zea', *Interventions*, 5, 1 (2003), 113–24

—— 'James Joyce and Spanish-American Fiction: A Study of the Origins and Transmission of Literary Influence', *Bulletin of Hispanic Studies*, 65 (1989), 23–39

—— *The Novels of Fernando del Paso* (Gainesville: University Press of Florida, 2000)

FISHBURN, EVELYN, ed., *Borges and Europe Revisited* (London: Institute of Latin American Studies, 1998)

FOKKEMA, DOUWE W., *Literary History, Modernism, and Postmodernism* (Amsterdam: John Benjamins, 1984)

FOUCAULT, MICHEL, *The Order of Things: An Archaeology of the Human Sciences* (New York: Vintage, 1973)

—— *The History of Sexuality: An Introduction* (New York: Vintage, 1990)

FREEDMAN, ARIELA, 'Did it Flow? Bridging Aesthetics and History in Joyce's Ulysses', *Modernism/modernity*, 13, 1 (2006), 853–68

FUENTES, CARLOS, *Cervantes o la crítica de la lectura* (Mexico: Joaquín Mortiz, 1976)

—— *Cristóbal Nonato* (Mexico: Fondo de Cultura Económica, 1987)

—— *Geografía de la novela* (Mexico: Fondo de Cultura Económica, 1993)

—— '*Hopscotch*: The Novel as Pandora's Box', *Review of Contemporary Fiction*, 3, 3 (1983), 86–88

—— *La nueva novela hispanoamericana* (Mexico: Joaquín Mortiz, 1969)

GARCÍA CANCLINI, NÉSTOR, *Hybrid Cultures: Strategies for Entering and Leaving Modernity*, trans. by Christopher L. Chiappari and Silvia L. López (Minneapolis: University of Minnesota Press, 2005)

GEIST, ANTHONY, and JOSÉ MONLEÓN, eds, *Modernism and Its Margins: Reinscribing Cultural Modernity from Spain and Latin America* (New York: Garland, 1999)

GIBBONS, LUKE, 'Race Against Time: Racial Discourse and Irish History', *Oxford Literary Review*, 13, 1/2 (1991), 95–117

—— *Transformations in Irish Culture* (Cork: Cork University Press, 1996)

GIBSON, ANDREW, *Joyce's Revenge: History, Politics, and Aesthetics in 'Ulysses'* (Oxford: Oxford University Press, 2002)

GIKANDI, SIMON, 'Poststructuralism and Postcolonial Discourse', in *The Cambridge Companion to Postcolonial Literary Studies*, ed. by Neil Lazarus (Cambridge: Cambridge University Press, 2004), pp. 97–119

GILBERT, STUART, 'El fondo latino en el arte de James Joyce', *Sur*, 122 (1944), 11–24

—— *James Joyce's 'Ulysses'* (New York: A. A. Knopf, 1930)

GONZÁLEZ, MANUEL PEDRO, 'Consideraciones sobre la novela', in *Notas críticas* (Havana: UNEAC, 1969), pp. 189–94

—— 'El *Ulysses* cuarenta años después', in *Ensayos críticos* (Caracas: Universidad Central de Venezuela, 1963), pp. 5–21

—— 'La novela hispanoamericana en el contexto de la internacional', in *Coloquio sobre la literatura hispanoamericana*, ed. by Fernando Alegría and others (Mexico: Tezontle, 1967), pp. 35–67

GONZÁLEZ ECHEVARRÍA, ROBERTO, *The Voice of the Masters: Writing and Authority in Modern Latin American Literature* (Austin: University of Texas Press, 1985)

GONZÁLEZ LANUZA, EDUARDO, 'Leopoldo Marechal: *Adán Buenosayres*', in LAFFORGE AND COLLA, eds, *Adán Buenosayres*, pp. 876–79

GORDON, AMBROSE, 'Dublin and Buenos Aires, Joyce and Marechal', *Comparative Literature Studies*, 19, 2 (1982), 208–19

GUILLÉN, CLAUDIO, *Literature as System* (Princeton, NJ: Princeton University Press, 1971)

HARDING, DESMOND, *Writing the City: Urban Visions and Literary Modernism* (London: Routledge, 2003)

HARSS, LUIS, and BARBARA DOHMAN, 'Julio Cortázar, or the Slap in the Face', in ALAZRAKI, ed., *Critical Essays on Julio Cortázar*, pp. 33–59

HARTMANN, WOLFRAM, JEREMY SILVESTER and PATRICIA HAYES, *The Colonizing Camera: Photographs in the Making of Namibian History* (Cape Town: University of Cape Town Press, 1998)

HEGEL, GEORG W. F., *Hegel's Phenomenology of Spirit*, ed. by Howard P. Kainz (University Park, PA: Penn State University Press, 1994)

——*Lectures on the Philosophy of History*, trans. by H. B. Nisbet (Cambridge: Cambridge University Press, 1975)

HEISE, URSULA, *Chronoschisms: Time, Narrative, and Postmodernism* (Cambridge: Cambridge University Press, 1997)

HENRÍQUEZ UREÑA, PEDRO, *Literary Currents in Hispanic America* (Cambridge, MA: Harvard University Press, 1945)

——*Seis ensayos en busca de nuestra expresión* (Managua: Nueva Nicaragua, 1986)

HOPE, A. D., 'The Esthetic Theory of James Joyce', in *Joyce's 'Portrait': Criticism and Critiques*, ed. by Thomas E. Connolly (London: Owen, 1964), pp. 183–203

HOWE, STEPHEN, *Ireland and Empire: Colonial Legacies in Irish History and Culture* (Oxford: Oxford University Press, 2000)

HOWES, MARJORIE, and DEREK ATTRIDGE, eds, *Semicolonial Joyce* (Cambridge: Cambridge University Press, 2000)

HUTCHEON, LINDA. *A Theory of Parody: The Teachings of Twentieth-Century Art Forms* (Urbana and Chicago: University of Illinois Press, 2000)

——'Rethinking the National Model', in *Rethinking Literary History: A Dialogue on Theory*, ed. by Linda Hutcheon and Mario J. Valdés (Oxford: Oxford University Press, 2002), pp. 3–49

HYDE, DOUGLAS, 'The Necessity of De-Anglicizing Ireland', in *The Revival of Irish Literature*, ed. by Charles Duffy and others (London: T. Fisher Unwin, 1894), pp. 115–61

INNES, C. L., 'Modernism, Ireland and Empire: Yeats, Joyce and Their Implied Audiences', in *Modernism and Empire*, ed. by Howard J. Booth and Nigel Rigby (Manchester: Manchester University Press, 2000), pp. 137–55

IRBY, JAMES E. 'La influencia de William Faulkner en cuatro narradores hispanoamericanos' (unpublished master's thesis, Universidad Autónoma de México, 1956)

JAMESON, FREDRIC, 'Modernism and Imperialism', in *Nationalism, Colonialism and Literature*, by Seamus Deane, Terry Eagleton, Fredric Jameson and Edward Said (Minneapolis: University of Minnesota Press, 1990), pp. 43–68

——*The Political Unconscious: Narrative as a Socially Symbolic Act* (Ithaca, NY: Cornell University Press, 1981)

——*Postmodernism, or, The Cultural Logic of Late Capitalism* (Durham, NC: Duke University Press, 1991)

JOYCE, JAMES, *A Portrait of the Artist as a Young Man*, ed. by Chester G. Anderson (New York: Penguin, 1968)

——*Finnegans Wake*, ed. by Seamus Deane (London: Penguin, 2000)

——*Occasional, Critical, and Political Writing*, ed. by Kevin Barry (Oxford: Oxford University Press, 2000)

——*Stephen Hero* (London: Granada, 1977)

——*Ulysses: A Critical and Synoptic Edition*, ed. by Hans Walter Gabler (London: Routledge, 1984)

JUAN-NAVARRO, SANTIAGO, 'Postmodernist Collage and Montage in Julio Cortázar's *Libro de Manuel*', in ALAZRAKI, ed., *Critical Essays on Julio Cortázar*, pp. 173–92

KADIR, DJELAL, 'Stalking the Oxen of the Sun and Felling the Sacred Cows: Joyce's *Ulysses* and Cabrera Infante's *Three Trapped Tigers*', *Latin American Literary Review*, 3, 8 (1976), 15–22

——*Questing Fictions: Latin America's Family Romance* (Minneapolis: University of Minnesota Press, 1986)

KANT, IMMANUEL, *Anthropology from a Pragmatic Point of View*, ed. by Robert B. Louden (Cambridge: Cambridge University Press, 2006)

——*Observations on the Feeling of the Beautiful and the Sublime*, trans. by John T. Goldthwait (Berkeley: University of California Press, 1960)

——*The Critique of Judgment*, trans. by J. H. Bernard (Amherst, NY: Prometheus, 2000)

KAUP, MONICA, 'Becoming-Baroque: Folding European Forms into the New World Baroque with Alejo Carpentier', *CR: The New Centennial Review*, 5, 2 (2005), 107–49

KELLY, JOSEPH, *Our Joyce: From Outcast to Icon* (Austin: University of Texas Press, 1998)

KENNEDY, LIAM, *Colonialism, Religion and Nationalism in Ireland* (Belfast: Institute of Irish Studies, Queen's University of Belfast, 1996)

KENNER, HUGH, *Dublin's Joyce* (Bloomington: Indiana University Press, 1956)

KERR, LUCILLE, *Reclaiming the Author: Figures and Fictions from Spanish America* (Durham, NC: Duke University Press, 1992)

KIBERD, DECLAN, *Inventing Ireland* (Cambridge, MA: Harvard University Press, 1996)

——'Modern Ireland: Postcolonial or European?', in *Not on Any Map: Essays on Coloniality and Cultural Nationalism*, ed. by Stuart Murray (Exeter: University of Exeter Press, 1997), pp. 81–100

——*Irish Classics* (Cambridge, MA: Harvard University Press, 2001)

KING, JOHN, *Sur: A Study of the Argentine Literary Journal and its Role in the Development of a Culture* (Cambridge: Cambridge University Press, 1986)

KLOR DE ALVA, JORGE. 'Colonialism and Postcolonialism as (Latin) American Mirages', *Colonial Latin American Review*, 1, 1/2 (1992), 2–23

KRISTAL, EFRAÍN, ' "Considering Coldly...": A Response to Franco Moretti', *New Left Review*, 15 (2002), 61–74

——*Invisible Work: Borges and Translation* (Nashville, TN: Vanderbilt University Press, 2002)

——'The Incest Motif in Narratives of the United States and Spanish America', in *Internationalität nationaler Literaturen*, ed. by Udo Schöning (Göttingen: Wallstein Verlag, 2000), pp. 390–403

LACLAU, ERNESTO, 'Politics and the Limits of Modernity', *Social Text*, 21 (1989), 63–82

LACLAU, ERNESTO, and CHANTAL MOUFFE, *Hegemony and Socialist Strategy: Towards a Radical Democratic Politics*, trans. by Winston Moore and Paul Cammack (London: Verso, 1985)

LAFFORGE, JORGE, and FERNANDO COLLA, eds, *Adán Buenosayres*, by Leopoldo Marechal (Madrid: ALLCA XX, 1997)

LARSEN, NEIL, 'Cortázar and Postmodernity: New Interpretive Liabilities', in *Julio Cortázar: New Readings*, ed. by Carlos J. Alonso (Cambridge: Cambridge University Press, 1998), pp. 57–75

——*Reading North by South: On Latin American Literature, Culture, and Politics* (Minneapolis: University of Minnesota Press, 1995)

LAWRENCE, KAREN, *The Odyssey of Style in 'Ulysses'* (Princeton, NJ: Princeton University Press, 1981)

——, ed., *Transcultural Joyce* (Cambridge: Cambridge University Press, 1998)

LERNOUT, GEERT, *The French Joyce* (Ann Arbor: University of Michigan Press, 1990)

LEVENSON, MICHAEL H., *A Genealogy of Modernism: A Study of English Literary Doctrine, 1908–1922* (Cambridge: Cambridge University Press, 1984)

LEVIN, HARRY, *James Joyce: A Critical Introduction* (Norfolk, CT: New Directions, 1960)

LEVINE, SUZANNE J., 'La maldición del incesto en *Cien años de soledad*', *Revista Iberoamericana*, 37 (1971), 711–23

——'Notes on Borges's Notes on Joyce: Infinite Affinities.' *Comparative Literature*, 49, 4 (1997), 344–59

LEVITT, MORTON, *Modernist Survivors: The Contemporary Novel in England, the United States, France, and Latin America* (Columbus: Ohio State University Press, 1987)

LEZAMA LIMA, JOSÉ, *Obras completas*, 2 vols (Mexico: Aguilar, 1977)

——*Paradiso*, ed. by Eloísa Lezama Lima (Madrid: Cátedra, 2001)

LITZ, A. WALTON, 'Pound and Eliot on *Ulysses*: The Critical Tradition', in *'Ulysses': Fifty Years*, ed. by Thomas F. Staley (Bloomington: Indiana University Press, 1974), pp. 5–18

LLOYD, DAVID, *Anomalous States: Irish Writing and the Postcolonial Moment* (Durham, NC: Duke University Press, 1993)

——*Ireland after History* (Notre Dame, IN: University of Notre Dame Press, 1999)

LOSS, JACQUELINE, *Cosmopolitanisms and Latin America: Against the Destiny of Place* (New York: Palgrave Macmillan, 2005)

LYONS, TED, and PJERS HANGROW, 'Heresy as Motif in the Short Stories of Borges', *Latin American Literary Review*, 3, 5 (1975), 23–35

MANGANARO, MARC', Dissociation in "Dead Land": The Primitive Mind in the Early Poetry of T. S. Eliot', *Journal of Modern Literature*, 13 (1986), 97–110

MANGIANELLO, DOMINIC, *Joyce's Politics* (London: Routledge, 1980)

MARECHAL, LEOPOLDO, *Adán Buenosayres*, ed. by Jorge Lafforge and Fernando Colla (Madrid: ALLCA XX, 1997)

——'Las claves de *Adán Buenosayres*', in Lafforge and Colla, eds, *Adán Buenosayres*, pp. 863–70

MARTIN, GERALD, *Journeys through the Labyrinth: Latin American Fiction in the Twentieth Century* (London: Verso, 1989)

MATERER, TIMOTHY, 'T. S. Eliot's Critical Program', in *The Cambridge Companion to T. S. Eliot*, ed. by David Moody (New York: Cambridge University Press), pp. 48–59

McDEVITT, PATRICK, 'Ireland, Latin America, and an Atlantic Liberation Theology', in *The Atlantic in Global History, 1500–2000*, ed. by Jorge Cañizares-Esguerra and Erik R. Seeman (Upper Saddle River, NJ: Prentice Hall, 2007), pp. 239–51

MELAS, NATALIE, *All the Difference in the World: Postcoloniality and the Ends of Comparison* (Stanford, CA: Stanford University Press, 2007)

MIGNOLO, WALTER D., *Local Histories/Global Designs: Coloniality, Subaltern Knowledges, and Border Thinking* (Princeton, NJ: Princeton University Press, 2000)

——'Occidentalización, imperialismo, globalización: herencias coloniales y teorías postcoloniales', *Revista Iberoamericana*, 61, 170/71 (1995), 26–39

——'Rethinking the Colonial Model', in *Rethinking Literary History: A Dialogue on Theory*, ed. by Linda Hutcheon and Mario J. Valdés (Oxford: Oxford University Press), pp. 155–93

——'The Geopolitics of Knowledge and the Colonial Difference', *South Atlantic Quarterly*, 101, 1 (2002), 57–96

——'The Many Faces of Cosmo-Polis: Border Thinking and Critical Cosmopolitanism', *Public Culture*, 12, 3 (2000), 721–48

—— *The Idea of Latin America* (Malden, MA: Blackwell, 2005)

MOLLOY, SYLVIA, 'Lost in Translation: Borges, the Western Tradition and Fictions of Latin America', in FISHBURN, ed., *Borges and Europe Revisited*, pp. 8–20

—— *Signs of Borges*, trans. by Óscar Montero (Durham, NC: Duke University Press, 1994)

MORAN, DOMINIC, *Questions of the Liminal in the Fiction of Julio Cortázar* (Oxford: Legenda, 2000)

MORETTI, FRANCO, *Atlas of the European Novel, 1800–1900* (London: Verso, 1999)

—— 'Conjectures on World Literature', *New Left Review*, 1 (2000), 54–68

—— *Graphs, Maps, Trees: Abstract Models for a Literary History* (London: Verso, 2005)

—— *Modern Epic: The World-System from Goethe to García Márquez*, trans. by Quintin Hoare (London: Verso, 1996)

MURILLO, LUIS, *The Cyclical Night: Irony in James Joyce and Jorge Luis Borges* (Cambridge, MA: Harvard University Press, 1968)

MURRY, JOHN MIDDLETON, '*Ulysses*', in DEMING, ed., *James Joyce: The Critical Heritage*, 1, 195–98

NAIPUL, V. S., *The Mimic Men* (New York: Macmillan, 1967)

NAVASCUÉS, JAVIER DE, 'Marechal frente a Joyce y Cortázar', *Cuadernos Hispanoamericanos*, 538 (1995), 45–56

—— 'Sobre la novela argentina: *Rayuela y Adán Buenosayres*', in LAFFORGE AND COLLA, eds, *Adán Buenosayres*, pp. 957–66

NOLAN, EMER, *James Joyce and Nationalism* (London: Routledge, 1995)

NOON, WILLIAM T., *Joyce and Aquinas* (Hamden, CT: Archon, 1970)

OCAMPO, VICTORIA, 'T. S. Eliot', *Sur*, 159 (1948), 7–10

—— *Testimonios* (Buenos Aires: Sudamericana, 1946)

O'Gorman, Edmundo, *La invención de América: el universalismo de la cultura de Occidente* (Mexico: Fondo de Cultura Económica, 1958)

ORR, LEONARD, 'Joyce and the Contemporary Cuban Novel: Lezama Lima and Cabrera Infante', *Neohelicon*, 19, 2 (1992), 17–25

ORTEGA, JULIO, *Poetics of Change: The New Spanish-American Narrative*, trans. by Galen Greaser (Austin: University of Texas Press, 1984)

ORTEGA Y GASSET, JOSÉ, *La deshumanización del arte y otros ensayos de estética* (Madrid: Alianza, 1981)

PALMER, PATRICIA, *Language and Conquest in Early Modern Ireland: English Renaissance Literature and Elizabethan Imperial Expansion* (Cambridge: Cambridge University Press, 2001)

PAZ, OCTAVIO, *Corriente alterna* (Mexico: Siglo Veintiuno, 1978)

—— 'La búsqueda del presente', *Vuelta*, 170 (1991), 10–14

PELLÓN, GUSTAVO, *José Lezama Lima's Joyful Vision: A Study of 'Paradiso' and Other Prose Works* (Austin: University of Texas Press, 1989)

PEÑUELAS, MARCELINO C., 'James Joyce tras el interrogante', *Cuadernos Americanos*, 91 (1957), 183–200

PÉREZ FIRMAT, GUSTAVO, *The Cuban Condition: Translation and Identity in Modern Cuban Literature* (Cambridge: Cambridge University Press, 1989)

PÉREZ SIMON, ANDRÉS, 'Borges' Writings on Joyce: From a Mythical Translation to a Polemical Defence of Censorship', *Papers on Joyce*, 7/8 (2001/02), 121–37

PICÓN SALAS, MARIANO, *De la Conquista a la Independencia y otros estudios* (Caracas: Monte Ávila, 1990)

PIGLIA, RICARDO, *The Absent City*, trans. by Sergio Waisman (Durham, NC: Duke University Press, 2000)

—— *Respiración artificial* (Barcelona: Anagrama, 2001)

POUND, EZRA, *Pound/Joyce: The Letters of Ezra Pound to James Joyce, with Pound's Essays on Joyce*, ed. by Forrest Read (New York: New Directions, 1967)

PRIETO, ADOLFO, 'Los dos mundos de *Adán Buenosayres*', in LAFFORGE AND COLLA, eds, *Adán Buenosayres*, pp. 897–907

RAMA, ÁNGEL, *Transculturación narrativa en América Latina* (Mexico: Siglo Veintiuno, 1982)

RANK, OTTO, *The Incest Theme in Literature and Legend: Fundamentals of a Psychology of Literary Creation* (Baltimore, MD: Johns Hopkins University Press, 1991)

RICE, THOMAS J., *Joyce, Chaos, and Complexity* (Urbana: University of Illinois Press, 1997)

——'Subtle Reflections of/upon Joyce in/by Borges', *Journal of Modern Literature*, 24, 1 (2000), 47–62

RIERA, GABRIEL, '"The One Does Not Exist": Borges and Modernity's Predicament', *Romance Studies*, 24, 1 (2006), 55–66

RODRÍGUEZ MONEGAL, EMIR, '*Adán Buenosayres*: Una novela infernal', in LAFFORGE AND COLLA, eds, *Adán Buenosayres*, pp. 923–29

——'Aspectos de la novela en el siglo XX', *Sur*, 159 (1948), 86–96

——*El boom de la novela latinoamericana* (Caracas: Tiempo Nuevo, 1972)

——'Borges and La Nouvelle Critique', *Diacritics*, 2, 2 (1972), 27–34

ROSENBERG, FERNANDO J., *The Avant-Garde and Geopolitics in Latin America* (Pittsburgh, PA: University of Pittsburgh Press, 2006)

ROSENBLUM, JOSEPH, '"The Immortal": Jorge Luis Borges's Rendition of T. S. Eliot's *The Waste Land*', *Studies in Short Fiction*, 18, 2 (1981), 183–86

ROSMAN, SILVIA, *Dislocaciones culturales: nación, sujeto y comunidad en América Latina* (Rosario, Argentina: Beatriz Viterbo, 2003)

ROUGHLEY, ALAN, *James Joyce and Critical Theory: An Introduction* (Ann Arbor: University of Michigan Press, 1991)

ROWE, WILLIAM, 'How European Is It?', in FISHBURN, ed., *Borges and Europe Revisited*, pp. 21–36

SAID, EDWARD, *Culture and Imperialism* (New York: Random House, 1993)

——*Orientalism* (New York: Pantheon Books, 1978)

SAINZ, GUSTAVO, *Obsesivos días circulares* (Mexico: Joaquín Mortiz, 1969)

SALGADO, CÉSAR A., '*Barroco* Joyce: Jorge Luis Borges's and José Lezama Lima's Antagonistic Readings', in LAWRENCE, ed., *Transcultural Joyce*, pp. 63–93

——*From Modernism to Neobaroque: Joyce and Lezama Lima* (Lewisburg, PA: Bucknell University Press, 2001)

SALOMON, NOËL, 'Cosmopolitanism and Internationalism in the History of Ideas in Latin America', *Cultures*, 6, 1 (1979), 83–108

SÁNCHEZ ROBAYNA, ANDRÉS, 'Borges y Joyce', *Ínsula*, 437, 1 (1983), 1, 12

SARDUY, SEVERO, 'El barroco y el neobarroco', in *América latina en su literatura*, ed. by César Fernández Moreno (Mexico: Siglo Veintiuno, 1972), pp. 167–84

——*Barroco* (Buenos Aires: Editorial Sudamericana, 1974)

SARLO, BEATRIZ, *Jorge Luis Borges: A Writer on the Edge*, ed. by John King (London: Verso, 1993)

SCHULMAN, IVAN A., 'Reflexiones en torno a la definición de modernismo', in *Estudios críticos sobre el modernismo*, ed. by Homero Castillo (Madrid: Gredos, 1968), pp. 325–57

SCHWARZ, ROBERTO, *Misplaced Ideas: Essays on Brazilian Culture*, ed. by John Gledson (London: Verso, 1992)

SCHWARTZ, LAWRENCE H., *Creating Faulkner's Reputation: The Politics of Modern Literary Criticism* (Knoxville: University of Tennessee Press, 1988)

SEGALL, JEFFREY, *Joyce in America: Cultural Politics and the Trials of 'Ulysses'* (Berkeley: University of California Press, 1993)

SENN, FRITZ, *Joyce's Dislocutions: Essays on Reading as Translation*, ed. by J. P. Riquelme (Baltimore, MD: Johns Hopkins University Press, 1984)

SHAW, DONALD L., 'El tema del incesto en Faulkner y García Márquez', *Anthropos*, 187 (1999), 100–05

——'More about Modernism in Spanish America', *A Contracorriente*, 4, 2 (2007), 143–52

——*Nueva narrativa hispanoamericana: boom, posboom, posmodernismo* (Madrid: Cátedra, 1999)

——'When Was Modernism in Spanish-American Fiction?', *Bulletin of Spanish Studies*, 79, 2/3 (2002), 395–409

Simo, Ana María, and others, *Cinco miradas sobre Cortázar* (Buenos Aires: Editorial Tiempo Contemporáneo, 1968)

Smith, Eric D., 'The Mimetic "Spirit of Denial": Buck Mulligan and the Cultural Limits of Mockery', *Papers on Joyce*, 9 (2003), 19–33

Sommer, Doris, *Foundational Fictions: The National Romances of Latin America* (Berkeley: University of California Press, 1991)

——*Proceed with Caution, When Engaged by Minority Writing in the Americas* (Cambridge, MA: Harvard University Press, 1999)

Sorensen, Diana, *A Turbulent Decade Remembered: Scenes from the Latin American Sixties* (Stanford, CA: Stanford University Press, 2007)

Spurr, David, 'Myths of Anthropology: Eliot, Joyce, Lévy-Bruhl', *PMLA*, 109, 2 (1994), 266–80

Thornton, Weldon, 'Authorial Omniscience and Cultural Psyche: The Antimodernism of Joyce's *Ulysses*', in *Irishness and (Post)Modernism*, ed. by John S. Rickard (Lewisburg, PA: Bucknell University Press, 1994), pp. 84–102

——*The Antimodernism of Joyce's 'A Portrait of the Artist as a Young Man'* (Syracuse, NY: Syracuse University Press, 1994)

Thiong'o, Ngugi wa, *Decolonising the Mind: The Politics of Language in African Literature* (Portsmouth, NH: Heinemann, 1986)

Torres Caballero, Benjamín, *Gabriel García Márquez o la alquimia del incesto* (Madrid: Playor, 1987)

Trejo Fuentes, Ignacio, 'El que despalinurice a Palinuro será un buen despalinurizador: entrevista con Fernando del Paso', *La Semana de Bellas Artes*, 138 (1980), 6–11

Uslar Pietri, Arturo, 'La tentativa desesperada de James Joyce', *Cuadernos Americanos*, 27 (1946), 256–65

——'Lo criollo en la literatura', in *Veinticinco ensayos: antología* (Caracas: Monte Ávila, 1969), pp. 39–50

Van Delden, Maarten, 'The Spanish-American Novel and European Modernism', in *Modernism*, ed. by Astradur Eysteinsson and Vivian Liska, 2 vols (Amsterdam: Johns Benjamins, 2007), II, 947–65

Vegh, Beatriz, 'A Meeting in the Western Canon: Borges's Conversation with Joyce', *European Joyce Studies*, 14, 1 (2002), 85–97

Venegas, José Luis, 'Exile, Photography, and the Politics of Style in Guillermo Cabrera Infante's *Tres tristes tigres*', *Latin American Literary Review*, 36, 72 (2008), 107–33

Vieira, Else, 'Ig/noble Barbarians: Revising Latin American Modernisms', in *Postcolonial Perspectives on the Cultures of Latin America and Lusophone Africa*, ed. by Robin Fiddian (Liverpool: Liverpool University Press, 2000), pp. 70–102

Viñas, David, *De Sarmiento a Cortázar* (Buenos Aires: Siglo Veinte, 1971)

——*Literatura argentina y realidad política* (Buenos Aires: Siglo Veinte, 1971)

Waisman, Sergio Gabriel, *Borges and Translation: The Irreverence of the Periphery* (Lewisburg, PA: Bucknell University Press, 2005)

——'Borges Reads Joyce: The Role of Translation in the Creation of Texts', *Variaciones Borges*, 9 (2000), 59–73

Walkowitz, Rebecca, *Cosmopolitan Style: Modernism Beyond the Nation* (New York: Columbia University Press, 2006)

Wells, H. G., 'James Joyce', in Deming, ed., *James Joyce: The Critical Heritage*, I, 86–88

WHYTE, NICHOLAS, *Science, Colonialism and Ireland* (Cork: Cork University Press, 1999)

WILLIAMS, RAYMOND L., 'Modernist Continuities: The Desire To Be Modern in Twentieth-Century Spanish American Fiction', *Bulletin of Spanish Studies*, 79, 2/3 (2002), 369–93

—— *The Modern Latin American Novel* (New York: Twayne Publishers, 1998)

—— *The Twentieth-Century Spanish American Novel* (Austin: University of Texas Press, 2003)

—— *The Postmodern Novel in Latin America: Politics, Culture, and the Crisis of Truth* (New York: St Martin's Press, 1995)

WOOD, MICHAEL, 'Cabrera Infante: Unruly Pupil', in LAWRENCE, ed., *Transcultural Joyce*, pp. 49–62

WOOLF, VIRGINIA, *A Writer's Diary* (New York: Harcourt Brace Jovanovich, 2003)

—— 'Modern Fiction', in *Selected Essays*, ed. by David Bradshaw (Oxford: Oxford University Press, 2008), pp. 6–12

WYNTER, SYLVIA, 'Unsettling the Coloniality of Being/Power/Truth/Freedom: Towards the Human, After Man, Its Overrepresentation: An Argument', *CR: The New Centennial Review*, 3, 3 (2003), 257–337

YOUNG, ROBERT, *White Mythologies: Writing History and the West* (London: Routledge, 1990)

ZAMORA, LOIS PARKINSON, *The Inordinate Eye: New World Baroque and Latin American Fiction* (Chicago: University of Chicago Press, 2006)

ZEA, LEOPOLDO, 'En torno a una filosofía americana', *Cuadernos Americanos*, 3 (1942), 63–78

—— *La filosofía como compromiso y otros ensayos* (Mexico: Tezontle, 1952)

—— *Dependencia y liberación en la cultura latinoamericana* (Mexico: Joaquín Mortiz, 1974)

INDEX

❖